THE MYSTERY OF BARABBAS

Exploring the Origins of a Pagan Religion

By the same author:

Who Lies Sleeping? The Dinosaur Heritage
and the Extinction of Man

ISBN 9521913-0-X

AskWhy! Publications

THE MYSTERY OF BARABBAS

Exploring the Origins of a Pagan Religion

M D Magee

AskWhy! Publications

Selwyn Frome

First published in Great Britain 1995
by AskWhy! Publications
Selwyn, 41 The Butts, Frome
Somerset, BA11 4AB

British Library Cataloguing-in-Publication Data
A catalogue record for this book is available from the British Library

ISBN 0-9521913-1-8

Typeset by PCS Typesetting, Frome
Printed in Great Britain by
Hillman Printers (Frome) Ltd, Somerset

For my children,
David Michael Magee, Helen Frances Magee
and Paul Evan Magee

CONTENTS

BARABBAS

BARABBAS

Now Barabbas was a robber.

John 18:40

The Mystery of Barabbas

The extraordinary incident of Barabbas gives us a glimpse through the distorting veils of time to the foundation of Christianity and the truth about its beginnings. All four gospels tell the story (Mk 15:6-15, Mt 27:15-26, Lk 23:17-25, Jn 18:39-40). In paraphrase it is this.

Jesus of Nazareth, a simple travelling preacher and healer, has been betrayed by the scheming Jews and stands before the Roman governor of Judaea on capital charges. The governor, Pontius Pilate, a just and kindly man, can find no wrong in Jesus, but is scared of offending the Jews. He tries to release him by invoking an old custom whereby, at festival time (in this instance, the Jewish Passover) a prisoner of the people's choosing is released. He offers the crowd, who had only days before been hailing Jesus as a king, a choice: they could release Jesus, or a thief called Barabbas. The fickle crowd pick the criminal. Not wanting to be associated with sending an innocent man to a cruel death Pilate theatrically washes his hands before the crowd to declare to them he is not responsible for the death of a good man.

For Christians this is simply another callous event in the narrative of the unjust and cruel death of the Son of God in atonement for the sins of mankind. The tale proves that the Jews, by their rejection of Jesus, were no longer the Chosen People of God. Instead the followers of Jesus were.

"So", you ask, "What's the mystery?"

The mystery, though rarely remarked upon by Christian scholars, is this...

Jesus always called God "my Father" using an affectionate Aramaic word for father, Abba. If God is the father then the man who calls God "my Father" is the Son of God, which is just what Christians believe. The Son of my Father was the Son of God. Now the gospels tell us the name of the robber Pilate offered to the crowd for release instead of Jesus was Barabbas.

Barabbas is not a personal name – in Aramaic it means "the Son of my Father".

This seems a strange coincidence. That's the mystery! It's too strange to *be* a coincidence.

Nor does it end there. Some old manuscripts of *Matthew*, confirmed by the writings of the church father, Origen, reveal the full name of the criminal – it is Jesus Barabbas!

The gospels ask us to believe that Pilate offers the crowd the choice of Jesus Barabbas, the crook, or Jesus "Bar Abbas", the son of his father, God. If we follow the gospel according to Matthew (27:17), Pilate asks the multitude: "Which Jesus will ye that I release unto you? Barabbas or 'Bar Abbas'?" The crowd replied, "Bar Abbas" – or, as Christians would have it, "Barabbas"?

It is as if the governor said: "Who do you want me to release, your king, Jesus, God's Son, or a criminal we just happen to have in the nick, Jesus Godson." "God's Son," they shout, so Pilate released Godson! Can we accept that God has such a wicked sense of humour?

That is not the only unbelievable aspect of the Barabbas incident.

First, Pontius Pilate appears in it as a most sensitive and understanding man. Yet the judgement of history is vastly different. He is known to have been an exceptionally cruel, greedy and callous man when, under the totalitarian regime of Imperial Rome, such men were common. He was so bad that the Romans eventually withdrew him in disgrace to Rome because of his excesses.

Second, even young children find it hard to accept that the Jewish throng, which had hailed and hosannahed Jesus as a king only a few days before, should have so completely turned against him that they now wanted him crucified. A man, who is a king leading his ecstatic people one day, does not suddenly become hated when the next day he is captured. His disciples and supporters, we are invited to believe, thought he was the Son of God. Would they have summoned God's wrath by turning against his son in his hour of need? Surely they would have expected God to intervene with a miracle as long as Jesus were alive, and they would have clamoured for their leader.

Third, the habit of the Governor at festival time of releasing the prisoner begged for by the crowd is not recorded outside the *New Testament* and was unknown anywhere in the Roman Empire, let alone in Judaea which was at the time a hotbed of unrest. Even granted that there had been until then such a custom, it again stretches credibility that Pilate would release one such as Barabbas – he would have committed treason against the Emperor if he had! For though *John*, the last gospel to be composed, describes Barabbas simply as "a robber", he was no ordinary criminal. In *Matthew* Barabbas is "a notable prisoner". We would say he was notorious. But both writers are being disingenuous. Mark, in the earliest gospel, frankly identifies him as **a rioter who had committed murder during an insurrection**, and *Luke* adds that the **insurrection had occurred in Jerusalem itself**! The gospels are here skating over something remarkable. At the very time that gentle Jesus of Nazareth was entering Jerusalem hailed as a king, by coincidence a fellow called Barabbas was leading a revolution!

By fomenting an insurrection Barabbas had committed a political crime against the Emperor and against the Roman state. Pilate would have had to report such a serious crime, and his response to it, to the Emperor himself. He could have found no excuse for letting such a man off – he had no say in the matter. Rebellion was a capital crime requiring the lowest form of death – crucifixion. Yet the Holy Book of Christianity tells us it was gentle Jesus of Nazareth who was unjustly crucified while Pilate himself committed treason against the Emperor by releasing the leader of a revolution.

What does it all mean?

This confusion can only be intelligently untangled if Jesus Barabbas and Jesus the Nazarene were the same person! The gospels are hiding the fact that the man worshipped as a deity by Christian believers for 2000 years was a Jewish rebel punished horribly but quite properly under Roman law for attempting to overthrow the civic authorities in Jerusalem.

Evidently an insurrection with popular support had occurred in Jerusalem at the Passover festival. Its instigator, Jesus the Nazarene, nicknamed Barabbas by the crowd from his habit of referring to God in Heaven as his father, had been caught by the authorities and promptly taken to Pilate with the Jewish crowds still milling around in a religious and nationalist fervour, expecting a miracle. They called out “Barabbas, Barabbas” asking for the release of the Nazarene, their leader, using their nickname for him. Pilate, who despised the Jews, realised the only way to curb the unrest was to dispatch the Jewish leader with no further ado... and that is what he did.

If, as the gospels say, Pilate did agree to release Jesus Barabbas, later known as Jesus Christ, then he deliberately duped the crowd. But that sounds more like the real Pilate, the rapacious, two-faced Pilate of history, and less like the kindly Pilate of the gospels. Faced with the excited and rebellious crowd, Pilate cunningly decides to give them their miracle – he agrees to release Jesus if the crowd would only disperse. Pilate has such a vile reputation that this *really does* seem like a miracle to the crowd – they disperse in wonder. Then Pilate crucifies Jesus as he always intended.

Later, when Christians passed on the story by word of mouth, it included the scene of the crowd assembled outside the official building calling “Barabbas, Barabbas”. When the oral tradition of the first Christians was being recorded by the gospel writers this was one of the many difficulties that they had to hide or explain.

Jesus was Barabbas, the rebel, but they wanted their incarnated god to be a saintly man. Jesus was condemned and crucified by Romans yet, for Christianity to prosper, it had to seek respectability within the Roman Empire. Jesus, himself a Jew, was hailed by Jews, a race which was widely scorned within the Roman world when they rebelled in 66 AD. They were trouble makers or even terrorists just as some in the world today might regard Libyans, Basques or Irish. And so gentle Jesus was invented and his true nature hidden.

The gospel writers pretended Barabbas was someone else and they invented the story of the Passover custom to explain who he was. The just Roman Prefect, Pilate, offered to let the mob have their choice of prisoner but the treacherous Jews picked the murderer, Barabbas. The gospel writers could use the Aramaic word Barabbas knowing that few of their Latin or Greek speaking gentile converts would know its meaning and question the coincidence. The Romans were depicted as fair and just; the Jewish supporters of the Jew, Jesus, were shown as treacherous villains. A Jewish incident was de-Judaised and the Jewish religion simultaneously discredited within the Roman Empire as a rival religion to Christianity.

You might feel that this is all very unlikely, especially if you cannot throw off the prejudices of a Christian upbringing. But if you look at the history of Palestine and the situation at that time you might be more inclined to accept it. If you look at the nuggets of evidence that remain unexpurgated by earlier Christians you might be convinced.

The Palestine of Barabbas

The Oppression of the Jews

Despite the impression given by the gospels, Palestine in New Testament times was not a rural idyll ruled by a benign foreign Emperor. The region was politically and socially unstable. Palestine was at the crossroads between Asia and Africa and its proudly religious Jewish inhabitants, who believed themselves the Chosen People of God, had been harassed by mighty armies moving in either direction at various times in history. As an important trade route between Egypt and Mesopotamia (modern day Iraq) the mighty empires that periodically arose in those countries plotted and fought incessantly over the land between. Add to that divisions within the nation, partly self-induced and partly fostered by foreign powers, and the sum was turmoil.

The land invaded by the Israelites a thousand years before when Moses led them out of Egypt seeking a Land of Milk and Honey was originally known as Canaan. Only later did the neighbouring countries in the Mediterranean world come to know it as Palestine when the Philistines occupied its coastal areas. Vowels were omitted in writing the languages of the Middle East in those days so the two words are the same.

The Israelites were not a unified nation from Egypt as the *Old Testament* story states, though the superpower of Egypt always had a strong influence on its smaller neighbour. Mainly the invaders of Canaan were a mixture of Semitic tribes from Arabia where they kept goats and spoke Hebrew. Possibly some tribes settled in Egypt had earlier been driven east accounting for the scriptural story. Joshua did not conquer Canaan in a swift campaign in which he knocked down the walls of Jericho. His exploits are an invention of the Jewish sages returning from exile in Babylon some seven hundred years later. Canaan was conquered by a long and slow process in which the Hebrew nomads adapted from a predominantly pastoral life to one which was largely agricultural. Only in about 1000 BC did the tribes unite under King David and complete the conquest of the new territory. A brief but well remembered golden period followed under David's son Solomon but thereafter the tiny kingdom, only about as big as Wales, split into the yet smaller kingdoms of Judah and Israel.

When the Babylonians under Nebuchadnezzar conquered Palestine in about 600 BC, they used it as a source of slaves and skilled labour and many Jews were carried away captive to Babylon. They were allowed to return when Babylon in its turn was defeated by the Persians under their king, Cyrus, in 538 BC. The Jews who returned were culturally different from those who had remained in Palestine, bringing with them the sophistication and scholarship of a mighty civilisation. Then it was that the early books of the *Old Testament* were set down in their present form, drawing upon Mesopotamian myth as well as previous Jewish works, and praising the kindness of the Persian monarch who had liberated them. Then also began the idea that their tribal god, Yahweh, one of many Semitic gods, was the one true god, absolute and universal, who had entered into a Covenant with the Jews, his specially Chosen People. And only from among them would he chose his Messiah, the human agent of his will. Under the umbrella of the Persians, the former exiles built a new Temple in Jerusalem and set up a theocracy in Judah – the holy people were to be ruled by God through his recognised priesthood. For the next few hundred years Jewish sages rewrote and reinterpreted Jewish legend creating the *Scriptures*, known to us as the *Old Testament*.

When the Greeks under Alexander and his generals took control of Palestine in 332 BC they attempted to unite different peoples under a common Hellenistic religion. The Jews objected strongly to this and began a period of rebellion. The family of the Maccabees successfully rose against their Greek masters and set up a Jewish state for a short time but the kingdom divided again and fell under Roman domination first under Pompey and then under the vassal monarch, Herod the Great, who reigned as a tyrant for 33 years. Herod was an Idumaean who adopted the Jewish religion and rebuilt the Temple among other large projects. He was a good soldier and a competent king but he was cruel and immoral and remained unpopular with his Jewish subjects.

Shortly after Herod died in 4 BC, a long period of civic unrest began, punctuated by rebellion and repression, culminating in the destruction of Jerusalem by the Romans in 70 AD. In 6 AD the Romans instituted direct rule over the southernmost part of Palestine, Judaea, replacing one of Herod's sons, Archelaus, who was just as bad as his father but only half as competent. For Jews this violated the Royalty Law of *Deuteronomy*. The sages who had compiled the *Old Testament*, conscious of the years of oppression under the Babylonians, had written in *Deuteronomy* (17:15):

> *One from among thy brethren shalt thou set king over thee; thou mayest not put a foreigner over thee, who is not thy brother.*

The Roman occupiers were hated. The Jews had happily submitted to the rule of the Persians for hundreds of years and less happily the Greeks but God's Law forbade the Jews to accept foreign rule and was a constant spur to Jewish nationalists to rise against their Roman rulers. Throughout New Testament times rioting and insurrection were commonplace in Judaea. A succession of Roman Prefects and Procurators were put in charge of Judaea to quell the discontent of the population.

And so we come to the time of Barabbas, with Pontius Pilate the Prefect of Judaea, when the events of the gospel occurred. Uprisings had been occurring regularly for over twenty years and would continue to occur even beyond the destruction of Jerusalem forty years in the future. In the midst of this the gospels tell us that a gentle wandering holy man was falsely picked on by jealous priests, unfairly turned over to the Romans as a pretender to the throne of Judaea and unjustly tortured to death on a cross.

The Messiah

The oppression of the Jews by the foreigner aroused in them thoughts of a Messiah.

Though the Christian idea of the Messiah, or in Greek parlance, the Christ, is one of a divine redeemer, it is quite different from the older, Jewish conception of a Messiah, a warrior who would free them from their enemies and institute the kingdom of God on earth in which the Jews would be the elite.

The Messiah is perfectly described in the Book of Daniel written about 200 years before Barabbas when the Jewish state was oppressed by the Greeks. Even then Jews were seeking a Saviour.

> *...and, behold, one like unto the son of man came with the clouds of Heaven, and came even to the ancient of days, and they brought him near before him. And there was given him dominion, and glory, and a kingdom, that all the peoples, nations, and languages, should serve him: his dominion is an everlasting dominion, which shall not pass away, and his kingdom that which shall not be destroyed.*
>
> Daniel 7:13 -14

In the non-canonical *Psalms of Solomon*, written not by Solomon, the king, but by unknown authors between 70 and 40 BC – only about 70 years before Barabbas, we get a detailed description (edited here for brevity). The Messiah of the house of David shall gather the nation together and evict the foreigners from Jerusalem.

O God, raise up unto them their king, the Son of David that he may reign over Israel thy servant. And gird him with strength that he may shatter unrighteous rulers, and that he may purge Jerusalem from nations that trample her down to destruction. He shall destroy the godless nations with the word of his mouth. At his rebuke the nations shall flee before him. All nations shall be in fear before him.

Wisely, righteously he shall thrust out sinners from the inheritance. He shall destroy the pride of the sinner as a potter's vessel. With a rod of iron he shall break in pieces all their substance and he shall reprove the sinners for the thoughts of their hearts. And he shall purge Jerusalem making it holy as of old.

And he shall gather together a holy people whom he shall lead in righteousness. And he shall divide them according to their tribes upon the land, and neither visitor nor stranger shall remain with them any more.

And he shall judge the tribes of his people which has been sanctified by the Lord. And he shall not suffer unrighteousness to lodge any more in their midst, nor shall there dwell with them any man that knoweth wickedness, for he shall know them that they are all sons of God.

And he shall be a righteous king, taught of God, over them, and there shall be no unrighteousness in his days in their midst, for all shall be holy and their king the anointed of the Lord. The Lord himself is king, the hope of him that is mighty is through his hope in God.

He will bless the people of the Lord with wisdom and gladness, and he himself will be pure from sin, so that he may rule a great people and relying on his God throughout his days he will not stumble; for God will make him mighty by means of his holy spirit, and wise by means of the spirit of understanding, with strength and righteousness.

His hope will be in the Lord: who then can prevail over him? He will be mighty in his works and strong in the fear of God; he will be shepherding the flock of the Lord faithfully and righteously and will suffer none among them to stumble in their pasture. He will lead them all aright, and there will be no pride among them that any among them should be oppressed.

He shall judge peoples and nations in the wisdom of his righteousness. And he shall have the heathen nations to serve under his yoke.

You will note that a mendicant pacifist preaching goodwill to all men was not the Jews' best idea of a leader suitable to free them from the yoke of their oppressors. The chief heathen nation was, by the time of Barabbas in the first century AD, the Romans. The political position of the Jews under the Romans seemed hopeless. Consequently popular Jewish hopes were of this imminent redeemer, this warrior king, born in the image of and of the line of King David, a supernatural being sent by God who would overthrow the foreigners, impose Jewish authority over the world and institute a kingdom of God on earth which he would rule assisted by the Jews as the elite. The Messiah had become a fervent belief.

These visions of God giving dominion of a kingdom to his Messiah, an everlasting kingdom which encompassed all peoples and nations, ignited the torch of Jewish nationalism for several centuries. Leaders of varying degrees of credibility were to step forward from the death of Herod to the defeat of Bar Kosiba claiming to be the Messiah of God.

Both the Hebrew word, Messiah, and the Greek word, Christos, mean one who is anointed, or rather it is always given as meaning one who is anointed. Actually Messiah is made up of the Egyptian root MS, as in Moses, meaning a child or, if the child is male, a son, and the Hebrew word, iah which is God. Thus Messiah means literally "Son of God". The Christian gospel writer Matthew identified Jesus Christ with Moses, whose name is also of course "a son". If Moses is the Egyptian word for a son who was he a son of? Was Moses also a Messiah? He was! Moses was adopted by Pharaoh's daughter who found him in the bulrushes. And a Pharaoh was a god!

Moses's brother, the priest Aaron, died and was buried at a place called Moseroth, Moserah or Mosera, the site of the Israelite camp near Mount Hor. Curiously Mosera can be read as Egyptian for Son of Ra or Son of God, Ra being the Egyptian word for god. The father of Moses and Aaron, according to the *Old Testament*, was Amram interpreted as the Hebrew for exalted people when it is plainly a corruption of the Egyptian Amun-Ra. Amun-Ra was the high God – Amun meaning the Hidden One – of the Egyptians. From the time of the pyramid builder, Cephren in the IVth dynasty all Pharaohs were considered to have been Ra's son, in other words they were Sons of God or Messiahs. Mosera is the purely Egyptian word from which the compound word Messiah was constructed. It is the same word, with roots in a different order, as Rameses, the name of several pharaohs – Sons of God. One of the inscriptions of Rameses the Great records Amun-Ra addressing the Pharaoh with words familiar to a modern Christian:

> *I am thy father. I have begotten thee like a god.*

The Pharaoh replies:

> *I am thy son. Thou hast given me the power of a god.*

Thus both Moses and his brother were considered Sons of God, both were literally Messiahs. Moses and Aaron combine the roles of king, priest and prophet. Later David was identified as the Great King and Moses took the single role of the prophet, but it is plain that, in leading the Israelites out of Egypt, his role was that of king as well as prophet.

Jochebed, Amram's wife was also his Aunt. This ties in with the practice of the Pharaohs whose title came through the female line. Thus they usually married their sisters to become king but could marry their mother's sister – their maternal aunt – or even their mother – to succeed to the throne. Plainly the Israelites led away from Egypt by Moses, a Messiah, were thoroughly Egyptianised and ruled by a Pharoah-like king, if not an actual dissident Pharoah. It seems the word Messiah, a Son of God, came into the Jewish religion from Egypt.

From the time of exile in Babylonia the word messiah took on the meaning of a God-sent saviour or deliverer. The Jewish concept was not of a divine Messiah: as the extract from the *Psalms of Solomon* makes clear, he was entirely human, though possessing God-given supernatural powers. Judaism had become strictly monotheistic – it had only one god and it was a heresy for Jews to think otherwise – even their Messiah could not be regarded as divine. A Jew proclaiming a Messiah a god at the time of Jesus would have been stoned for blasphemy. But it was no blasphemy to claim to be a Messiah, a man. Under the Romans most Jews felt they had suffered enough and were expecting a man of power backed by the supernatural might of God to lead the people to freedom. The idea of a saviour Messiah spurred Jewish nationalism. From 4 BC to 135 AD several Messiahs were proclaimed as the Jews yearned for an end to the trials and indignities of Roman rule. Each led an unsuccessful revolt and died.

Failure fertilised the growth of another concept, the suffering servant. The despised and rejected servant of God in *Isaiah* would suffer to redeem the world in a spiritual rather than physical sense. The suffering servant was a personification of the sufferings of the Jewish people rather than a model for their Messiah. But the Messiah had to be demonstrably of the highest morals as the moral judge of mankind. Possibly some Jews thought that suffering ensured great virtue and gave supernatural power. A suffering Messiah could have been part of God's plan to save the people. They expected the Messiah to suffer as the Jewish nation had. There is evidence of this in the *Dead Sea Scrolls*.

The contradiction of *Daniel* which pictured a glorious Messiah was resolved by the Messiah's glorious second coming when the world would end and the faithful would be saved. From this probably came the Christian idea of Christos meaning a divine redeemer, an incarnate God who deliberately suffers, dies and is resurrected to atone for the inherent sins of mankind. Certainly the importance of the suffering Messiah concept largely emerged out of the events of the intertestamental years rather than before – many scholars believe it only reached prominence as a justification of Christianity.

Most ordinary Jews, though, were fed up with suffering. They had incessantly been humiliated by foreign rulers with only the Maccabees providing any hope. Submission had got them nowhere. Gentle Jesus could not have fitted their preferred image – a warrior, a king David, a superman on the lines described in *Daniel*.

Jewish Sects

Hardly surprisingly in the chaos of the times, the Jews could not agree among themselves what they should do to help god in his aspirations for them. Pious Jews were set on obeying God's commandments to the letter but this led to sectarianism – the commandments were not always clear; interpretation was needed and with it came disagreement. Encouraged by the occupying forces Jews had split into several sects each believing its approach was the right one. The Christian gospels introduce us to some of them.

Particularly prominent in the gospels are the Pharisees who are depicted as the arch enemies of the Son of God. But other sects, the Sadducees, the Herodians, and the Zealots are mentioned with decreasing levels of interest. Indeed the Zealots are effectively not mentioned because they are introduced only as an appellation of one of the disciples, Simon the Zealot. Amazingly the Essenes, the keepers of the *Dead Sea Scrolls*, are not mentioned at all in the *New Testament* though they must have been an important influence on the lives of people living in small towns and villages such as those preferred by Jesus and his disciples. The Nazarenes were of course the sect considered to have been founded by Jesus, the hero of the gospel stories. As a sect they are mentioned once only in *Acts*.

In fact we have excellent descriptions of these sects from sources other than the *Bible*, particularly Josephus, the Jewish historian, who lived in these turbulent times. Josephus tells us the three main "philosophies" of the Jews are the Pharisees, Sadducees and Essenes. Though essentially these were religious groups, equally important to understanding them is their political dimension – their attitude to the invader. Religion and politics could not be separated for Jews at that time.

1. The Sadducees were wealthy families, mainly of priests, who were blatant collaborators, fearful of their position if there should be any unrest. The Boethusians of the Rabbinical literature were the family and descendants of one Boethus, the Egyptian, who had assumed the role of High Priest under Herod the Great. They might have been the Herodians of the gospels of Mark and Matthew, Herod having rebuilt the Jerusalem Temple, the source of their influence.
2. The Pharisees were not active collaborators in general but on several previous occasions they had invited foreign powers into Israel to quell civil war and they were unwilling to risk reprisals against Israel by

organising against Rome. However the Pharisees were not monolithic and the pragmatists were opposed by more nationalistic factions.

3. The Dead Sea Essenes were opposed to the invader and spent time preparing themselves for an apocalyptic bust-up but believed god would only support them if they were absolutely ritually pure, hence this became their main interest. Village Essenes had a similar apocalyptic outlook but lived more practical lives in the community at large. It is inconceivable that these latter communities did not have some impact on the events of the gospels. Here is another mystery – why are they not mentioned by the gospel writers?

Josephus in *Antiquities* adds a fourth sect of Jewish philosophy, but does not give it a name, merely saying it was founded by Judas the Galilaean and that it accepts Pharisaic notions but adding that they accept God only as their Lord. Scholars generally regard these men as Zealots, firebrands incensed by the invader and ready to join in armed struggle against them. The Sicarii were a branch of the Zealots whose aim was political assassination.

The Pharisees

Rabbinical literature depicts the Pharisees as just, humane and adaptable. "Well it would, wouldn't it?" you might say. After all, the Jewish religion that survived the destruction of Jerusalem and the Temple in 70 AD was the religion of the Pharisees. It metamorphosed into Rabbinical Judaism. But the tradition of the rabbis is confirmed by Josephus.

The Pharisees arose in the period of about 160 BC when the Jews were rebelling against the Seleucid Greeks. They opposed the imposed priesthood for political as well as religious reasons. They wanted to get rid of foreign oppressors and their agents and to return the priesthood to its simple function of being ritual officials in the Temple rather than political quislings. When the Jews did succeed in throwing off the foreigners it was to set up the Hasmonaean dynasty which combined the roles of High Priests and monarchs. Naturally the Pharisees' opposition continued. Thus the Pharisees opposed the oppressors, the sacrilegious and collaborationist Sadducees. But they were pragmatic. If they believed hostility was futile they would not advocate it.

The Pharisees accepted the *Torah* as inspired by God but, unlike the Sadducees, were not fundamentalists. They believed that the body of oral interpretation, carefully recorded by the scribes, was more immediate, pertinent and alive. They point out that the *Torah* itself says: "The Torah is not in Heaven". It is therefore not perfect and needs interpretation by men. This oral tradition was immensely flexible. The age of the Prophets had long gone so no one could claim to know God's will – it could be expressed through anyone. No one could be certain that their own interpretation was what God intended and so all views and interpretations were respected by all: humanity and understanding were built into the system. Perhaps this was just as well because the Pharisees were far from a homogeneous body. They certainly divided into a Left Wing and a Right Wing, and perhaps there were finer subdivisions. The famous disputes between the Rabbis Hillel and Shammai in the century before the crucifixion testify to this.

In matters of law where a clear cut decision was needed, a vote was taken and dissenting rabbis were obliged to hold to the view of the majority until the matter was raised again. A change of vote did not perturb the assembly because changes of circumstances were recognised as part of life – decisions would change as the circumstances did. Dissenting views as well as majority decisions were recorded for future reference thus becoming akin to precedent so that when changes occurred a new generation of scholars could refer back to the dissenting views of their predecessors. Decisions were not divine but human and were therefore fallible – rejected views might turn out to be more correct. This was how God wanted it: the work required in considering, reasoning and interpreting was necessary to the seeking of truth:

According to the effort is the reward.

The conclusion is that Pharisees had no need to quarrel when they disagreed, nor to persecute dissenters. Disciplinary action only came when someone refused to abide by the majority decision, and even then on matters of the Law not on matters of theology. Punishment was simply a period of ostracism. Different views on the Messiah could be and were voiced perfectly acceptably including the one that there could be no Messiah because he had already been manifest as the virtuous king, Hezekiah. The Pharisees *did* regard as heretical refusal to accept oral law.

Pharisee sages came from all levels of society including the poorest, unlike the hereditary priesthood. They were not paid but, like Jesus the carpenter of the *Bible*, had to develop a practical skill with which to earn a living. They were admired for their fairness as judges of the Law, their knowledge and their originality of expression in preaching. Though they practised Temple worship, the centre of their lives was the synagogue.

The sages and later, the rabbis, thought of themselves as heirs to the prophets, who also came from the people rather than from dynasties, and especially Moses, though they claimed no prophetic abilities themselves. Prophecy had ceased with the biblical prophets and would start again only with the age of the Messiah. Theirs was an interpretive and analytical role not a sacerdotal one – that was the priests' role. The Pharisees regarded the priests only as functionaries with no authority to speak on the Law or religion. The sages were progressive whilst the Sadducees were conservative.

The Sadducees

The Sadducees on the other hand followed the priests. The Sadducees were families of vast wealth and power and their hangers on. They allied with the topmost priesthood and the ruling power to retain their wealth: they were collaborators. The Romans appointed the High Priest as did Herod before them. Failing to understand the diffuse nature of Judaism, Romans thought that control of the Temple would control the people. But the separation of the sacerdotal and the teaching functions in Judaism is one reason why it has been able to survive – destruction of the ceremonial centre never affected the religion as a whole.

Sadducees were fundamentalists needing no interpretation of the *Bible* and therefore no scholars: atonement through Temple ritual was sufficient. Yet their tradition stemmed only from the time of the successors of Alexander the Great. The priesthood was properly the function of the caste descended from Aaron, Moses's brother, but under Alexander's successors, the Ptolemies, the priestly line was broken. The High Priests were established as agents of foreign rule – and so they remained under the Romans. Many Jews were distressed by the situation but continued to tolerate it believing it to be god's will. Others such as the Essenes, to judge by the *Dead Sea Scrolls*, were training a pure priesthood in waiting ready to replace the unclean upstarts they considered ran the Temple. In the meantime the Chief Priests and their Sadducaean supporters serviced the Temple financed by supposedly voluntary tithes that were often extorted.

The two sects disagreed over the resurrection of the dead, the Sadducees denied it and the Pharisees accepted it. In the Christian *New Testament* the Son of God takes the view of the Pharisees but the Essenes too believed in resurrection.

The Essenes

Why are the gospels silent about the Essenes and the Zealots, though they introduce us to the Pharisees, the Sadducees and the Herodians? Could it be that the people at the centre of the story were Essenes? Neither Paul nor any of the other writers of epistles in the *New Testament* mentions the Essenes – they might as well have not existed. But we know they did. Three writers from the first century AD describe the Essenes – Pliny, Josephus and Philo. We now also have the evidence of the excavations at Qumran and the *Dead Sea Scrolls* – but a clear understanding of the Essenes still eludes us.

Pliny is describing the region around the Dead Sea and says that on the western shore, where they had been for thousands of centuries, live the Essenes, a solitary people who renounce women and money. They maintain their numbers by accepting those driven by the vicissitudes of fortune and weariness of life. "Below" them are the ashes of Engedi and "beyond" is the fortress of Masada. If the words "below" and "beyond" imply direction towards the south then the

Essenes lived at the most northerly of the three sites mentioned. Indeed there is a ruin in just that position that could have been the Essene's centre: it is at Qumran. If Pliny indicated relative altitude when he wrote "below", the Essene community was in the hills behind Engedi from the Dead Sea but there is no sign of any such community there.

Pliny's "thousands of centuries" is an exaggeration but one which might suggest an association between this community and a much older one. Josephus, who gives us the most complete account of the Essenes, puts the rise of the community in the previous century, during the first century BC. Josephus suggests he was initiated into the order so one assumes he knows what he is talking about. He writes that the Essenes, all Jews by birth, were a closely knit brotherhood which had something in common with the Pythagoreans. There were about 4000 of them.

They regarded pleasure as evil and disciplined themselves in continence and self control. They did not marry but propagated the sect by adopting other people's children. Not that they were against marriage in principle – they realised it was necessary for the continuation of mankind – but they felt that women were wanton and unfaithful. Josephus goes on to say that there is another order of Essenes, the village Essenes, who differ in accepting marriage though maintaining strict rules about intercourse. The Essenes were Zadokites, naming themselves after Zadok the priest, suggesting they were a dissident priestly order. Objecting to the debasement of the Temple and the venality of the Sadducees, they had left them to adopt a largely frugal and monastic life uncorrupted by the scandal of collaboration. Their purpose was to keep themselves ritually pure because they were expecting the apocalypse when God would endow a Messiah to purge and judge the world.

The Zealots

The Zealots, first mentioned by Josephus as the fighters against the Romans in the Jewish rebellion of 66-73 AD, apparently based themselves on the example of Phinehas whose zeal for the Law turned God's wrath from the Israelites in *Numbers* 25:10-13. A copycat incident led to the outlawing of the Maccabees in the second century BC. Scholars assume Zealotry essentially stems from then. Judas of Galilee and a Pharisee, Sadduc, according to Josephus, combined to resist the numbering of the people by the Romans when they conducted their census of 6 AD. Since the Essenes called themselves "the Sons of Zadok", this association of Galilaean and Zadok in the founding of the Zealots should be noted. (Sadduc and Zadok seem to be the same word varyingly rendered in our alphabet.) Their "zeal for the Law of Moses" and veneration of the *Torah* led them to hate foreigners, whence their leading role in the war against the Romans. They were of major significance in Palestine during the whole of the period of the gospels so the single reference to them (Simon, the Zealot) looks suspicious. However, Josephus often uses the word "robber" as equivalent to "zealot". *John* describes Barabbas as a robber.

The failure of the gospels to mention either the Zealots or the Essenes while mentioning the other Jewish parties suggests that Essenes and Zealots have deliberately been left out of the story. Is it because the Nazarenes were a branch of the Essenes or the Zealots? Hyppolytus, writing about 230 AD, confirms that the Zealots were indeed a branch of the Essenes. Are the gospels narrating, in a distorted or coded way, a sequence of Zealot incidents! The Zealot leader – none other than Barabbas!

A Revolution in Jerusalem

The Rebel

Uprisings had been occurring with alarming regularity. The gospels tell us there had just been one in Jerusalem at the time of Jesus's crucifixion. The freedom fighter specifically mentioned was Jesus Barabbas. Yet it was the Christian god, gentle Jesus, who was charged with treason! The conclusion is forced. Jesus was a freedom fighter leading a revolution against the Roman occupiers of Judaea, just as Reimarus pointed out two hundred years ago. This was why Jesus was arrested by the authorities. No other interpretation even of the evidence in the gospels makes sense.

The evidence of the gospels is this:

- the authorities viewed Jesus with suspicion for gathering large crowds which they regarded as potentially subversive;
- Jesus had strong associations with Galilee, a place which had a reputation for breeding rebels;
- many of Jesus's followers sound, from their nicknames, more like men of violence than men of peace;
- Jesus's supporters greeted him openly as king as he entered Jerusalem;
- An insurrection had occurred in which men had died;
- Jesus was charged, tried and crucified as a rival to Caesar's rule in Palestine, claiming to be the king of the Jews, and he chose not to deny these charges unequivocally at his trial.

The Suspicions of the Authorities

Control of Judaea was vested by the Emperor of Rome in Prefects and later Procurators who he appointed to govern the province on his behalf. They had to report to him all significant events that occurred. Imperial policy centred on raising revenue through taxation and, to do so effectively, maintaining peace, the Pax Romani. So a governor's duties included keeping law and order and raising taxes. Since they were unpaid free lance agents, governors had to obtain their own income out of local revenue. By milking the province to get rich they created their own source of unrest. They had a small garrison of about 3000 soldiers based at Caesarea on the coast but some were deployed in Jerusalem especially when it was crowded with pilgrims at the Passover.

The governors left non-political matters to a council of senior Jews called the Sanhedrin. The principle force in it was the High Priest and his party of Sadducees and they controlled the Temple Guard which had limited powers. The death sentence for purely civil matters could only be declared by the Roman Governor. The Sanhedrin could possibly declare a sentence of stoning for a religious misdemeanor, but, if so, it rarely did. The Romans would have disapproved of and, most probably never allowed, a concession which could have been used by the national authorities against collaborators.

Some of the Sanhedrin shared with the Romans a distaste for rebel movements – they posed a threat to the whole Jewish nation from Roman reprisals. Centuries before the Romans had razed under the plough the great city of Cathage, an enemy of Rome. Later they were to raze Jerusalem. There was reason for Jews to worry if Rome became incensed. Josephus says that Herod Antipas killed John the Baptist, not because of the plottings of his wife, but because he saw a threat of an uprising in the large crowds that John was attracting. Herod's fear of the multitude is declared in *Matthew* (14:5) but as a reason for *not* killing John, though this fear did not deter him from killing John when Salome requested it. Repeatedly in *Mark*, *Luke* and *Acts* the fear of the authorities for the people is expressed. In *John* 18:14, the High Priest, Caiaphas, directly expresses the fears of the rulers of the Jews when he says it is expedient that one man should die for the people. A general outbreak of rebellion would bring retribution on the Jews by the Romans. If it could be nipped in the bud by disposing of the leader of the insurgents, the state would be preserved.

Galilaeans

At the time of Christ, Galilee was ruled by a Tetrarch, a Roman title for a minor king. Antipas (4 BC – 39 AD) was a son of Herod the Great. But from 6 AD, when Antipas's brother, Archelaus, ruler of Judaea, was banished to Gaul, Judaea was ruled directly from Rome under a Prefect, a Roman governor. Galilee was a land of fertile soil and industrious people: it exported olive oil and had a thriving fishery on the Sea of Galilee. It was wealthy and well populated, though many people had been impoverished by being turned off their land to become day labourers and resentment was high.

The sayings of Jesus in the gospels reflect a rural background in agriculture and fishing; Galilaean city life hardly figures in them. Sepphoris, the main city in Galilee, is never mentioned in the gospels even though it was only four miles from Nazareth. Tiberias is hardly mentioned even though it was a magnificent new town built in honour of the reigning Emperor. The local town that *is* mentioned is Capernaum, a custom post which was little more than a village. Indeed Josephus described it merely as "a highly fertilising spring".

The regional accent of Galilaeans was strong and their gutturals almost disappeared making it difficult to distinguish certain words. Lazarus (Lazar), for example, is the Galilaean dialect pronunciation of Eleazar. In the *New Testament*, Peter is recognised by his accent as being a follower of Jesus (Mt 26:73). Many in the more southerly state of Judaea saw native Galilaeans as ignoramuses or clowns.

Galilaeans' ignorance or neglect of the Jewish laws of purity and decorum also offended devout Jews in Judaea. Even eminent Galilaean rabbis were not free of criticism. Galilee in gospel times was almost surrounded by pagan countries. Indeed it had been pagan itself not long before. The victory of the Hasmonaean king, Aristobulus I, over Iturea, and his threat to the Galilaeans that they should become circumcised and live according to Jewish Law or be dispersed, made Galilee a Jewish province about 100 BC. Anyone who had been forcibly converted could hardly have been the most devout Jews and a certain tradition of laxity must have emerged from them, and persevered even when their descendants had become otherwise Judaised.

By the time of Jesus, Galilaeans regarded themselves as thoroughly Jewish, if somewhat unorthodox, but their southern co-religionists were snooty about them. Judaeans would call the northerners "peasants" not primarily because that is what they were but because they were thought to be ignorant. In the *New Testament* (Jn 7:14) the Jerusalem crowd whisper among themselves, "Surely the Messiah is not to come from Galilee?" and when Nicodemus, a Pharisee, defends Jesus to the Chief Priests and Pharisees, they say, "Are you a Galilaean too?...Prophets do not come from Galilee". Jesus was just what the Jews of Judea expected of a Galilaean: he kept company with publicans and whores; he seemed to deride Levitical purity; he did not avoid defilement through contact with a corpse. Being a Galilaean, in practice, he seemed to flout the Mosaic purity laws.

The Pharisee Party had little support in the North. The only first century rabbi known to be a northerner was actually called "the Galilaean" suggesting that it was unusual. In *Mark*, Pharisees in conflict with Jesus are twice described as visitors to Galilee. Josephus specified that the Pharisees were influential in the cities, leading one to infer that they had little influence in the countryside. Thus, beside the political suspicion of Jesus, there were also some religious doubts and the snobbery of urban sophisticates toward rural simpletons.

Though, under Antipas, Galilee was generally peaceful, it was the source of much of the Jewish rebelliousness against Rome. To be a Galilaean was synonymous with being an agitator and the Herodian and Roman authorities often mistrusted them as potential rebels. Galilaeans were even quarrelsome among themselves according to Rabbinical sources. Galilaeans were linked with Jewish nationalism from the time that the brigand, Ezekias, was executed in 47 BC. Judas, considered the founder of the Zealots, was referred to as Judas of Galilee. He and his disciples broke into the king's arsenal in 4 BC and instituted a reign of terror in the region. When Roman rule was declared in Judaea after the banishment of Archelaus, a census was announced to assess the population for taxes. It was carried out by Quirinius, the Legate of the Roman Province of Syria, which included Judaea, in 6 to 7 AD. The followers of Judas believed the only master of the Jews was God. It was improper to pay taxes to a foreign god – the Emperors were beginning to claim divinity. Furthermore the Law of Moses forbade not only foreign rulers, it forbade numbering the people. For some this was the final straw. Judas and his followers urged the Jews not to pay taxes to Rome, and eventually rebelled. Thus it was that Judas of Galilee teamed up with Sadduc to form a religious and political movement of fanatical nationalists.

Josephus in Book 18 of *Antiquities of the Jews* describes the philosophy founded by Judas of Galilee as the "fourth sect of Jewish philosophy" but leaves it to us to deduce he means the Zealots. As followers of Judas of Galilee it would have been quite logical to call them Galilaeans and that is the approach of Rev. Matthew Black writing in *Peake's Commentary on the Bible*. Josephus tells us Galilaeans endured pain with resolution, were "ready to suffer any manner of death" and they put honour before wealth. They believed:

> *God would not otherwise be assisting to them, than upon their joining with one another in such counsels as might be successful, and for their own advantage; and this especially if they would set about great exploits, and not grow weary in executing the same.*

In other words God helps those who help themselves through daring deeds and persistence.

To what extent the sect of the Galilaeans was Pharisaic as Josephus maintains is a moot point. Hyppolytus believed the Zealots were Essenes. In the *Jewish War* Josephus tells us that Judas of Galilee was a teacher of a peculiar sect of his own then proceeds to describe at length the Essenes, a hint perhaps that the one was a branch of the other. The word from which we get "Pharisee" means "separated", a description which would apply perfectly to the Essenes. So it is conceivable that Josephus wrote in Aramaic "the notions of the Separated Ones" meaning the Essenes but his amanuensis mistook him to mean the Pharisees. His description of Judas's ally, Sadduc, as a Pharisee in the same chapter seems to repeat the error. But whether Pharisees or Essenes were nearest to the Galilaeans' general outlook, they added their own particular beliefs:

- having an inviolable attachment to liberty;
- holding God to be their only ruler and Lord;
- not calling any man Lord even though threatened with death or torture.

Judas's Galilaeans became very large and active especially among the young who "were zealous for it". Josephus blamed them for the troubles of the Jews leading up to the Jewish War, saying

> *The nation was infected with this doctrine to an incredible degree and it had a great many followers, filled our civil governments with tumults and laid the foundations of our future miseries.*

Many people, some of whom must have had allegiance to one or other of the other Jewish sects became attracted to the Galilaean sect as the troubles progressed. It had then factionalised internally. Ultimately, as far as Josephus was concerned, the Zealots became gangsters, killing for personal gain, killing Jews rather than gentiles and fighting amongst each other. And so it transposed, like the Mafia, from a liberation movement into gangs of criminals. Zealots indeed became robbers.

Judas of Galilee and his family nevertheless commanded wide respect for later we find his sons also leading rebellions against Roman rule. Tiberius Julius Alexander, a Romanised Jew, Procurator of Judaea from 46-48 AD and the nephew of Philo of Alexandria, crucified two of them, Jacob and Simon. A third son, Menehem, captured the stronghold of Masada from the Romans but subsequently died in faction fighting among the rebels. Eleazar, a nephew of Menehem, with only a few hundred zealots, held Masada against the Romans for three years after the fall of Jerusalem in 70 AD. John of Gischala, also a Galilaean, was another leader of the Jewish revolt of 66 AD.

Jesus's Followers

Judas of Galilee and his followers were barjonim, ones who live on the outside. We would say guerrillas or an underground movement. Barjonim and Zealots were effectively synonyms. The barjonim avoided the towns, preferring wilderness and mountains, and only visiting towns and villages to commit robberies or political murder.

The evangelist, Mark, wrote his gospel at about the time of the Roman triumph in 71 AD when the captured leader of the Jewish Zealots was led in chains through the streets of Rome. Naturally neither Jews in general nor Zealots in particular were popular and Mark was faced with a few problems. Describing the Apostle Simon, he deliberately uses the obscure Aramaic expression, the Cananaean, without explaining it, though Mark normally explains Aramaic words for the benefit of his gentile readers. Luke, writing at least ten years later when feelings were running less high, openly uses the Greek equivalent, understood by all – the Apostle is Simon the Zealot!

Other words are disguised by the gospel writers. For example there is another strange coincidence, like that of Barabbas. When Jesus reveals to Simon Peter his messiahship in *Matthew* 16:17, he calls him Simon Bar-jona as if Bar-jona were Simon's surname. In *John* (Jn 21:15) this is rendered as bar Jonah, as if it were a patronymic, Son of Jonah. It is beyond a coincidence that Barjona as we saw above is a guerrilla or extremist. What was originally intended? Furthermore the nickname, Peter, in Aramaic – Cephas, given to Simon means "rock". Today we would call him "Rocky". Then as now it signified a tough guy. How tough? Well later in the story he slices off a man's ear and later still murders a man and a woman for holding back money. He seems pretty ruthless.

Judas is named as Judas Iscariot, said to mean "of Kerioth" but no such place seems to have existed at the time, though there had once been a town Kiriathim in Moab across the Dead Sea. The word "Sicarii" meaning Knifemen seems more identifiable with Iscariot. Judas would therefore have been a member of the assassins branch of the Zealots. However, a Syrian word Skariot meaning "I shall deliver up" could be an equally appropriate root. Were the Sikari the Deliverers of Israel, a branch of the Zealots or even an alternative name for them? The *Talmud* names the leader of the barjonim in Jerusalem during the siege as Abbas Sikari, implying that the Knifemen or Deliverers were closely allied to, or a branch of, the Zealots.

The two "Sons of Thunder", John and James, already sound menacing enough but the expression, "Boanerges", a meaningless word, is probably "bene reges" meaning "Sons of Tumult" or "bene regaz" meaning "Sons of Wrath". Or another reading is "Sons of the Wild Ox", which signifies untameable wildness according to *Proverbs*. Patently these were not boy scouts. One suspects that the word "Boanerges" only survives because in his original gospel Mark used it without translation like the word "cananaean" used of Simon the Zealot. A few years later an editor felt able to explain it and so it comes down to us today – serving no purpose except as a clue to the nature of the Nazarene band. Finally, five of the Apostles had previously been with John the Baptist. According to his disciple, Mark, John the Baptist taught that to seek God people had to "leave the towns". He was urging them to become barjonim! It has been suggested that the Sadduc who teamed up with Judas of Galilee to form the Zealots was none other than John the Baptist.

Is all of this simply to be regarded as trivial coincidence? Largely from the gospels themselves we learn that between five and ten of gentle Jesus's twelve leading disciples were tough guys. Can anyone seriously deny that the band of Jesus the Nazarene sound more like the band of Jesus Barabbas, the Zealot?

The Crowd Acclaims Jesus as a King

When Jesus entered Jerusalem the crowd hailed him as a king:

> *Blessed is the King that cometh,*

wrote Luke (19:38).

> *Blessed is the kingdom that cometh, the kingdom of our father, David,*

wrote Mark (11:9). And Matthew (21:9) wrote:

> *Hosannah to the Son of David,*

as though the non-existent word "hosannah" meant something like "greetings" or "three cheers". The crowd actually shouted "osanna", an Aramaic word which means "free us". The crowd was actually calling: "Osanna, Son of David" – "Free us, Son of David". The correct expression was used in the Gospel of the Hebrews, an Aramaic version of *Matthew*, and in the *Nazarene Gospel* as Jerome writing in the latter part of the fourth century tells us.

On entering Jerusalem, the gospels tell us, Jesus is immensely popular. The Pharisees observe (Jn 12:19):

> *Look, the world has gone after him.*

He is widely acclaimed as a king, the heir to the throne of David and now Jesus does not refute these acclamations as he had done earlier, according to the gospel writers.

Beginning the descent from the Mount of Olives we find people shouting (*Luke* 19:38):

> *Blessed is the king that cometh in the name of the Lord!*

Even after the crucifixion the hopes of the disciples are expressed (Lk 24:21) in the same terms:

> *We had hoped that it was he who would deliver Israel,*

and meeting the resurrected Jesus they ask (*Acts* 1:6):

> *Lord, will you at this time restore the kingdom of Israel.*

There are other clues to Jesus's kingship in the gospels but rather more subtle ones. Jesus is described often in the synoptic gospels as teaching "as one having authority". We get the impression it means he knew what he was talking about. But reference to *Ecclesiastes* 8:4 gives the true meaning of this odd sounding phrase:

> *the king's word hath authority; and who may say unto him,*
> *What doest thou?*

Similarly the priests in the Temple ask Jesus by whose authority he had overthrown the tables, inviting him to admit he is a king. These passages are simply saying that people recognised Jesus as being a king according to the *Scriptures*. Those that had ears to hear would understand!

Explaining to the Apostles how they should pray, Jesus tells them in *Matthew* and *Luke* to say the Lord's prayer. It includes the lines :

> *Thy kingdom come. Thy will be done in earth, as it is in*
> *Heaven.*

The prayer was for God to inaugurate the messianic age of God's kingdom on earth. It clearly says "...in earth" yet the argument of the gospel writers is that the kingdom referred to is not of this world but in Heaven, and *John* has Jesus himself saying so (Jn 18:36). Jesus's followers did not understand this because they were stupid. And, indeed, the gospel writers go to some trouble to depict the Apostles as complete morons even though they had been personally selected by Jesus. This is manifest rubbish. We can be sure that the Apostles, as well as the Jerusalem throng, knew exactly what kingdom Jesus meant. And the Christian interpretation is plainly refuted in the principal prayer of Christendom.

All of the expectations of the Jerusalem crowds were of a restored Jewish kingdom, a new kingdom of David and Solomon on earth, a Jewish state strong enough to expel the invaders and establish a new world order. We know this because it is exactly what Jews expected of their Messiah as described in the extended quotations from the Psalms of Solomon above.

Jewish religion led Jews to believe that they were God's "Chosen People", having a special role in his plans and under his care. Anointment of ancient Jewish Kings made them God's appointed ruler. The Messiah of the Jews was an ideal Jewish king sent by God and those anointed as kings or priests became Sons of God. The ritual of anointing required the priest, acting as God's agent, to acknowledge his Son explicitly. At his baptism and Transfiguration, Jesus becomes a "Son of God" (and therefore a king or a priest) when "God" (the acting priest) announces (Mk 1:11, 9:7; Mt 3:17, 17:5; Lk 3:22, 9:35):

> *Thou art my beloved Son, in thee I am well pleased.*

The gospel writers are not lying when they say God spoke these words. God had spoken them – but through his earthly agent – just as today he speaks through books written by men! These ceremonies were effectively coronations.

The gospels offer little evidence that Jesus claimed to be a divine redeemer, the Christian idea of a Messiah, rather than a human saviour. They are consistent with Jesus, a Jew, initially denying – but later accepting – the appellation Messiah, convinced he had been chosen by God to prepare The Chosen People for the kingdom to come, God's kingdom on earth, and to lead them into it. As a Jew, he could have had no illusions about being a god or of being a divine world redeemer, nor would he have had any intentions of forming a new religion. These blasphemous thoughts were given to him later by the founders of the Christian church.

The Insurrection

In *Luke* 23:40 one of the "thieves" crucified alongside Jesus, rebuking the other, says they are all in the "same condemnation" implying they had all been found guilty of the same crimes at the same trial. Of course they were not "thieves" any more than Barabbas was simply a "robber". This is a cover up, the best rendering of the word being terrorists or rebels! They were members of Jesus's rebel gang.

The gospels admit that Jesus was not as peaceful as Christians like to make out but do so as quietly as possible. In *Matthew* 10:34 Jesus addressing his followers says:

> *Think not I came to send peace on the earth: I came not to send peace but a sword.*

Contrasted with peace, sword here plainly means conflict in the struggle for the coming kingdom and subsequently the judgement of God. In *Luke* Jesus says he would cast fire on the earth and that the kingdom of God had to be entered violently. This was certainly not a pacifist talking. But, in *Luke*, a later gospel than *Matthew*, "sword" is replaced by "division". The writer or an editor had realised the words did not match the desired image!

Luke 22:36 also has Biblical commentaries thrashing around in discomfort because gentle Jesus, the pacifist Son of God, urges his followers to buy arms – though two swords turn out to be enough! This looks like a prime example of a difficult passage for Christians being toned down by Christian editors. Both instances belie the gentle Jesus image revealing instead some of the truth hovering beneath the extant text.

Elsewhere in *Luke* (11:50) Jesus preaches in an impassioned speech that the blood of all the prophets which was shed from the foundation of the world, may be required of this generation. This sounds like Shakespeare's Henry V rallying his troops, though supposedly spoken to Pharisees. Is it coincidence that Luke is soon writing (Lk 13:1) of Pilate's troops mixing Galilaean's blood with their sacrifices, and then of the death of many when the Tower of Siloam collapsed (Lk 13:4)? Though misleadingly placed in the gospel, these sounds like tantalising references to a battle.

Had Pilate's troops counter attacked and slaughtered Galilaeans in the Temple while they were offering sacrifices? Were those killed when the Tower of Siloam fell on them resisting an attack by Pilate's soldiers using battering rams? Since Roman troops were normally housed in the Antonia fortress adjacent to the Temple and would therefore have easy access to the Temple and the city it is possible that the Jerusalem garrison had been overpowered, or had strategically withdrawn, and the insurgents had been attacked by a stronger force sent from Caesarea on the coast. Neither of these incidents are mentioned in the extant works of historians of the time.

After the Roman counter attack when the Galilaeans were killed, the Temple was lost and the Tower of Siloam had collapsed, Jesus withdrew to take a meal with his closest associates similar to the messianic meal of the Essenes. We know it as the Last Supper. They had been beaten but were not yet ready to surrender. Jesus repeatedly urges the disciples to repent, obviously believing still that God would intervene if they were all sufficiently pure of spirit. They went, still armed, to the Mount of Olives overlooking the city to wait for God's miracle, prophesied in *Zechariah* 14:4. Jesus Barabbas and his band had played their part and had temporarily freed the Holy City from its enemies. Now it was up to God to complete the task as he had promised. Barabbas wants his men to wait and watch for the signs of the miracle but they are exhausted.

The miracle never comes but instead soldiers, a detachment of Romans or some of the Temple Guard, arrive to capture him. God had forsaken him and the Jews.

Lest anyone should doubt that the followers of Jesus had been involved in bloody rebellion in which many had died, let them turn to the *Acts of the Apostles* (6:1-3) where the surviving Nazarenes have to appoint as many as seven men to ensure that no "widows were neglected in the daily ministration". Did you ever wonder why the Nazarenes had to make special provision for widows just after Jesus's crucifixion?

Jewish Charges

In Palestine, the years in which Christianity was founded were totally anarchic. Uprisings or tumults were commonplace, Messiahs were commonplace and hatred of the Romans was almost universal among ordinary Jews. Most of the *New Testament* was written during or just after this chaotic period and the authors plainly knew the true circumstances. Yet the books of the *New Testament* try to give an impression of this rustic idyll inhabited by gormless yokels led by a mendicant pacifist for whom overthrowing a table is a violent act, where the Roman administrator is a just and competent judge and where the Jews are cowardly and treacherous.

"And so they were," you might say. "Perhaps Pilate was cruel, and perhaps Jesus was not quite as pacifist as the later Christians made out, but it was the Jews who betrayed him and set him before Pilate because Jesus taught a new religion which the Jews thought was blasphemous."

The trouble is it is not true. All of it is concocted!

Who were these "Jews" anyway. Don't forget Jesus, himself a Jew, had such a following of Jews when he entered Jerusalem that the priests thought the whole world followed him. The *New Testament* distinguishes the "Jews" because when it was written the Christians did not want to be associated with Jews. Gospel writers wanted to impress that their martyred god was hated by the Jews.

In some places the writers are more specific, referring to Pharisees rather than "Jews". The gospels portray the Pharisees as the main opponents of Jesus. He calls them hypocrites and oppressors. They try to trick him into blasphemous statements or into false teaching but Jesus always gets the better of them. The gospels imply that the Pharisees, aiming to rid themselves of his criticisms, brought various religious accusations against him. Yet an objective scrutiny shows that the Pharisees could not have brought these religious charges. They were not valid charges!

Claiming to be the Messiah, a God

If Jesus claimed to be the Messiah, was he committing a blasphemy? The answer is "no" because only a claim to be God was blasphemous and, unlike Christians, the Jews did not regard the Messiah as an aspect or a title of God. The Messiah was a claimant to the throne of Israel and was, therefore, a political threat to the Romans – the claim was a political crime not a religious one, especially in view of the Jews' reputation as rebels constantly hankering after a warrior Messiah to save them from their oppressors.

Other claimants to Messiahship were not accused of blasphemy whether Judas of Galilee, before Jesus, or Bar Kosiba, after Jesus, both militant rebels, or Theudas or "the Egyptian" mentioned in the *New Testament*, who would save the Jews with a miracle from God.

The Messiah's aim might have been to liberate Israel from foreign occupation or to inaugurate an era of peace for the whole world – perhaps both. But these were not blasphemous ideas. Later, Christians thought Christ, Greek for Messiah, was a divine title and that Jesus was claiming divinity. That would have been blasphemous – but Jesus made no claim to divinity. That Jesus kept his claim to divinity secret, "the Messianic Secret", is a later idea. On the other hand, knowing what the Roman attitude was to royal claimants, Jesus must have preferred not to attract premature attention from the authorities by initially refusing to accept acclamation from the multitudes.

In the synoptic gospels, note, it was the High Priest who accused Jesus of blasphemy not the Pharisees, tying in with his roles, under the Romans, of magistrate and policeman because the title was a danger to his own position as well as his Roman masters. The gospel editors played down the political implications of Messiahship so as not to spoil their message: Romans – good; Jews – bad; Jesus, a divine innocent – yes; Jesus, a threat to Caesar – no.

Threatening to Destroy the Temple

At the hearing a charge was brought, not by Pharisees, that Jesus had threatened to destroy the Temple, the House of God. That sounds fairly blasphemous! The gospel of *John* (Jn 2:19) records that Jesus had said:

> *Destroy this Temple and in three days I will raise it up,*

meaning, *John* maintains, the "temple of his body" which he would raise up after three days – a prediction of his resurrection. The Jews deliberately misunderstood him to get him crucified.

Now the Temple was built by Herod the Great, the hated foreign king. Though many Jews continued to accept the ritual of the Temple they did not approve of this particular one, built by an Idumaean, or its functionaries, the collaborating priestly caste. The Temple of Herod would not have been tolerated by any credible Messiah, nor would the Jews have expected it to continue to exist in the messianic age. To destroy it and rebuild it is what any Messiah would promise. So such a threat was the sort of promise that messianic Jews would have liked to hear. Since it implied defiance of the state it represented the view of the nationalists.

If Jesus had said, "Destroy this temple and in three days I will raise it up," he meant the collaborationist Temple organisation controlled by the Boethusians and the Sadducees and not the bricks and mortar of the Temple. He was simply saying that he could replace the unpopular priesthood with an acceptable alternative by the end of the Passover weekend. In short he had an alternative priesthood at the ready. The priests Jesus had in mind must surely have been members of the Qumran Community, guardians of the *Dead Sea Scrolls*, who maintained themselves specifically as an alternative priesthood. The implication is that Jesus had links with the Essenes. If he had, then the threat to the Chief Priests would be even more transparent and their attitude toward Jesus thoroughly explicable.

Though most Pharisees would not object to Jesus's words, the Sadducaean priesthood could not be expected to take them lying down. They feared a direct threat to their position of power – and with justification. At a later date the Sicarii murdered a High Priest and, during the Jewish War, the rebels actually did appoint one of their own.

The charge of making the threat to the Temple was therefore again a political threat – this time to the ruling Jewish caste. No blasphemy was incurred.

Abrogating the Law of Moses

The gospels relate that Jesus rejected the old Hamurabi principle of an-eye-for-an-eye, which the Pharisees accepted, and replaced it with that of "turning the other cheek" when one suffered a wrong. In fact the Pharisees did not literally approve of an-eye-for-an-eye. Remember the Pharisees believed in interpretation not fundamentalism. They made no virtue of tearing out eyes. They took an-eye-for-an-eye to be a law of equivalence for compensation of wrongs. It gave a measure of the recompense needed when someone had suffered an injury. But whatever rights the principle gave anyone, the Pharisees favoured a merciful response. Effectively they also advocated the principle of "turning the other cheek". A man who had suffered a theft by a desperate man might, in mercy, wish to waive the compensation to which he was entitled under the Law. He could "turn the other cheek" by refusing compensation to which he was entitled. But he would defend another man's right to insist upon such recompense before the Law. To turn the other cheek as a manifestation of God's love invited others to do the same but it did not require them to do so.

What of the food laws? Scholars accept that the declaration of all food as clean in *Mark* 7:19 is a later addition, and it is contradicted by the *New Testament* itself in other books. In *Matthew* 5:17-19 Jesus is emphatic that he had not come to destroy the Law but to fulfil it. And not just its general principles but each "jot and tittle". It is certain that Jesus is referring to the laws of Moses because he mentions it in conjunction with "the prophets" showing that he meant the teachings of the *Old Testament*. If not a "jot or tittle" could be omitted, then the food laws too had to be obeyed. In the later gospel of *Luke* (16:16-17) the contradiction had been realised and the editor pretends it is sarcasm.

Inasmuch as Christians considered rejection of the Law of Moses a crucial issue, Jesus's supposed teaching on it was remarkably slow to sink in. That was because the disciples themselves were slow according to Christian apologists! Peter for example was totally bemused by it all. In *Acts* 10:14 some time after the death of Jesus, Peter says he had *never* eaten anything that was unclean. It is a vision from God that tells him that formerly unclean items are now clean, not the teaching of Jesus. But according to the *New Testament* he changes his mind more than once. James the Just, the brother of Jesus and leader of the church after Jesus's death, never accepted the Law had been rejected. He rebuked Paul for ignoring the Law and made him do penance.

Jesus, as a Galilaean, might have been lax in his own adherence to the strictest interpretation of the Law. He might also have made a genuine point about the relative merits of purity of spirit and ritual purity. But he did not reject the Law of Moses. The truth is that the abrogation of the Mosaic Law was not a novelty of Jesus but of the evangelist, Paul, so that he could recruit gentiles.

Breaking the Sabbath

The *New Testament* maintains that the main disagreement between Jesus and the Pharisees was Jesus's healing on the Sabbath. The Pharisees are depicted as holding so strongly to the Sabbath that even healing was forbidden. *John* (7:23) has Jesus defending Sabbath healing while *Mark* (3:6) and *Matthew* (12:14) have the Pharisees plotting against Jesus because they were so offended by his healing on the Sabbath.

Mark (2:23-28) relates an incident when the disciples pluck corn on the Sabbath only to invite the criticism of the Pharisees. Jesus replies,

> *The Sabbath is made for man not man for the Sabbath.*

Now the Pharisees *did* forbid labour on the Sabbath, but tempered the rule with exceptions. Thus they allowed healing on the Sabbath when human life was at risk. In justification they used the same arguments as Jesus and even the same expression as Jesus. Jesus's reply was simply a well known maxim of the Pharisees.

In the substance of his answer to the Pharisaic critics in the gospel, Jesus quotes from scripture the instance when king David and his men ate consecrated bread from the Temple – something only priests were allowed to do. King David and his men, on that occasion, were fleeing from king Saul – they were tired and hungry. Now when life is at stake it is no sin to devour the Temple shewbread. The implication of Jesus choosing this particular quotation from scripture was that Jesus and his men were in an equivalent situation – they also were starving. One concludes that this was no peaceful stroll in the cornfields on a balmy summer day. An exhausted group of refugees took the only sustenance at hand. The inference is they were fleeing Herod Antipas and were justified, in Pharisaic interpretation of the Law, to pluck corn as food on a Sabbath because life was at stake.

Then, as now, taking someone else's corn without permission was theft but the gospels do not raise this as an issue because it had no implications of blasphemy. It also spoils the divine image being created – the Son of God condoning thieving! Remarkably, the Pharisaic interpretation of the Law did not unequivocally forbid theft. Indeed the *Babylonian Talmud* makes it a duty to steal to save life. Jesus was behaving not like a god but like a desperate man following an interpretation of the Law acceptable to the Pharisees.

The gospel account is best understood if Jesus was actually giving an explanation of why plucking corn on the Sabbath was allowed, just as any rabbi would, with a quotation from scripture and a well known saying. Jesus's final words are

> *...therefore the Son of Man is sovereign even over the Sabbath.*

Though this reads to a Christian as an assertion that the Divine Christ could do what he liked, to a Jew he is simply saying that mankind is sovereign over the Sabbath. In Aramaic the expression "Son of Man" simply means "Man" or, as the Queen would say, "one", or an Irishman, "Your man". It merely restates that the Sabbath is for men. The gospel writers omit half the story to avoid the conclusion that Jesus was a wanted man. They aimed to show that the times were tranquil not the reality which was rebellion, and to create falsely an opportunity for Pharisaic criticism.

If Pharisees opposed Jesus on Sabbath healing, why did they not bring this charge at the hearing in the court of the Sanhedrin? Indeed why were no charges brought specifically by the Pharisees at the hearing? Because the hearing was not before the Sanhedrin but before the court of the High Priest acting as a Roman stooge in his capacity as Chief of Police. In the later trial of Peter which was before the Sanhedrin because the grounds were religious, Gamaliel, the leading Pharisee, defended Peter.

The Pharisees and the Jesus of the gospels had more in common than dividing them. In religious terms Jesus would not have seen the Pharisees as ultra pious as the gospels make out but as ultra-lax. They sought not to address problems posed by the requirements of the law by building a wall around it to prevent anyone transgressing it inadvertently. For Jesus this would have been avoiding the issue. Jesus would have regarded the law as sacrosanct and would not break it unless there were sound precedents in the *Scriptures* which could justify it. Pharisees would have seen Jesus as a fundamentalist. Jesus's principal disagreements with the Pharisees in the gospels were political not religious. A nationalist extremist like Jesus would certainly have regarded Pharisees as hypocrites – Jesus's favourite word for them. Pharisees professed to be against the foreigner but were much more pragmatic about it and so they often seemed hypocritical. Some Pharisees were fed up with madmen claiming to be messianic leaders. Like any other Jew Pharisees hoped for a Messiah but too many mountebanks had failed to do anything except stir up trouble with the Romans. They might have thought of him as another madman they should discredit before he caused trouble. They certainly seemed to enjoy trying to embarrass him but there is little evidence of a Pharisaic plot against him. The Pharisees tended to be cautious, not knowing how God might reveal himself. They dared not take peremptory action for fear of offending God but would have been happy to test God's servant by posing him legal conundrums. That appears to be just what they did to Jesus.

For all Jews the greatest commandment was "to love God". Jesus ranks the next one as "to love your neighbour", a commandment that Hillel, the noted Pharisee teacher and leader, called the great practical principle. Jesus's Pharisaic inquisitor in *Mark* (12:28 – 34) comments that these principles are more important than burnt offerings, an expression of Pharisaic opposition to the Sadducees whose emphasis was on ritual rather than piety. Pharisees accepted sacrifice only as a token of sincere repentance. Jesus concludes by telling the scribe that he is not far from the kingdom of God. The liberal treatment of the story in *Mark* is because it was the first gospel, written while the church was still evolving. It was edited in later gospels to leave no credit to the Pharisee.

Imperial policy was to leave local matters in the hands of local chiefs. In Judaea the Romans entrusted civic authority to the Sanhedrin, the council of 70 Jewish elders. But Sadducees, who were collaborators, dominated this council and knew they had to denounce a man claiming kingship or be tried as traitors themselves. The gospels try to make the judicial hearing held at night before the High Priest into a meeting of the Sanhedrin when it could not have been – no Pharisee would have broken the Law to attend.

Elsewhere in the *New Testament*, the Sanhedrin seems to concur with the High Priest's persecution yet the Pharisees on the Sanhedrin oppose the priestly faction. The Pharisaic opposition to the High Priests, under the leadership of Gamaliel, even succeed in defeating the Sadducee faction intent on persecuting the Nazarenes in the trial of Peter. The *Acts of the Apostles* quite often favours the Pharisees by depicting them as being liberal about religious differences and factions. If *Acts* were an early work, the later need to discredit the Jews would not have been so intense and many remnants of the original sympathy of the Pharisees for the Nazarenes would remain.

It seems then that the enemies of Jesus were the priests and their supporters, the collaborating Sadducees, rather than the Pharisees as the gospels try to make out, though Jesus would have willingly criticised the latter too. It was the High Priest who held the initial hearing into Jesus's crimes; they were the ones who stood to lose if an uprising were successful and they did not like the idea of inviting Roman antagonism even if it were not. After the fall of Jerusalem the Temple no longer existed and therefore the Sadducees had lost their *raison d'etre*. Judaism survived through the Pharisees. The Pharisees therefore became the targets in the Christian gospels.

The Trial Before Pilate

Having been turned over to the Romans by the priests, Jesus was quickly brought for trial before the Roman Prefect, Pontius Pilate, the highest official in the province. The charges were serious. In *Luke* (23:2) they were charges of treason:

- claiming to be "Christ, a King".
- perverting the nation;
- refusing tribute;

Claiming to be a King

The gospels record the trials of Jesus as if they were in a play or as if there were a visitors' gallery in each of the courtrooms. Ordinary Jews or supporters of Jesus could not have been present at either of the two hearings. It is not clear therefore how accurate records of the proceedings of the Roman Court or the Court of the High Priest could have reached us. If the story were related at second hand by others who were present then distortions are more likely. A brief report of the trial by Pilate must have been posted and could have formed the basis of subsequent romanticised versions by the disciples.

Pilate puts before Jesus the charge that he claimed he was a king and asks how he wishes to plead: "Are you the King of the Jews?" Jesus replies: "Thou sayest", an ambiguous reply. It might be agreement, meaning "As you say". On the other hand it could be a defiant and surly, "So you say", but otherwise meaning "No" which is Pilate's interpretation.

John has the defendant agreeing but explaining that his kingdom was not of this world, a later addition because the idea of another-worldly kingdom of God was developed by Christianity, the Jews believing firmly that the kingdom of God would be here on earth. However, in *John* that explanation is sufficient for Pilate to find Jesus innocent.

Yet even if *John*'s defence of Jesus were true history Pilate could not have found Jesus innocent because his acts had shown him to be guilty. If we take the gospels at face value, Jesus had deliberately arranged a foal so that he could ride it into Jerusalem in fulfilment of prophecy. In *Zechariah* 9:9 we read:

> *Rejoice greatly, O daughter of Zion; shout, O daughter of Jerusalem: behold, thy King cometh unto thee: he is just, and having salvation; lowly, and riding upon an ass, and upon a colt the foal of an ass.*

This passage is purely messianic. It states unequivocally that the king will ride into Jerusalem on a foal. For what purpose? It is worth quoting succeeding passages in *Zechariah*.

When I have bent Judah for me, filled the bow with Ephraim, and raised up thy sons, O Zion, against thy sons, O Greece, and made thee as the sword of a mighty man.

Zechariah 9:13

And they shall be as mighty men, which tread down their enemies in the mire of the streets in the battle: and they shall fight, because the Lord is with them, and the riders on horses shall be confounded.

Zechariah 10:5

The student should read the whole of the prophecies of *Zechariah* to understand what Jesus the Nazarene was up to. The two passages quoted serve to prove that Jesus's intentions were not peaceful when he ordered a foal of an ass to enter Jerusalem. He intended to destroy the enemies of Israel and institute a Jewish kingdom to bring peace to the world. By deliberately entering Jerusalem on a foal, Jesus was declaring himself King of the Jews, and declaring his intention to follow the prophecy of *Zechariah*. No Jew could have mistaken the symbolism and they shouted, "Free us, Son of David" as he entered the city.

Even if Pilate had been a humane person, and he was not, he would himself have invited a charge of treason to have ignored a challenge to the authority of the Emperor. Pilate undoubtedly knew this but *John* (19:12) has the Jews reminding him of his duty:

If you release this man you are not Caesar's friend: everyone that maketh himself a king speaketh against Caesar.

Here the gospel writer puts the indefensible case against Jesus in a nutshell. It is absurd to imagine that the Roman Prefect of Judaea needed reminding of Roman law, or of his own duty. That this line should be included proves that the gospel writer knew that Pilate had no option but to crucify the defendant. All that had gone before was pure fiction composed to absolve Romans of the guilt of murdering a god.

You might ask: "How do we know that Pilate was not a kind man? Perhaps he was so kind that he was willing to risk everything because he considered this man innocent. If this is all known to be out of character, what is the basis of his sinister reputation?"

The Emperor Tiberius wanted to keep peace and order in a sensitive but politically important area of the empire. To get the confidence of some at least of the population he allowed the Jews religious privileges: they were free to pursue their own religion; they were exempt from military service; Roman soldiers were not allowed to insult the Jewish religion on pain of death and were subject to the Jewish penalty of death if they violated the Holy of Holies.

But Pontius Pilate was singularly crass in his treatment of the Jews, offending them repeatedly. He was spiteful, unjust, greedy and indiscreet.

- He carried Roman standards bearing the image of Caesar into Jerusalem knowing the Jews would have been incensed.
- He took the Temple treasure to build an aqueduct into the city, an action that one might have thought would be welcomed – but the Jews put God before any beneficent actions of the foreigner.
- He strongly favoured the Priestly Party of the Sadducees – disliked by the masses – and its leaders, the Annas family.

Such obduracy led to a series of uprisings. One of these was the uprising of Simon Magus, an Egyptian Jew who was hailed as Messiah in Samaria. After savagely putting down the uprising the complaints of the Samaritans to the Roman Legate in Syria, Vitellius, led to Pilate's recall to Rome where he disappears from history.

Perverting the Nation

Roman law had the crime of "laesae majestatis" whereby the assumption of the power of the government without authority was punishable by death. The gospels state clearly that Jesus defied the civic authorities. He overthrows the tables in the Temple Court and controls access into it because he refuses, according to *Mark*, to allow anyone to carry anything through it. Yet the High Priests had absolute power in the Temple precinct and would have set the Temple Police on to anyone disrupting Temple activities in such a manner. Instead they merely asked Jesus on whose authority he carried out these acts. Of course they might well have asked this question to get Jesus to incriminate himself, but whatever his reply he would have been swiftly arrested. Why did they not do it?

The gospels admit the High Priests feared the people, confirming the immense support Jesus had. But ordinary Jews, though they hated the collaborators, would have respected their rights within the Temple because they would have felt they had them by God's will. The only explanation is that Jesus and his followers had forcibly occupied the Temple and almost certainly the city as well. Under his regime Jesus taught daily in the Temple implying a continuous period of occupation of at least several days. The parable of the vineyard and the husbandmen told the enthusiastic audience that Israel would soon be under new management.

Some fragments of an unknown gospel and of Josephus say that Jesus officiated as a priest, entering the Holy Place, implying both that Jesus had the role of an alternative priest and that he was in a position to play it because the

Temple had been captured. The only people who maintained a priestly tradition outside the Temple Priesthood were the community at Qumran, guardians of the *Dead Sea Scrolls*.

The *Gospel of John*, the last gospel written, blatantly seeks to dissociate the events in the Temple from Jesus's arrest. It puts them at the start of a four year ministry instead of at the end of a shorter one as do the other gospels. The raising of Lazarus is unconvincingly substituted as the reason for Jesus's arrest. *John* also fails to make it clear that the Sanhedrin, as the civic authority, had issued a formal warrant for Jesus's arrest, as they must if they were to remain within the laws laid down by Rome and not leave themselves open to accusations of incompetence in Pilate's eyes, and, most importantly, that Jesus's band had resisted arrest.

Refusing Tribute

What of Jesus's attitude to the money required as tribute to Caesar (Mt 22:15-22). The gospel story seems to refute the idea that Jesus was a nationalist because his answer seems to acknowledge Caesar's political power and imply that Jesus would have paid the tribute. Yet in *Luke* (23:2) he was accused of refusing!

The question was a trick like "Have you stopped beating your wife?". Whatever reply he gave would have discredited him. To have denied the tribute money would have suited Jewish nationalists but would have been treasonable to the Romans; to have recognised Caesar's right to tribute would have pleased the Romans but lost support from most Jews. The answer in the gospels:

> *Render unto Caesar the things that are Caesar's and unto God the things that are God's,*

is considered to be very clever by Christians, implying that the tribute money is merely this-worldly whereas God was interested only in other-worldly matters.

This interpretation is nonsense. If the reported words were those of Jesus, he was openly defying Caesar and the Romans. He was telling Romans they had no right to be there and he had no intention of paying them tribute. When Jesus spoke of "the things that are God's" no Jew could mistake his meaning – it was Israel itself. There could be no mistake in the context in which it is spoken – what is God's is contrasted with what is Caesar's. He is saying "Judaea is God's land; the Jews are God's Chosen People. Caesar is welcome to what is his, the rest of the Roman Empire, but he can have no claim to what is God's". That this is the correct interpretation explains *Luke*'s charge of refusing to pay the tribute money.

This episode occurred in the Temple. But Pharisees would not defile the

Temple with unclean coin – it was against the Law of Moses. In the same episode related in *Luke* (Lk 20:19-26) it was the Chief Priests who posed the question. This seems more likely. The Sadducees were out and out collaborators, kept wealthy out of the Temple tax, paid by all Jews, and the sale of sacrificial animals. As agents of the occupying power they were the real enemies of Jesus.

Jesus's hatred of the Romans is revealed also in the miracle of the withering of the fig tree (Mt 21:19-21; Mk 11:20-21). This episode has offered difficulties for Christians because Jesus is considered to be acting uncharacteristically. The gospels of *Matthew* and *Mark* report the incident as an actual event – a miracle but it was plainly a parable. Elsewhere (Mt 24:32; Mk 13:28) a parable of a fig tree is mentioned again but we get no parable only a short metaphor. Plainly the original parable later rendered into a miracle is being referred to.

The story in *Matthew*'s gospel is that Jesus was hungry...

> *And seeing a fig tree by the way side, he came to it, and found nothing thereon, but leaves only; and he saith unto it, Let there be no fruit from thee henceforward forever. And immediately the fig tree withered away.*

The disciples were amazed at this but Jesus goes on to say (Mt 21:21) that they could throw "this mountain" into the sea if they had faith. Christians have generally regarded the fig tree as Israel which Jesus cursed because they had failed as the Chosen People. In fact, the fig tree was the Roman Empire. What was "this mountain" other than the might of Rome. The fig tree was the symbol of Rome because, in the myth of the foundation of the city, the abandoned twins Romulus and Remus are sheltered by a fig tree while being suckled by a she-wolf and a woodpecker. Those who had ears to hear would have recognised the fig-tree as Rome. Jesus was urging his followers to take arms against the enemy of Israel. They would succeed through their faith in the coming of the kingdom so that God would assist them with a miracle.

In *John* Jesus sees Nathanael under a fig tree, meaning that he accepted the power of Rome – he was a collaborator. Jesus wins him over to the cause of the revolution.

Jesus The Christ

Was Jesus a Jewish Nationalist?

In interpreting the gospels, we apply the rule that a statement which contradicts the later teaching of the Church is a fossil of the original Nazarene doctrine. Conversely a statement which supports the later Church but contradicts the doctrines of Judaism at the time is safer considered a Christian editor's "improvement". Jesus said God made the sun rise on good and bad alike and the rain to fall on the just and the unjust. Which means everyone deserves equal treatment by each other and should love each other, just as God does. And so the Church has taught until today though few Christians take any notice. Yet if Jesus really said, "Love everyone", he meant it only for the Jews. No one else counted!

Jesus was a nationalist, sent for the Jews alone. Why otherwise would he bluntly refuse to help the Syro-Phoenician woman, a gentile, whose daughter was possessed and call her a dog? His words were (Mt 15:24):

> *It was only to the lost sheep of the house of Israel that I was sent...It is not fair to take the children's bread and cast it to the dogs.*

He eventually responds to her humility when she rejoins:

> *...even the dogs eat of the crumbs which fall from the Master's table.*

So he rewards the gentile woman by helping her. In similar vein Jesus says (Mt 7:6):

> *Do not give dogs what is sacred and do not throw pearls before swine, in case they trample them underfoot and turn to gore you.*

Here he unequivocally states that gentiles, described as swine and dogs, are not fit for the holy. Persisting with the theme he told his Apostles (Mt 10:5):

> *Do not go among the gentiles, and do not enter a Samaritan town, rather make your way to the lost sheep of the house of Israel*

And as a final example, having cured the gentile demoniac of Gerasa, he tells him to go home to his own people. That these commands go against the Church's later teaching suggests that they are genuine and indeed the *Acts of the Apostles* confirms them in the case of the family of Cornelius.

Cornelius was a gentile godfearer who sought an audience with Peter. The audience is granted but Peter tells the gentiles they knew it was against the Law of Moses for a Jew to mix with those of another nation. In this case, though, God had told Peter, in a dream, it was all right. So, though Jesus supposedly taught that Jews and gentiles were equal, Peter apparently did not accept it until God told him in person! Jesus's teaching must actually have been to love everyone – as long as they were Jews. Thus when Jesus says his work is for the Children of Israel alone we can accept it as the truth, for why should a Christian editor want to insert something so contrary to the message of a Church trying to get gentile converts. It could only be there because it was there in the first place – it could not have been added. When he says his message is for gentiles also, we incline to the view that an editor of the later gentile Church has thought it important to insert this message.

Glimpses such as these show that the real Jesus was a Jewish nationalist. He did not believe that God had abandoned the Jews in favour of the hoi polloi of the Roman Empire. Indeed he gave his life believing that God was about to establish a new Jewish kingdom which would rule the earth.

Did Jesus Think he Was Christ, a God?

All scholars agree that in the gospels Jesus never asserted that he was the Messiah. Of the five instances when he mentions it, three are later interpolations (Mk 9:41; Lk 24:26,46), one is improbable (Mk 13:6) but if true either implies that the Messiah was yet to come or to return (but Jesus never suggested he would – see later) and the final one (Mk 12:35-37; Mt 22:41-46) is part of a scriptural discussion the rest of which is omitted. Had there been other instances the gospel writers and editors would have used them. Other references to Messiahship, those in the nativity stories, those in the titles of *Matthew* and *Mark* and those in an editorial clause in *Matthew* are plainly added by editors.

Messianic words only get used in the gospels after the troubles began in Jerusalem. Jesus silences a demon who reveals who he is; he does not admit it even to Peter when he replies to Jesus's direct question, "You are the Messiah". The congratulation to Peter, not present in *Mark*, looks like an interpolation to get rid of this embarrassing silence. In exchanges with the High Priest, Jesus answers coyly, his replies do not mean "yes" and could mean the opposite. Similarly, the answer to Pilate's question: and in fact *Luke* implies that Pilate takes it to be a denial. In *Acts* Jesus definitely is the Christ though the claim is still not attributed to Jesus, and the book implies that Jesus became the Messiah on his resurrection. In *Acts* Peter (3:17-18) and Paul (17:3;26:23) both cite the *Scriptures* as evidence that Jesus was the Messiah through his suffering but do not give a source. *John* is written with the premise that Jesus is the Messiah and introduces him as such in Chapter 2 when Andrew announces, "We have found the Messiah".

Jesus's earthly leadership was transformed to a heavenly one after his crucifixion, possibly because ideas of a pre-existent Messiah and a suffering Messiah were becoming popular. Jews hoped for a Davidic redeemer with soldierly powers, righteousness and holiness. But there were also other speculations:

- about a priestly or prophetic Messiah,
- that the Messiah had already come,
- that he pre-existed in Heaven,
- and even about a "slain" Messiah.

2 Baruch 30:1 provided the idea of a heavenly Messiah who would "return" in glory to Heaven after his mission on earth but there was never a suggestion that he was divine: he was always human. In *Zechariah* 2:10-12 there is a suggestion of a "slain" Messiah, "him who they have pierced..." Though this is discussed in the Rabbinical literature, it is not mentioned before the second Jewish War when bar Kosiba is killed suggesting that it might be a reference to him. Equally it could be a reference to the Essene Teacher of Righteousness.

One school of thought based on the *Scriptures* was that there would be three men sent towards the end of days, a prophet, a royal Messiah and a priestly Messiah; all were equals. The scriptural meaning of "prophet" is that of a man with special insight. But the title was also used of men who were admired for their miraculous deeds. The Essenes thought that their Teacher of Righteousness was the prophet. John, the evangelist, and Peter give the title to Jesus. After Jesus's resurrection, a disciple, Cleopas, described him as "a prophet mighty in deed and word before God and all the people". Jesus also claimed to be a prophet himself and compared himself with Elijah and Elisha. Other holy men, the Hasidim, did the same.

Yet the era of prophecy had ended with Haggai, Zechariah and Malachi. Even Daniel was not regarded as a prophet, and his book was not included among the *Prophets* in the *Jewish Bible* but in the *Writings*. Even if a man were worthy of the holy spirit the belief was that men generally had become unworthy of prophecy. Though the great teacher Hillel was considered worthy, his generation was not. In *Against Apion* Josephus explains that prophecy had not ended but no Jew could trust a prophet any more because the exact line of succession from the *Old Testament* prophets had been lost so no one could distinguish true prophets from false prophets.

Such was the thinking of learned men, but the ordinary people still believed in saints and prophets and a prophetic revival was expected based on *1 Maccabees*. Both views are expressed in the gospels. The Chief Priests could not arrest Jesus after his entry into Jerusalem because "they were afraid of the people, who looked on Jesus as a prophet". After they do capture him the High Priest's more sceptical followers hit him and asked mockingly, "Now prophet, who hit you?"

The people expected miracles, but the Pharisaic intellectuals could not accept them – though they could accept insight. Hillel and Shammai on opposite wings of the Pharisaic party, and founders of modern Judaism, were not accredited with any miracles despite their acknowledged insight. Josephus, a Pharisee himself, considered wonder workers to be charlatans. In The *Jewish War* Josephus angrily notes the "impostors and deceivers, pretending divine inspiration, provoking revolutionary actions and provoking the masses to madness. They led them out to the wilderness so that God would show them signs of impending freedom".

The gospels (Mk 13:22; Mt 24:24) issue similar warnings but the Palestinian poor eagerly followed one after another, desperate for signs that their tribulations were nearing an end. Repeated failure led to a degradation of the term prophet and it ceased to be used of Jesus.

What then of the titles Son of God and Son of Man? Surely these mean that Jesus was claiming to be the Messiah and, indeed, a god? The title Son of Man occurs over 60 times in the synoptic gospels and very often in *John* but otherwise it occurs only three times in the *New Testament*, once in *Acts* and twice in Revelations.

It occurs nowhere in the Epistles!

Curiously no one but Jesus uses the expression in the synoptics, and it is never used as a form of address to the prophet as it is by God addressing Ezekiel. No one, not even a Pharisee, is puzzled or offended by Jesus's use of the expression. The reason is, as scholars agree, that in Galilaean Aramaic at that time it simply meant "a man" or "the man" and was used as equivalent to "one" or "someone". This usage is known in documents from the second century but it seems from the gospels that it was also used in the first century. It was a modest circumlocution used to avoid the use of "I" which might have seemed arrogant. Furthermore since God gave his name to Moses with the words: "I am who I am", pious Jews would not have wanted to risk saying the name of God even inadvertently. The Essene punishment for so doing, even accidentally, was banishment, which meant death. Jesus would therefore have avoided the first person singular of the verb "to be".

There is no evidence that "Son of Man" was used as a synonym for "the Messiah" as *John* (Jn 12:34) implies. The expression is used in *Daniel* (7:13) where a supernatural being "like a son of man" is described, but the Jewish scholar, Geza Vermes, points out that the expression "like" is common in describing dreams (which Daniel's was) and it is used of beasts in the same description. The being, "like a son of man", is a symbolic representation of Israel and implies no title to a particular person, though some later rabbis did identify this representative figure with the Messiah. The difference from the Messiah of the gospels was that this one was a glorious figure not a humble one.

Finally, in Hebrew even the two uses are not the same: the prophetic title is ben Adam; the everyday use was bar nash, showing that it was not identifiable with the title. The gospel passages that refer to *Daniel* 7:13 are later interpolations intended to identify the everyday expression with a messianic prophecy. Further there is contemporaneous evidence in *4 Ezra* 13 written after the destruction of the Temple in 70 AD. There the Messiah is described not as the "son of man" but as the "form of a man". In the *Parables* of the *Book of Enoch*, verses 46 to 71, the expression "son of man" is used 16 times but always as is clear with the meaning "man" and not as a title. Fragments of the *Book of*

Enoch from Qumran lack the Parables. Some scholars believe they were second century additions, possibly by a Jewish Christian!

There can be no doubt that since the expression was a way of saying simply "man" it could not also have been a title of honour since the two meanings were too apt to be confused with embarrassing consequences. The two meanings offer problems to translators of the *Bible* into Aramaic and ungainly constructions have to be used to circumvent the ambiguity.

The title Son of God today implies divinity because, from the Council of Nicaea, that is how the Christians defined it. Yet scholars largely agree that Jesus never referred to himself as Son of God and the concept never played a part in his teaching. In the gospels it never occurs in narration but only in confessions. In the extract from the *Psalms of Solomon* already quoted, everyone led in righteousness as the Holy People of the Messiah are Sons of God. Thus it was used of the just or saintly men known as Hasidim. Hanina ben Dosa was a Son of God. Correspondingly, the Hasidim were likely to call God Abba, father. The *Psalms of Solomon* have every indication of deriving from the Qumran Community and it is not impossible that the New Covenanters thought of themselves all as Sons of God. Jesus, if he were an Essene, might therefore have been a Son of God in this diluted sense. The formula for anointing a king or a priest, as we have seen, was to use the term "only begotten" or "beloved" son, so in this sense Jesus certainly was the Son of God. Many *New Testament* cases of the use of "Son of God" occur in descriptions of miracles and it seems it was a title used of miracle workers.

If Jesus had the title Son of God as a Hasid, a miracle worker or an anointed king it is possible that his followers extended the meaning to that of Messiah. But he would still not have been thought of as a god, that was blasphemy, and none of the synoptic gospels do so. However, from Messiah Jesus would easily have been identified then with the pre-existent Messiah, already accepted by some Jewish thinkers, then after the dispersal of the Jerusalem Church, the step to divinity would have been easier for the remaining gentile followers. Nevertheless even Paul and the epistle writers were hesitant, using expressions like "the image of god" rather than leaping in with full blown divinity. Ignatius of Antioch, at the turn of the first century AD, felt able to refer to Jesus as "our god".

"All right," you might say, "but what about the use of the word "Lord". Surely that means that Jesus was a god?"

Certainly the expression "the Lord" was an important religious title to the Jews from the time of Daniel to the intertestamental period. It was used as an alternative to Yahweh and as an absolute address for God. The *Wisdom of Solomon* uses it for God 27 times. Lord and God are used interchangeably in one of the scroll fragments. Josephus says the Galilaeans would not call any man Lord and nor could they if they used it as a title for God. The Greek word for Lord – Kyrios – was imported into Aramaic as Kiri in the Hellenistic period as an alternative.

For those who were less dogmatic "Lord" was used in a lesser sense as an address for a person with some degree of power, perhaps a father or husband as well as people of higher rank. In this sense "Lord" used of Jesus, as a person of authority, was to be expected. Rabbi is a title of a teacher of authority but Vermes shows us that "Lord" is the higher title: a first century Hasid, Abba Hilkiah, is addressed "Lord" by rabbis sent to him whereas they refer to each other as rabbi only – yet the holy man was only a farm worker! "Lord" was also used in respectful speech to replace "you" when addressing a senior figure or a holy man.

Jesus could have been addressed as "Lord" in any of these latter senses without any implications of divinity. In the synoptic gospels there is a progression in the usage of the word "Lord". In the earliest gospel, Mark's, the form "Lord" is used rarely of Jesus. It is a form of address to him usually by strangers, though in one instance it is rendered absolute as "the Lord". All of the vocative uses are in the context of miracles suggesting that it was an honourable form of address for a wonder worker. In *Matthew* the usage is slightly extended, it being used by Jesus's followers and in some cases with a prophetic implication. *Luke* applies it less in the context of miracle working, more in the context of a teacher of authority and most commonly in the absolute sense of "the Lord". Finally in *John* where the usage is largely in the context of a teacher of authority there is eventually a clear identification of "Lord" and god (Jn 20:28).

The conclusion is that there is little direct evidence in the gospels that Jesus thought of himself as the Messiah. That might have been expediency, so as not to attract undue attention to himself while he built up support. – the Messianic Secret. That he thought of himself as divine is a non-starter. No one brought up in the most strictly monotheistic of religions could possibly consider it. Yet, if the symbolism of the entry into Jerusalem on the foal is not a gospel writer's device, then he certainly believed he was the Messiah by the time he attempted an insurrection in Jerusalem and was willing to state it theatrically.

Kings of the Jews

It was a capital offence to act against the Empire or Caesar; it was a capital offence to assume the actions of an official without authority; it was a capital offence to join an armed body in capturing a public place. The gospels are clear that Jesus was unequivocally guilty of each of these offences. Pilate had no discretion in the matter of sentencing. Under the laws of Rome Jesus was guilty of treason. Simply being acclaimed a king without an insurrection would have been sufficient for the Roman authorities to have found him guilty. There is no argument about this! The punishment for these crimes could only be crucifixion.

Nor did Pilate imagine that Jesus was innocent as the gospels make out. Pilate insisted that the inscription on the cross should read "The King of the Jews" rather than "They said he was King of the Jews". Pilate intended the execution and the inscription to serve as a lesson to any future nationalists similarly claiming kingship over the Jews. Thus ended the career in life of Jesus Barabbas, the Zealot, better known later as Jesus Christ.

The crucifixion of Jesus however did not have the effect desired by Pilate. After Pilate's disgrace in 36 AD Roman Prefects came and went until Agrippa, the grandson of Herod the Great, was instated for a few years until 44 AD when Roman rule resumed under the Procurators. Immediately there was an uprising under a Messiah called Theudas who was slain. A High Priest was murdered by the Sicarii. Simon Magus assembled a crowd at the Mount of Olives to see a miracle. The revolt of Lazarus continued for twenty years until he was captured and sent to Rome. James the Just, brother of Jesus, was stoned to death in 62 AD.

The Jewish War began in 66 AD with astonishing successes. The leader of the Zealots, Menehem, a son of Judas of Galilee, and Eleazar, the captain of the Temple Guard, revolted at the same time. The Zealots captured the fortress of Masada and murdered the Roman garrison; the Captain of the Temple Guard refused to allow a daily sacrifice for the Emperor, a blatant outrage to the Romans; the Roman garrison in Jerusalem surrendered and was butchered. The Legate of Syria had to send an army of twenty thousand men which the rebels promptly defeated.

Then it began to go wrong – the rebels began to quarrel among themselves. Menehem declared himself king only to be murdered by the Sadducees. John of Gischala, another Galilaean, leader of the Zealots, then murdered the High Priest, Annas, and overthrew the Sadducees.

It took a large force from Rome under the generalship of Vespasian, soon to be Emperor, and his son Titus to put down the rising, taking advantage of the disunity of the Jewish factions. With the fall of Jerusalem after a siege of five months, the Jewish state was crushed. The Temple was shattered and with it the party of the Sadducees; Jews were taken captive to Rome; Jewish wealth was plundered; the Sanhedrin was disbanded; the Rabbis and the Pharisees were scattered to re-establish Judaism centred on the synagogue; most important of all from the viewpoint of Christianity, the Jewish followers of Jesus in Jerusalem were also dispersed, a few remnants taking to the desert. Even after Jerusalem and the Temple had been razed, Jewish spirit was not destroyed. There were to be further messianic uprisings in 116 AD and 136 AD when, with the slaying of Bar Kosiba, the flame of revolt was finally extinguished.

Something powerful had fanned these flames for two hundred years. What was it?

SOLDIERS OF GOD

...the kingdom of heaven suffereth violence, and men of violence take it by force.

Mt 11:12

The Essenes

Josephus on the Essenes

In his two famous books the *Jewish War* and the *Antiquities of the Jews* Josephus describes in considerable detail the cult ignored in the gospels – the Essenes.

Essenes renounced riches and kept no servants, ministering to one another, eating only the simplest food and wearing their clothes and shoes to shreds. They held their goods in common yielding their possessions to the order when they joined and contributing all their earnings. Failure to do this was a grave dishonesty and was severely punished. In return they received all that they needed. Stewards looked after the common affairs of the group. Their lives were fully regulated by guardians or bishops who directed their daily duties leaving them able to do only two things of their own free will – to assist those in need and to show mercy.

Oil was a defilement but being sweaty was not considered impure. They wore white garments. They settled in all towns in Palestine living apart in organised communities based on a centre where they congregated for meals. Someone was appointed to look after strangers for they offered hospitality to any visiting brother just as if he were part of the family. And so they never needed to take any provisions with them except weapons to protect themselves against robbers. There was no commerce between them, everything being given willingly to brothers who had need, once the guardian approved.

Their first act in the morning, before dawn, was to pray as if in supplication for the sun's rising. Then they took to their tasks until the fifth hour when they returned, clothed themselves in delicate white raiments, bathed in cold water and assembled in a room into which only the initiates were allowed for a sacred meal. Following grace said by the priest they partook of bread and a single type of food and concluded with another prayer in praise of god as the provider of the food. They then changed back into their working clothes and resumed their labours until the evening when they repeated the cleansing ritual in preparation for the evening meal after the same manner. Conversation at the meal was orderly, each speaking in turn, otherwise silence prevailing, and they ate and drank only what they needed thus maintaining their "perpetual sobriety".

Having sworn the solemn ritual oaths of their initiation they were bound then no longer to swear on oath believing that those who are untruthful were in any case condemned by God. Thus they were faithful, peaceful and restrained. They spent much time studying the writings of the ancients taking from them what was good for their body and soul including medicinal knowledge based on roots and stones.

To be admitted, a proselyte must first live in the manner of an Essene for a year to prove he is capable of it. Then he is baptised but is still not admitted to the order – he has to continue to live in their fashion for two more years to prove his worthiness. It is at this stage that he takes the solemn oaths to become a full member and participate in the sacred meal. He has to swear piety toward God, justice toward men, not to harm anyone of his own accord or at the command of another, to hate the wicked and assist the righteous, to show faith to all men especially those in authority but not to abuse his own authority or try to outshine others in garments or other finery, to love truth and reprove those who lie, not to steal or covet, not to conceal from others in the sect nor divulge their doctrines to others on pain of death, to pass on the rules to proselytes just as he received them, and to preserve the books of the sect and the names of the angels.

If anyone was guilty of sin he was cast out eating only grass since he could accept no succour from anyone without the permission of the guardian and thus he wasted away to die of starvation. Excommunication therefore meant death because no Essene would forgo his vows even though he had been excommunicated. In practice the community usually accepted them back when they felt they had been punished enough. Their judgements were just, not being passed by a court of less than a hundred, and usually permanent. Josephus writes that, after God, they revered most the name of their legislator, it being a capital offence to blaspheme him. Scholars naturally have assumed this to be Moses but, since all Jews revere Moses, it is tempting, in the light of the scrolls, to wonder whether Qumran's Teacher of Righteousness was meant.

They obeyed their elders and accepted majority decisions. They avoided spitting in public and were stricter than other Jews in observing the Sabbath, preparing all their food on the day before and not even defaecating on the Sabbath. They carried with them a small hatchet to dig a pit as a latrine then filled the pit again when they had finished. While in the act of defaecating they wrapped themselves with their white robe so that they did not offend, not simply other people because their toilets were well away from habitation, but the divine rays of light. Afterwards they washed themselves thoroughly.

The full members were split into four classes. Seniors considered junior members to be as unclean as a gentile and had to undergo purification if they touched one. Their regular and simple lifestyle and diet made them long lived, often living to over a hundred years old.

They believed in an immortal soul locked in a corruptible body. The body is a prison for the soul which rejoices when it is freed of it. Heaven has no storms, snow or intense heat but is refreshed by a cool breeze always blowing gently from the ocean. Hell is a dark and stormy pit full of torments. These act as enticements to men to be good in life for fear of being punished after death. Unlike other Jewish sects they did not offer sacrifices at the Temple, indeed were excluded from it though, Josephus says, they were favoured by Herod.

Some Essenes foretold the future and apparently were rarely wrong.

Another account of the Essenes by Philo of Alexandria broadly matches Josephus's but sometimes he disagrees and occasionally adds something new. Thus he says that only mature men were admitted. He agrees with Josephus that the Essenes lived all over Judaea but maintains that they preferred to live in villages. The sick and elderly were cared for. Josephus tells us they practise husbandry but Philo enlarges saying they are farmers, shepherds, cowherds, beekeepers, artisans and craftsmen, but they did not make weapons, would not engage in commerce and were no sailors. They believe brotherhood to be the natural relationship of men but that it has been spoiled by covetousness. Though they read a great deal they were not interested in philosophy in general but only morals. They ignored the weather and never used it as an excuse not to work. They returned from work rejoicing, as if they had been partying all day.

Though Josephus gives the impression they were pacifist adherents of the Law, he invites the opposite conclusion when he says that they were above pain and gloried in death rather than the misery of life, as they showed in the war with the Romans when they could not be broken by the victors though they be "racked and twisted, burnt and broke". Though they were tortured, they did not shed a tear, indeed laughed at their tormentors rather than blaspheme their legislator or eat forbidden food. They sound more like Zealots!

The Dead Sea Scrolls

Shortly after the second World War ancient scrolls were found in caves at Qumran near the Dead Sea. Even in the dry climate of the Judaean wilderness the scrolls had mainly crumbled to powder. But, amazingly, several were found complete and there were thousands of fragments, mainly small, some of which could be pieced together. Complete scrolls – the *Manual of Discipline*, the *Damascus Document*, the *Rule of the Congregation*, the *Habakkuk Commentary*, the *War Scroll*, the *Temple Scroll* – have been translated but scholars' comparative work has been hindered by restrictions on access to the fragments. The scandal of such restrictions on scholarship has forced more openness and now two US scholars, Eisenman and Wise, have published translations of 50 Qumran fragmentary texts not previously open to public scrutiny. With the discovery of the *Dead Sea Scrolls* we have, according to Eisenman and Wise, "nothing less than a picture of the movement from which Christianity sprang in Palestine".

Ruins near the caves of the scrolls, and in just the place described by Pliny as the home of the Essenes, apparently were the headquarters of the community that had hidden the scrolls. Excavations seemed to confirm that the ruins had housed a monastic religious order similar to that of the Essenes described by Pliny, Philo and Josephus. The *Damascus Document* however refers to marriage and children – showing that Essenes in general were not celibate monks – and to other affiliated communities in Palestine, showing that the Qumran Community was not the only Essene settlement.

The *Damascus Document*, copies of which had amazingly already been found in 1897 in a Cairo synagogue, was plainly important to the sect because portions of as many as nine copies were found in the caves. In part it tells the story of a group of Jews who with their "Teacher of Righteousness" went to a place in the wilderness – which they seemed to call Damascus – to uphold the Law. They became barjonim: outsiders. They had entered into a New Covenant with God. "Damascus" seems to be Qumran, the name of Qumran at that time being otherwise unknown to us. With this knowledge Paul's trip to Damascus in the *New Testament* takes on a new meaning and several problems can be explained. The New Covenanters called it Damascus after a staging post of the Jews on the way to and from exile under the Babylonians.

When the First Temple was destroyed in 586 BC and the Jews were deported to Babylon, many saw it as a divine punishment for laxity in observing the Mosaic Law. Thenceforth they resolved to follow the Law to the letter. When Cyrus the Persian allowed the Jews to return to Palestine many preferred to stay behind. They had been taken as captives because of their skills, had set themselves up as scribes and artisans and were doing quite well in their new environment. Babylonia ever after had a high Jewish population.

The *Damascus Document* tells us of those who had returned from exile in "the land of Damascus" having gone "out of the land of Judah" and with whom:

> *God established his Covenant with Israel forever, revealing to them the hidden things in which all Israel had strayed*

where "all Israel" means the whole nation whereas "Israel" means the select few who are pure enough and observant enough – the sectarians themselves. Here the reference to the Land of Damascus cannot be to Qumran because the *Damascus Document* clearly says it was "out of the land of Judah" whereas Qumran is only a few miles from Jerusalem. The *Damascus Document* explicitly quotes, apparently by way of explanation, *Amos* 5:26-27 which describes the place of exile as beyond Damascus. Babylon is, of course, beyond Damascus. But Babylon had been destroyed 300 years earlier by the Persian King, Xerxes, and the Jews must have migrated to neighbouring cities including Damascus. Perhaps some had been heading back to Israel but had found Damascus comfortable. It seems quite likely, that having settled at

Qumran the former exiles nick-named it Damascus after their place of origin. The exilic origin of the group is supported by many rules which pertain to life among the gentiles, a situation that scarcely applied in Judaea despite it being under foreign rule, but obviously would apply to Jews living in a foreign country.

This interpretation is confirmed from an unusual source. The *Damascus Document* implies that not all the New Covenanters in the land of Damascus returned when the Jewish free state was set up. What happened to them? We have noted that there was after the original banishment into captivity always a large Jewish population in Mesopotamia, many Jews choosing to stay put. Among them evidently were some of the New Covenanters.

Around 800 AD a Mesopotamian Jewish reformer, Anan ben David, called for a return to the basics of Judaism and a rejection of the *Talmud*. He wanted, like the Essenes, a literal interpretation of the Mosaic Law, and he founded a sect called the Karaites. Scholars had noticed the astonishing similarities of the Karaites and the Essenes, separated as they were by almost a millennium. However, the discovery of the *Cairo Damascus Document* in 1897 seemed to them the source of Karaite beliefs. Evidently the *Cairo Damascus Document* was a holy book of the mediaeval Karaites who were strong in Egypt around 1000 AD when that version was transcribed. The Karaites opposed Rabbinic Judaism and proved to be very successful in the near and Middle East in mediaeval times. Now only a few thousand remain. The New Covenanters must have maintained their identity for over a thousand years in Mesopotamia before emerging as the Karaites.

The New Covenant evidently was founded by Jews in exile. The New Covenanters had returned expecting the purity of the Temple to be restored by the Maccabees. When it was not they decided to withdraw into the wilderness, to set up a pure people ready for the Judgement of God.

The Influence of Exile

The Persian religion, founded by Zoroaster (or Zarathrustra) and whose priests came to be called the Magi, has had an influence on the world which today is unrecognised. The Neo-Pythagoreans owed much to Magian belief. Indeed Pythagoras himself was said to have learnt from the Magi of Babylon. The apocryphal *Book of Tobit* seems to contain a lot of Magian teaching. There seem to be links between the Jewish philosopher, Philo of Alexandria, and Zoroastrianism. The Neo-Platonist leader, Appolonius, came from Tyana, a Cappadocian city where Persian influence was strong. Gnosticism was also indebted to Persian religion. Plainly the *Dead Sea Scrolls* of the Qumran Community had an astonishing flavour of Persian religion, and so does Christianity. The appearance of the Wise Men of the East, considered to be Magi, in the gospel of Matthew offering gifts to the infant god seems to be a symbolic assertion that this new Christian god was superior to those of the Persian religion. It certainly implies that the writer was aware of a link, and a need to demonstrate to others who might notice it that is was not a debt.

Zoroaster was a real person but when he lived is unsure, not because there is doubt that he did but, because the evidence of the date is contradictory. It could have been any time between 1400 and 700 BC. Thus Zoroaster either preceded or was a contemporary of the prophets of Israel, Buddha, Confucius and Lao-Tse. Probably about 1000 BC is the best guess because the *Gathas* of Zoroaster have certain things in common with the *Vedas* of India which are dated about then.

Before anyone other than the Pharaoh Akhenaton, Zoroaster introduced monotheism. The various tribes of Persia worshipped a pantheon of lesser gods and spirits, called Ahuras, but Zoroaster declared Ormuzd or Ahura Mazda, the Lord of Light, to be the single true God above all others. Ormuzd is the same as Varuna of the Vedas. Like Varuna, he has a surrounding court of ministering spirits. Ormuzd was "Lord", "The Wise Lord", "The First and the Last", "The Father of the Good Thought". He created Right. He promised eternal life to good people:

> *in eternity shall the souls of the righteous be joyful.*

To follow goodness or evil was one's personal choice. In the later development of the religion, Ahriman, the Devil, becomes identified with the Evil Spirit, but in the *Gathas* of Zoroaster the Evil Spirit is actually one of the two aspects of Ormuzd himself, the other being the Holy Spirit. When Ahriman became identified with the Evil Spirit, Ormuzd became a purely Holy Spirit. But man had free will to refuse evil in both stages of the religion.

> *Bliss shall flee from them that despise Righteousness. In such wise do you destroy for yourselves the spiritual life.*

Either Zoroaster was a High Priest or "Zoroaster" later became a title meaning High Priest for he is sometimes referred to as the best or highest "Zoroaster" suggesting a hierarchy of priests or possibly a group of them at community level led by a "pontifex maximus". Later the priestly caste were called the Magi (like the Brahmins of India) whose leader was considered a direct successor to Zoroaster. They introduced new elements into the Persian religion and revived some old ones.

Zoroaster, like Christians, wanted to convert everyone: he sent missionaries as far as Hindustan. It has been said that Zoroaster taught nothing about God which a Christian would not endorse and much that a Christian should add. He was threatened with death by a king as a baby, started his ministry at 30, underwent a period of temptation, healed and taught. He championed the oppressed, lived an ascetic life and finally he was murdered. He described Heaven as a green place, a beautiful meadow or a Royal Park – in Persian, paradise.

Alexander's conquests (330 BC) led to the destruction of many Zoroastrian texts. According to Diodorus, the historian, the Persian archives were held at Persepolis yet Alexander burnt the city and murdered many of Persia's leading scholars. In the second century BC a king called Valkash collected the remaining scattered manuscripts and the oral tradition and tried to reconstruct the holy works. Fortunately Zoroaster's *Gathas*, being particularly sacred, seem to have survived essentially unaltered.

At the time of the Jewish exile in Babylonia, much Zoroastrian thought had the chance to enter Judaism and surely did. Scholars once took this for granted. Thus, in *Jeremiah*, Rab-Mag was the chief of the Magi. *2 Chronicles*, *Ezra* and *Deutero-Isaiah* show how close Persian and Jewish thought was. Darius Hystaspes, the Persian King of about 550 BC, worshipped Ormuzd. He was probably a Zoroastrian, as was his father Cyrus. Jewish history is dated from the reign of Persian kings and the Persian king Cyrus is seen as a Deliverer. He rebuilt the Jerusalem Temple as we know from inscriptions as well as the *Old Testament* and was much admired by the prophet, Isaiah. Herodotus confirms that he was a noble king.

Zoroastrianism was the source of Jewish monotheism, brought from exile on the return. It has been said that the concept of Ormuzd is closer to that of the Jewish God than that of any other eastern religion. Yet prior to exile the Jewish god was a tribal god – one of many Semitic tribal gods. After the return from exile, when the sages wrote down the holy books, they introduced ideas from Zoroastrianism. Their tribal god became a universal God but one which still favoured his Chosen People. Ahuras became Angels and Demons.

Ancient Judaism knew of no Last Judgement. Before the exile the Jewish concept of death was Sheol, a dark and dismal place with no memory of God. After it the concepts of Heaven and Hell had emerged and the Jews had a doctrine of resurrection and Judgement for all. The "dry bones" of *Ezekiel* seems to be based on the Persian custom of leaving the dead to be picked by birds in towers, so that they do not defile the earth, after which they could be resurrected. The Persians, like the post-exilic Jews, believed the soul remained with the body for three days – a dead person was not really dead until the fourth day when the soul had departed. This explains why Jesus was to rise on the third day. It also shows that the raising of Lazarus was an afterthought. The greatness of the miracle of raising Lazarus in the fourth gospel is that he had been dead for *four* days. His soul had departed and he was beyond recall. One would have thought that Jesus would have saved this exceptional miracle for himself.

Zoroastrian parallels with the Qumran documents are huge. The *Damascus*

Document condemns those who enter the New Covenant but then leave to join the Liar. The *Habakkuk Commentary* enlarges on the theme of the Liar, telling of trouble within the community when the Liar secedes from the order and comes into conflict with the Teacher of Righteousness. In *2 Corinthians* 11:31, Paul is insistent that he "does not lie" apparently answering an unpleasant criticism of him. The choice of language in these instances stems from Zoroaster. For Zoroaster the enemy was within, the Druj or the Lie.

> *Let none of you listen to the Liar's words;*

and the "Followers of the Lie":

> *...at the last the Worst Existence shall be the followers of the Lie, but the Best thought to him that follows Right. Of these twain Spirits, he that followed the Lie chose the worst things; the Holiest Spirit chose Right...*

Zoroaster had a doctrine of free will and individual responsibility for all actions, writing:

> *Whoso worketh ill for the Liar by word or thought or hands, or converts his dependents to the Good, such men meet the will of Ormuzd to his satisfaction.*

Herodotus, writing about the Persians of his day, recorded:

> *They teach boys, from five years to twenty, three things only – to ride, to shoot and to be truthful...Most disgraceful of all is lying.*

The Qumran Community was an apocalyptic sect. They were expecting the end of the world. The apocalyptic movement arose with the death of classical Jewish prophecy when the Israelites were carried off to Babylon which soon became absorbed into the empire of the Persians. The Enoch Literature is Persian of about the fourth century BC. Apocalypticism seems to owe a great deal to Persia and the influence of Persian religion on Judaism stems partly from the apocalyptic writers. The Qumran library proves that Apocalypticism was a considerable movement in Judaism not merely a fringe interest. Christian theologians used to believe that the anticipation of God's kingdom to come was uniquely Jesus's message. Now we see it was hundreds of years old, had come out of Persia with the exiles and had been perpetuated by the Essenes.

The Jewish messianic ideal of a Deliverer also came from Persia. In Persian religion Ahriman and his angels rose out of the Abyss to attack the Good spirit and the Angels of Light. Neither good nor evil was victorious but eventually Ahriman will be defeated by a Deliverer sent by god, the Saoshyant. The Saoshyant, of the line of Zoroaster or perhaps the prophet himself reincarnated, heralds the beginning of a new age. There follows a "Day of the Lord" and trial by ordeal for mankind when the earth will be flooded with molten metal which burns up the wicked but allows the righteous to bathe in it as in warm milk. The earth would be levelled into a great plain just as it is in *Isaiah* 40. Finally Ahriman will be cast back into the Abyss and mankind will ascend to the realm of light to dwell with Ormuzd. There will be no repentance or pardon – in life, evil deeds can only be cancelled out by good deeds, and judgement is on this balance.

Such a dualistic doctrine was unknown to the ancient Hebrews. But the Qumran documents speak of Good and Evil; Light and Dark, the Way of Darkness and the Way of Light, the Spirit of Darkness and the Spirit of Light, The Children of Darkness and the Children of Light, Truth is Light, Falsehood is Darkness. The Teacher of Righteousness is opposed by Belial, the Demon of Evil. The Way of Good leads to salvation, the Way of Evil leads to torment. Of the four gospels, *John* reflects this terminology most accurately showing its Essene links. In *2 Corinthians* 11:12-15, Paul criticises the Archapostles as disguising themselves as "Servants of Righteousness" and uses the sentence "Satan disguises himself as an Angel of Light" both betraying Qumran influence and apparently deliberately used against the upholders of the Community tradition.

The Zadokite Priesthood

The Macedonian Greek, Alexander the Great, conquered Palestine in the fourth century BC. After his death his empire was immediately split among his generals and Palestine became part of Egypt under the dynasty of the Ptolemies. In 200 BC however it became part of the Seleucid kingdom centred on Syria and Mesopotamia. All of these former Alexandrian territories were Greek in culture and the process of Greek cultural imperialism was called Hellenisation. During his reign the Seleucid king, Antiochus IV Epiphanes (175-163 BC), pressed ahead with an aggressive policy of Hellenisation in Israel until 165 BC. The Jews had had enough – they revolted.

The Zadokite line of Jewish priests had been founded by Solomon and had continued unbroken since. But the Greeks opposed an inherited priesthood: they wanted anyone to have a chance of being a priest. In 172 BC Antiochus IV Epiphanes murdered Onias III, the High Priest, breaking the line of traditional Zadokite priests in Jerusalem. He put the office up to the highest bidder.

At first the Zadokites retained the office by submitting the highest bid but later Jesus, the Zadokite High Priest, lost his bid to a non-Zadokite and civil war broke out. The Jews had little chance and many were massacred. The victorious Greeks desecrated the Temple, dedicating it to Jupiter and sacrificing swine. Jerusalem became a Greek city. Baby boys went uncircumcised, priests exercised naked in the gymnasium and the king's officers went around forcing

Jews to make pagan sacrifices. But at one village the local priest, Mattathias Maccabaeus, refused. Another Jew stepped forward to offer the sacrifice. The story is continued in the apocryphal book of *1 Maccabee*(2:24-28):

> *When Mattathias saw it he burned with zeal, and his heart was stirred. He gave vent to righteous anger; he ran and killed him upon the alter. At the same time he killed the king's officer, as Phinehas did against Zimri the son of Salu. Then Mattathias cried out in the city with a loud voice, saying: 'Let every one who is zealous for the Law and supports the Covenant come out with me!' And he and his sons fled to the hills and left all that they had in the city.*

Eventually the Maccabaean rebellion succeeded. Judas Maccabaeus, son of Mattathias, proved a brilliant general and defeated the Greeks setting up the Jewish dynasty of the Hasmonaeans. Judas (165 -160) was followed by his brother Jonathan (160 – 143) and another brother Simon (143 – 134). The victory of the Maccabees is still celebrated by Jews at Hanukkah.

These victories of the Maccabees induced more Jews to return from Mesopotamia including many who were zealous for the Law and were impressed by Mattathias's stand. In Palestine they were doomed to disappointment. Hellenisation had not ceased. The Hasmonaeans did not return to strict tradition. Judas was keen to secure Rome as an ally against the Seleucids and signed a treaty with the Roman senate. To effect this he made Hellenised Jews his diplomats.

Nor did the Hasmonaeans reinstate the Zadokites: Jonathan Maccabee claimed the High Priestly office for himself. It was possibly at this point that the sect which was to become the Community of Qumran was first founded largely by zealous returners from Babylon disappointed by the turn of events. Josephus first mentions the Essenes in his description of the reign of Jonathan Maccabaeus implying that they were founded then. However many Jews at this stage still supported Jonathan. He remained in conflict with the Seleucids throughout his reign and would have been given the benefit of the doubt while he was engaged in throwing off the foreigner.

Such regard would not have been shown to his brother, Simon Maccabaeus, whose son in law killed him and his eldest and youngest sons while they were drunk on a visit to Jericho. Another son, John Hyrcanus, escaped. Meanwhile the Seleucid king, Antiochus VII Sidetes, took the chance to reassert Greek authority. One Qumran document apparently alludes to *Joshua* 6:26 where a "Cursed One" loses his eldest and youngest sons. In the *Habakkuk Peshar* we read that this priest "...walked in the ways of drunkenness ...but the cup of God's wrath will swallow him up... " Other Qumran *Testimonia* seem to identify this priest with Simon Maccabee. Why then did the Qumran Community hate this man so much?

Under Simon in 140 BC an assembly of Priests and Elders (Pharisees) decreed that Simon was High Priest "until a faithful prophet should arise" (1 Macc 14:30-39). The decree recognised its own illegality by making it sound only temporary through the quoted phrase about the prophet, but it removed the Zadokites permanently from office in practice because the age of prophecy had ended. Opposition was to be severely punished. An American Jewish scholar, Lawrence Schiffman, believes that the Sadducees were the Zadokites who lost control of the Temple when the Maccabees refused to return the High Priesthood to them. Later some compromised accepting back their priestly positions but under a non-Zadokite High Priest. Others refused to compromise and joined the sectarians founded earlier by a Zadokite New Covenanter, the Teacher of Righteousness, who had retreated with his followers into the wilderness to lead ritually pure lives, observing the Law strictly and following the solar calendar. The Pharisees supported the Maccabees throughout.

Another episode might also be important in the setting up of the Essene camp at Qumran-Damascus. Some scroll fragments mention three or possibly four historical people in a list of priestly courses – Aemilius, Shelamzion, Hyrcanus II and possibly Aristobulus II though only the beginning of the name can be read. The manuscript seems hostile to Scaurus and the gentiles, to Antipas, Hyrcanus and the Arabs and to Shelamzion. One deduces it favoured Aristobulus. Aemilius Scaurus was a general Pompey left as governor of Syria, which included Palestine, when he returned to Rome after his conquest of Palestine in 63 BC. Scaurus was a close associate of Herod's father Antipas, one of the first Roman administrators of Jerusalem, a thoroughly Hellenised Idumaean married to an Arab princess. Scaurus helped Antipas in a campaign against the Arab King of Petra – Arabia to the Apostle, Paul. Antipas had assisted Hyrcanus, the eldest son of Shelamzion (Salome Alexandra (d 67 BC), wife of Alexander Jannaeus), who, the fragment tells us, "rebelled" against someone unknown, opposed Aristobulus and through his machinations and his Roman influence succeeded in securing the throne for Herod, his son, who executed Hyrcanus in 30 BC. Presumably the unknown person that Hyrcanus rebelled against was the person that he opposed, Aristobulus.

Hyrcanus was a collaborator willing to yield to the outside powers rather than take risks by opposing them. The Pharisees who supported him sided with Pompey and Scaurus. Hyrcanus and his mother Shelamzion were happy to allow the invaders to appoint the High Priests if it meant less trouble. Aristobulus on the other hand was a nationalist and gained the support of the ordinary people. The split between them allowed the Roman intervention and the eventual crowning of Herod through the cunning of his father, Antipas. The Romans attacked Aristobulus's men who, through zeal to resist foreign rule, held out against the Romans in the Temple. Onias, called the Just by Josephus, otherwise Honi the Circle Drawer or Honi the Rainmaker, refused to condemn the followers of Aristobulus. But he did condemn the Pharisees who supported

Aristobulus's brother, Hyrcanus, who welcomed the Romans and the dynasty of Herod they imposed. The defenders of the Temple astonished their attackers by continuing to carry out their Temple duties even as they were being cut down, such was their dedication. Aristobulus finished up in chains in Pompey's triumph in Rome and was eventually poisoned by Sadducees who supported Pompey in 49 BC. The following generation saw the two sons of Aristobulus, Alexander and Antigonus, defeated and beheaded by Mark Antony who put the priests in power under the patronage of the Herodians.

Robert Eisenman identifies Aristobulus as a Sadducaean nationalist and Hyrcanus II as a Pharisaic collaborationist and believes the split in the Sadducees which led to the setting up of a priesthood in exile based on Qumran occurred at this point and not in the earlier period of Simon Maccabaeus. The pro-intervention Sadducees became the Herodian Boethusians of the *Talmud*, the Sadducees of the *New Testament*; the anti-interventionist, zealous Sadducees became the Qumran Essenes.

Whatever their origins, the Essenes of Qumran scorned the illegal priests of Jerusalem. Josephus says they rejected the Temple as unclean and "offered their sacrifices by themselves". The Communities of the Essenes were the True Israel and the priesthood they maintained at Qumran the true Zadokite priesthood. Following *Isaiah* they had gone into the wilderness to "prepare the way of the Lord in the wilderness". God's Covenant with Israel in the desert brought down by Moses had been replaced by the New Covenant with God's Elect in the desert. The military preparations the Children of Israel made to enter the promised land were now being made by God's Elect to enter the kingdom of God. God's soldiers had to be pure, whence the celibate regime, baptism and exemplary lifestyle. Josephus says the Essenes were pacifists but many Qumran sectarian documents are warlike in their phraseology and content. Josephus himself mentions a John the Essene who was a general in the Jewish war.

The New Covenant

Jews were the Chosen People with whom God had made his Covenant. If a male Jew had been circumcised at eight days old then he was one of the Chosen. The sect of the Scrolls however was exclusive. They believed in a New Covenant between God and the remnant of Israel that was righteous. The New Covenant was exclusive of all but those individuals who having reached the age of twenty undertook the solemn vows of the sect. Nowhere are they called Essenes but the curators of the scrolls knew themselves by many names: they were the Keepers of the Covenant, Joiners for War, Holy Ones or Saints, the New Covenanters, the Perfect of the Way, the Sons of Zadok, the Sons of Light, the Poor Men, the Righteous and the Doers of the Law.

From the scrolls we know the sect of Essenes was organised into two branches:

celibate monks at Qumran and lay members in all the villages and towns of Palestine. Many of the scrolls are holy orders for the various classes of Essene initiates. Geza Vermes, an Emeritus Professor of Jewish Studies, assures us that there are no precedents in ancient Jewish literature for the lists of rules given in the Qumran documents like the *Manual of Discipline* but such literature was common in Christian communities of the early centuries as exemplified by the *Didache*. This cannot be coincidence and shows that Christianity stemmed from one particular type of Judaism, the Essenes, and not Judaism in general.

The Rules of the New Covenant

From the *Manual of Discipline* we discover the rules the members of the Monastic Community were required to live by and they agree remarkably with Josephus. Monastic Essenes were to:

- be admitted to the Community only after a lengthy procedure;
- obey the Laws of Moses – indeed vow to be "Zealous for the Law" ... "until there shall come the prophet and the Messiahs of Aaron and Israel" (apparently suggesting that three people were expected, the prophet, the Priestly Messiah and the Kingly Messiah, but it seems the two Messiahs at least were the same person);
- love God and each other, and hate the wicked (but leave it to God to punish them);
- hold their property in common under the control of a "custodian of property";
- bathe daily in holy water;
- eat each day a sacred meal and pray together;
- be ruled by a Community Council which shall "preserve the faith in the land with steadfastness and meekness and shall atone for sin by the practice of justice and by suffering the sorrows of affliction";
- maintain total self-control – members were fined if they showed anger;
- organise themselves in a strict hierarchy of members and speak only in order, keeping silent when others are speaking and respecting the wishes of the majority;
- follow meticulously the appointed times which is to say the official schedules and solar calendar;
- separate from the ungodly;
- follow liturgy precisely.

The complicated procedure for admission was as follows.

- Appear before the full congregation to be examined by the Master of the whole sect for suitability; on acceptance swear to follow the Community's interpretation of the Law of Moses – any transgression to be punished by expulsion; enter a long period of instruction by the Master in the rules of the community;
- appear for a second time before the congregation for acceptance as a novice; on acceptance spend a year as a novice regarded by members still as impure and not worthy of the sacred meal;
- appear for the third time before the congregation; on acceptance leave all possessions with the bursar who would keep them distinct from the possessions of the Community; complete a second year as a novice still unable to partake of the drink of the congregation;
- submit yet again for examination and if accepted enter fully the congregation allowing all possessions to be taken into the Community and partaking fully of the sacred meal.

The Priests blessed the Perfect who were admitted to the New Covenant with the prayer:

> *May God bless you with all good and preserve you from all evil. May God lighten your heart with life-giving wisdom and grant you eternal knowledge. May God raise his merciful face towards you for everlasting bliss.*

All priestly blessings of the Most High were to be concluded with calls of Amen, Aramaic for "Truly" or "Verily" as it is often translated in the gospels. The curses of Satan and backsliders by the Levites which followed were similarly concluded with cries of Amen, Amen.

Such was the admission procedure for the monastic body. For a village Essene matters were less rigid but many requirements were the same as those for the monastic order. Both branches:

- considered themselves the true Israel;
- followed the Zadokite priesthood – every group of ten or more had to include a priest;
- partook of a common meal;
- arranged themselves in a strict hierarchy;
- insisted on a correct interpretation and strict adherence to the Laws of Moses;

- swore to uphold the New Covenant;
- followed a solar calendar precisely so as not to deviate from his appointed times, including holding an annual congregation.

Particular rules for village Essenes were given in the *Damascus Document* and the *Rule of the Congregation*, or the *Messianic Rule* as Vermes has renamed it.

- Members had to cleave to the laws of Moses but commerce with the impure and the imperfect was allowed;
- Temple sacrifice was permitted and demanded absolute ritual purity;
- full maturity was reached according to the Rule of the Congregation only at the age of 30;
- the Guardian of the "camp" or village community was its head, its teacher and its father figure – he had absolute power over members' contacts with the impure, permitting commercial transactions but not casual relationships;
- observance of the Sabbath was strict, the rule expressly forbidding the picking and eating of fruits from the fields;
- members were not allowed to bear witness in the courts of the gentiles – the Romans. The punishment was death but since the Community had no powers of capital punishment it is plain that expulsion was meant. Expulsion was eternal death, but for a strict Essene was often physical death too.

Village Essenes, unlike the monastic variety, owned their own property. Instead of holding goods in common they donated two days' wages a month into a common fund to provide for orphans, the old and needy and widows. The Community whether in the monastery or the camps was bonded by a common meal. Only the perfect were allowed to partake of it and in particular to partake of the "new wine" which is to say the unfermented grape juice of the congregation.

The Essene organisation was arranged to reflect Israel as a whole being split into twelve tribes whence the distinction between Israel and "All Israel". Hierarchy was strictly enforced. Priests preceded Levites who preceded Israel who preceded Proselytes – the four ranks of membership spoken of by Josephus – and within each rank everyone had his place which was reassessed annually. The *Manual of Discipline* and the *Damascus Document* describe the hierarchy of the organisation as being in thousands, hundreds, fifties and tens. Indeed the *War Scroll* refers to groupings of myriads. Of course they could not have been so numerous that there ever were divisions of myriads or even thousands because Josephus tells us there were only 4000 all together. Scholars inform us that there could never have been more than 200 Essenes in permanent occupation at Qumran. One concludes that they were providing for bigger numbers than they ever achieved but numbers they expected to achieve. The *Commentary on Nahum* explains that the ranks of the sectaries would be expanded by the conversion of the "simple of Ephraim", Jews who had been led astray by the smooth things of the Pharisees, prior to the battle with the Sons of Darkness. And the *Rule of the Congregation* is written specifically for all the congregation of Israel that will join the Community in the end days.

Each year all the camps – the village communities – assembled probably at Qumran for the "Feast of the Renewal of the Covenant", the principle Holy Day of the year, to renew the Covenant and to allow initiates to be regraded. It occurred on what we call Pentecost the chief of the agricultural festivals which were held every 50 days (whence Pentecontads from the Greek for fiftieth). The Pentecost of the Essenes was the Feast of the New Wheat, the Jewish Feast of Weeks, held about the beginning of June. Unfortunately the parts of the *Damascus Document* describing this have been lost or exist only in fragments. The leader of the monastic Community, the Master, was evidently the leader of the organisation at large because he presided over this annual gathering.

At this festival, initiates were questioned on all matters to assess their progress. First they assembled in their ranks, the Priests, then the Levites and after them "all the people one after another in their thousands, hundreds, fifties and tens, that every Israelite may know his place in the Community of God..." Priests and Levites respectively relate God's kindness to Israel and Israel's failings before God. Acknowledgment of guilt is followed by public repentance for their sins. The confessions having been heard the Priests call upon God to bless the congregation, to "preserve them from evil" and to grant them wisdom and knowledge. Lastly Belial – the name the Community preferred for the Devil – is cursed and apostates of the sect equally cursed, the congregation calling out Amen to each blessing and curse.

The *Damascus Document* refers to three particular sins which concerned the Community, the "Three snares of Belial". They were wealth, polluting the Temple, and "fornication" which included certain types of improper marriage such as taking more than one wife or marrying a niece. Another complete scroll, the *Temple Scroll*, echoes the *Damascus Document* in forbidding a king of Israel from marrying his niece. Since the only dynasty for which this was common practice was that of the Herodians, the scroll seems to refer to them. If so these scrolls must date from the time of Herod, in other words in the period of the gospels. It also negates the good terms Josephus said were shared by the Community and the Herodians. (The *Temple Scroll* also establishes that the Community was interested in the affairs of the Temple at Jerusalem.)

Though fornication is one of the three snares of Belial, the early characters of the *Old Testament* were unselfcritical fornicators. King David had many wives.

How was this to be justified? The Qumran Community did so by arguing that the Law had not yet been revealed to them or had not yet been fully revealed. They could not live according to standards that God had not yet provided. Paul, showing familiarity with Essene reasoning, uses a similar argument in *Galatians* 3 and *Romans* 4 to back up his rejection of the Law. Abraham could not have been restricted by a Law which did not exist yet he remained good because of his faith. Thus, Paul cunningly and evidently deliberately uses the Essenes' own argument to maintain that faith is superior to the Law.

The three snares of Belial help us to understand Jesus's outlook. He also identified wealth with sin so that it was easier for a camel to go through the eye of a needle than for a rich man to enter into the kingdom of God. He rages at the pollution of the Temple and refuses to allow divorce. *Acts* 15 and 21:25 depict James, the leader of the Jerusalem Church, as objecting to people indulging in "Blood", "fornication " and "food or things sacrificed to idols" – the latter expressing concern at the pollution of the Temple by offerings from abroad.

The Final Battle and Judgement

All Essenes, like Zoroaster, believed that all men walk in two spirits appointed by God, the spirits of truth and falsehood. The cosmic balance between the spirits is equal until the final age and God has set an everlasting hatred between them. But:

> *God has ordained an end for falsehood, and at the time of the visitation he will destroy it forever. Then truth, which has wallowed in the ways of wickedness during the dominion of falsehood until the appointed time of judgement, shall arise in the world forever.*

With the visitation the kingdom of God would dawn when mankind will be purged of falsehood, individual humans being judged on the balance of the spirits within them. A cosmic battle would be fought between the forces of Light and Good and the forces of Darkness and Evil; between Truth and Lies; between God and Belial. Good men would be saved and the wicked condemned. The Essenes were God's New Covenant ready to join battle against the forces of Evil at any moment. They were in a perpetual state of readiness. They were spiritually and ritually pure through repentance and baptism. They practised the messianic meal every evening. They had the Holy Spirit with them. God's prophets had written down the signs of the End Time and they, the possessors of the Holy Spirit, had the power to understand these writings. Thus they scoured the *Scriptures* for these signs, indications that the wicked would be destroyed and they. God's Elect upon earth would be chosen to rule, They wrote pesharim or commentaries explaining scripture in terms of the events of the End Time – their own time because the signs were there.

Armageddon had begun, the devout were being oppressed by The Lie. The End Time was nigh. God would soon intervene on their behalf.

At the appointed time the *War Scroll* explains that there will be a preliminary battle between the Righteous and the armies of the Kittim allied with the "Ungodly of the Covenant" in some specific but unknown (because of scroll damage) place. Then the "Exiles of the Desert" would move to Jerusalem for the final battle of the first week of years. Following victory over the Romans, the Temple would be cleansed and correct Temple worship would be restored. The war would continue for another 33 years before final victory. While the Righteous pitted themselves against the Ungodly on earth the heavens would be echoing to a mighty conflict between the archangel Michael, the Prince of Light and Belial, the prince of Darkness and their hosts of "gods" (Angels and Demons). The battle is indecisive because the forces of good and evil are evenly matched and victory is given to the Righteous and the Angels through God's intervention. There seems to be no role for the leader of the Elect except simply to lead out his forces. Beyond that victory is assured by God. The reward for the Righteous is explained in the *Manual of Discipline*:

> *...eternal joy in life without end, a crown of glory and a garment of majesty in unending light.*

This unending light and eternal joy were simply a continuation of life on earth whereas the punishment for sinners was:

> *eternal torment and endless disgrace together with shameful extinction in the fire of the dark regions.*

The literature of Qumran describes a messianic elite who have chosen to follow the command of *Isaiah* 40:3 to "make a straight Way in the wilderness for our God". They lived in desert camps waiting to be joined by a Heavenly Host of Angels to engage in a Holy War against their enemies. They are preparing themselves for "the End Times" by living a life of extreme purity. They sought The Way of Perfect Righteousness, The Work of the Law, and The Way in which the Law works. *Acts* 9:2 calls members of the early church the followers of The Way. The scroll of the *Habakkuk Commentary* tells us that the Council of the Community was located in Jerusalem, offering a potential link with the Jerusalem Church.

John the Baptist

Zacharius in the gospel of Luke (1:76-78) describes his unborn son, John the Baptist, thus:

> *[You will] be called the prophet of the Most High, for you will go before the Lord to prepare his ways... when the day shall*

> *dawn upon us from high... to shine upon them that sit in darkness...*

There seems to be a good deal of the Essene in this language. *Luke* continues:

> *And the child grew, and waxed strong in spirit, and was in the deserts until the day of his shewing unto Israel.*

What is meant by "the child... was in the deserts" other than that he was brought up at Qumran. Zacharius was a priest and he and his wife were both elderly according to the *New Testament*. The Qumran community took in waifs, strays and orphans according to the classical writers. One of the thanksgiving hymns in the Scrolls appears to confirm this having:

> *...Thou wilt care for me; for my father knew me not and my mother abandoned me to thee.*

So from *Luke* (1:5) we know John the Baptist came from a priestly family. In the Hebrew and Arabic versions of Josephus, John the Baptist is called the High Priest. Since he could not have been the High Priest of the Jerusalem Temple a position reserved at that time for a few aristocratic priestly families, the opponents of the regime must have had an alternative hierarchy with their leaders paralleling those in Jerusalem. The centre of the alternative organisation was at Qumran and John could have been a High Priest of the alternative priesthood.

John the Baptist has many similarities with the Essenes.

- The word of God came to him, says *Luke*, in the wilderness which is the desolate land between Qumran and Jerusalem.

- His ministry was in all the regions around Jordan, in other words not far from Qumran.

- He baptised those who repented. People had to repent urgently and be baptised by John to be ritually pure because a "greater one" than he would come to baptise with the Holy Spirit and with fire.

- He advocated communism, saying: "He who has two coats, let him share with him who has none; and he who has food, let him do likewise". The Essene monks had to give all their goods to the Community, as did the Nazarenes in the *Acts of the Apostles*.

- He expected a Messiah, quoting *Deutero-Isaiah* (40:3-4): "...the voice of one crying in the wilderness: prepare the way of the Lord, make his paths straight." The Qumran community justified their withdrawal to the wilderness with the same quotation.

The obvious difference was that John seems to be a solitary ascetic not a member of a community. Plainly though this is not true. John the Baptist had disciples as all four gospels tell us and *Acts* further explains that his disciples had spread far and wide. Christian baptism was rivalled by the baptism of John.

Baptism was a special rite to the Jews, a ritual purification before going to war, a soldier's oath of allegiance, a "sacramentum" and is still so called by the church. For the Elect, like those at the Qumran community, it was a cleansing of the body, the soul having already been purified by righteousness. The Essene *Manual of Discipline* prescribed washing in water for those who had repented:

> *They shall not enter the water to partake of the pure meal of the saints, for they shall not be cleansed unless they turn from their wickedness – for all who transgress his word are unclean.*

And all Israel had transgressed in allowing the foreigner to rule. Thus even the Messiah, to the Jews a man – with supernatural powers maybe – but not a god, had to be washed clean of this sin by baptism.

The first gospel written, *Mark*, does not tell us that John the Baptist recognises Jesus as the Messiah. *Matthew* introduces it and it is strengthened in *Luke*. But when John baptised Barabbas he simultaneously crowned him a king or a High Priest because a voice acknowledges him as a Son of God.

In the gospels Jesus has the highest praise for John as the forerunner of the Messiah but otherwise the gospels play him down to a sort of compere for the main act. Nonetheless they acknowledge that John heralded not just the Messiah but a whole period of violence:

> *In the days of the Baptist and until now the kingdom of Heaven has suffered violence, and the men of violence take it by force.*

Though John, like Jesus, was not a miracle worker, his own disciples, like Jesus's, became convinced *he* was the Messiah after his death. Rivalry between John's followers and those of Jesus was apparent even in the *New Testament*. Mandaean tradition has it that John arrived in Jerusalem and exposed Jesus as an imposter, an incident that might be reflected in the *New Testament* when John in prison no longer believes that Jesus is the Messiah and sends a message asking whether he is the one or whether another is to be expected. This might have reflected John's disappointment in Barabbas's preparations for an uprising.

John the Baptist referred to himself as "Enosh", the reborn grandson of Adam, and so he was known by the Mandaeans who revered him. Enosh in Hebrew means "Man", so we have the curiosity that John the Baptist was the Man and Jesus was the Son of Man! This might have been a Jewish joke. If John the Baptist played the role of the priest at Jesus's baptism as seems likely then it would have been his voice announcing his "beloved son" as the coronation liturgy required. Thus we have the irreverent titles: the "Man" and the "Son" of "Man" or, in Aramaic pronunciation, "nash" and "bar nash".

Did John the Baptist live longer than Jesus? The latest year of Jesus's death is 33 AD. The Tetrarch Philip died in 34 AD on the day that John interpreted a dream for him. Herod Antipas killed John and later was defeated in battle in 36 AD by Aretas, king of the Petraean Arabians, an event considered to have been retribution for John's murder. John must therefore have been killed within a year of 35 AD, the very year that Simon Magus, a disciple of John, led a rebellion on Mount Gerizim in Samaria. Antipas was probably more absorbed by John's potential for inflaming rebellion than he was by Salome's dance or John's criticism of his marital arrangements.

Note that Matthew's Gospel associates John's initial appearance with the return of Joseph and Mary from Egypt ("in those days..."). Since the Holy Family had fled from Herod and returned when he died, "those days" must have been about 4 BC. The apocryphal *Gospel of the Twelve Apostles* says that John came baptising "in the days of Herod, king of Judaea". Thus John was at least 60 years old and more likely nearer 70 when he was murdered.

The Essenes as Revolutionaries

The Star

The thrust of the *War Scroll* like many of the Qumran fragments is markedly apocalyptic. It anticipates a battle between the Kittim, the "Sons of Darkness" and the "Sons of Light". We have the familiar expression, "Sons of Light", from Persian religion for the members of the Community but who are their enemies, the Kittim? The answer seems to be the Romans. But are the scrolls referring to the Romans of Pompey's invading armies of Republican Rome in 63 BC or the Romans of the time of Christ, soldiers of Imperial Rome?

The *War Scroll* says the Kittim invaders had a king, which seems to count out the invasion of Pompey because Rome was a republic – unless they regarded Pompey as a king. The *Habakkuk Commentary* says that the Kittim offered sacrifices to their standards. Professor Driver of Oxford University tells us this was a practice of Imperial Roman soldiers but not Republican ones. They could not have been Pompey's troops but must have been those occupying the country from 6 AD till the destruction of 70 AD. And these scrolls must have been written or edited during or after this period in the first century. Elsewhere appears the "slain of the Kittim" and the "falling of the Cedars of Lebanon". The Cedars of Lebanon mean the Priesthood or the Temple because the Hebrew root of Lebanon means white signifying the white linen of the priests (the same imagery is used of the Community itself who also wore white). These passages seem to be referring to the Jewish War and the destruction of the Temple.

The leader of the Elect in the struggle against the Kittim is the Messiah prophesied in *Numbers* 24:17:

> *There shall come forth a star out of Jacob, and a sceptre shall rise out of Israel,*

a quotation which occurs in several Qumran sources. It seems "The Star" was another name for the Messiah. This is the true source of the Star of Bethlehem in *Matthew*. The Star of Bethlehem has nothing to do with stars in the sky, comets or supernovas but is simply a metaphor based on the "Star" prophecy – the Star of Bethlehem means The Messiah. The Messiah is also referred to as a star in *Revelations* 2:28 and the *Second Epistle of Peter* 1:19.

A related scroll fragment ends with an explanation of Jacob's blessing on Judah (Gen 49:10):

> *The sceptre shall not pass from Judah, nor the staff from between his feet until the coming of Shiloh to whom the people will gather.*

It interprets the sceptre as sovereignty and the staff as the Covenant of the kingdom given to the branch of David in perpetuity because he kept the Law with "the men of the Community"! Shiloh is the Messiah of Righteousness and is the same as the branch of David. The feet are the leaders of Israel. Now in the *Damascus Document* the sceptre is the Nasi, the Princely Leader of the Community who will smite all the children of Seth (the enemies of Israel) and the staff is the Law which has to be followed until the One who pours out Righteousness stands up – is resurrected – at the End of Days. Thus the Messiah of Righteousness and the One who pours out Righteousness are the same – the branch of David. Nowhere in the *Scriptures* is Shiloh used as a messianic name except here and modern scholars tend to seek other readings. But here its interpretation is plain. Note also that, though the messianic leader will smite Israel's enemies, he is not himself the Messiah.

The Star prophecy, supported by other messianic readings, was the key to the persistent troubles in Palestine in the intertestamental period. Josephus in the *Jewish War* says the prediction that a world ruler would come out of Palestine was the inspiration for the Jewish revolt. Suetonius and Tacitus, apparently following him, make the same assertion. Josephus cannily gained favour with Vespasian, the invading Roman general, by telling him the prophecy had been fulfilled in his victory – he was the sceptre and would rule the Empire, which later he did. The uprising in 132 AD was evidently grounded in the same prophecy because the leader of the uprising, one bar Kosiba was renamed bar Kochba, the Son of the Star, a pun – the words have almost the same pronunciation.

The *Cairo Damascus Document* and the *Manual of Discipline* seem to imply that there would be more than one Messiah – a Kingly Messiah and a Priestly Messiah. Other texts suggest just a single Messiah. Thus the Qumran *Damascus Document* reads that there is one Messiah "of Aaron and David" and the Cairo version describes the Messiah as "the Root of Planting out of Aaron and Israel". Thus the Root of Planting is one Messiah out of the two lineages of Aaron and Israel, the one is both Priest and King – the Melchizedek, the name used for Christ in the *Epistle to the Hebrews*! Fragmentary material at Qumran confirms this. Interestingly the Cairo document indicates that the Messiah had already come and later references to "arising" and "standing up" must therefore indicate resurrection. *Daniel* 12:13 uses the Hebrew for "standing up" in just this sense.

There are a plethora of fragments containing parts of *Daniel* which writings were among the most inspirational for messianic Jews at the time of Christ. Josephus in *Antiquities of the Jews* tells us that the Jews of the time considered Daniel as

> *one of the greatest prophets... for the books that he wrote are left and read by us still today... he did not only prophecy future events, like the other prophets but specified the time of their accomplishment.*

Prophets were seen as diviners and soothsayers in the first century and the Essenes themselves had a reputation for reliable prophesy. They would certainly have been trying to divine the signs that the End was Nigh. Fragments of a letter in the Qumran caves explain the "End of Days" which it mentions repeatedly, sometimes using the unusual description the "End Time". The letter also repeatedly mentions "the Way". It describes how at the "End Time" a particular concatenation of events occurs by which it can be recognised. The people of Israel then had to return to the Law "never to turn back" if they were to be judged as Righteous or Justified at the Day of Judgement.

At the start of the Jewish War readers of *Daniel* might have interpreted the 70 years of wrath (Dan 9:3) as beginning with the death of Herod (though hated enough himself, his building the Temple might have been seen as blessed compared with what followed) in 4 BC – the presumed date of the birth of Jesus – and lasting until 66 AD, the start of the ultimately failed rebellion. Furthermore the prediction in *Daniel* 12:7 of "the time, two times and a half" which preceded the "End Time" tied in with the three and a half years from the stoning of James the Just in 62 AD to the outbreak of the war. Thus the patriots had sufficient to convince them that the "End Time" had arrived and the battle should commence.

But thirty years earlier, the followers of the Nazarene band of Barabbas probably counted the last seventy years from the time of Herod's taking Jerusalem in 37

BC. They were expecting the End Days round about 33 or 34 AD. Jesus's mission according to *John*, lasted about three years and he had probably allowed the three and a half years of Daniel's prophecy to build up to his revolution. If Barabbas timed his mission according to the prophecy of Daniel to correspond with the "End of Days" or "End Time" he got it wrong, but then so did the diviners at the time of the Jewish War, and at many other times.

Hate your Enemies!

A Jewish scholar, Yigael Yadin, thinks he detects a reference to the Essenes in the Sermon on the Mount when Jesus says: "Ye have heard it said... hate thine enemy. But I say to you love your enemies." Yadin assures us that there is nothing in Rabbinic Jewish tradition which urges hatred of enemies. The Essene *Manual of Discipline* on the other hand says new members have to swear to hate the Sons of Darkness for all eternity:

> *that they may love all the sons of light, each according to his lot in God's design, and hate all the sons of darkness, each according to his guilt in God's vengeance.*

Nonetheless initiates were to pray:

> *I will pay no man the reward of evil; I will pursue him with goodness. For judgement of all the living is with God and it is he who will render to man his reward.*

In practice this is turning the other cheek. Hatred of the Ungodly was required but no one could judge another man with a view to handing out punishment. He had to pursue him with goodness. All this sounds odd in the light of the *War Scroll* and many other texts but it was a command which would be lifted when God set about purging the world. And it was a rule which would not have applied to gentiles in any case once the End Time began. The net effect was that initiates of the Essene order had to hate the Sons of Darkness but could do nothing about it until God indicated that the end was near.

The Essenes hated foreigners. The writer of one fragment urges his readers not to give their inheritance to foreigners for "they will come to dwell among you and become your masters..." Another fragment includes the sentence "The Lord is ruler... to Him alone belongs sovereignty" which recalls Josephus who wrote of the followers of Judas of Galilee, they call no man Lord but God, thus allowing no recognition of rulers other than God. A High Priest, Joezar, son of Boethus, the Egyptian that Herod made Priest, had persuaded the Jews to pay tax to Rome which the Herodians collected. This was not popular, nor were tax collectors. An opponent of Herod, Sadduc, joined Judas of Galilee in revolt against the tax. Josephus also explains in the *Jewish War* that the acceptance of gifts, which was an innovation introduced by the Boethusians, helped spark the War. The Zealots were so incensed by foreign gifts to the Temple that they wanted them banned. It was the eventual refusal of the junior priests to offer foreign sacrifices that helped trigger the war.

The attitude of the Qumran Community exactly matched this. The Community was not anti-Temple but it was anti-the polluted Temple. It was zealous for a pure Temple and that was an important symbol of Jewish nationalism. The Temple was at least in part polluted by foreigners and their unclean contributions presented in "skins" of animals which had been "sacrificed to idols". These problems are unlikely to have applied at the earlier period of the Maccabees implying that they pertain to the time of Barabbas.

Dogs were also banned from the Temple as unclean flesh eaters. The Elect referred to gentiles as dogs along with the deaf and the blind, metaphors for their opponents. (Those who were really crippled or infirm were considered to be under the protection of the Angels of Holiness). In this respect the Herodians were equally foreign as collaborators and in the war the rebels torched their palaces and those of the Boethusian High Priests.

The Qumran use of the word "fornication" is also relevant to the question of foreigners. It was applied to those who married outside Jewry. The essential aim was to keep Israel, a Holy People, separate from others. The command in the *Manual of Discipline* was to "separate yourselves" to prepare a way in the wilderness. Thus another theme arose – how to recognise purity and separateness. Separateness extended to crops in the field and fibres in a cloth – no mixing was allowed in either. In the *Damascus Document* the separateness of pure and impure in the Temple is considered inadequate because "they" sleep with women during their periods and "they" marry their nieces. Who are "they"? Those who sleep with women during their periods are the gentiles because Jews considered this grossly impure. Those who marry their nieces are, of course, the Herodians for whom marriage of nieces was common. The Temple was therefore itself grossly impure.

Jesus had nothing to do with foreigners. He was interested only in Jews. Even the Syro-Phoenician woman only won him over through her humbleness. Several of Jesus's remarks show disdain if not hatred for foreigners. Jesus in saying "love your enemies" spoke to Jews and knew they understood him to mean *only* Jews. He wanted Jews to love each other so that God's kingdom could begin. Partly this involved uniting them against the foreigner because God helped only those who help themselves. It was necessary to rid the land of the pollution of the foreigner to bring in the kingdom of God.

The Qumran sectarian documents refer to some of their enemies as "Ephraim", "builders of the wall" and "spouters of false things", the latter a play on the words "halakhot" (religious laws) and "halaqot" (false things or falsehoods). These are the Pharisees who according to the *Talmud* held dominance under the

Maccabees. The sectarian documents refer to the Sadducees as "Manasseh". Manasseh and Ephraim were the names of the two sons of Joseph blessed by Jacob. Ephraim signifies fertility and Manasseh signifies forgetfulness. The Pharisees' fertility was in creating new laws and the Sadducees forgetfulness was over the promise of Solomon to Zadok of the priesthood forever. Furthermore King Manasseh was a reformed idolater and Manasseh in *Ezra* signified those who had married foreign women, strong hints of Hellenisation of the official Priesthood.

The Pharisees were not entirely the men of the people depicted by later Rabbinic tradition, though they possibly had the best interests of the people at heart. The Pharisees had a reputation as surrenderers. They were the "seekers after smooth things" of the Qumran writings, so called because they took the path of least resistance so that the people would suffer least. Josephus writes that two prominent rabbis, "Pollio and Sameas" – probably pseudonyms for Hillel and Shammai – convinced the people to surrender to Herod and the Romans in 37 BC. Herod remained forever in the Pharisees debt. At a later period Josephus says that it was the "principal men of the Pharisees, the Chief Priests (Herodian Sadducees) and the men of power" (the Herodians) whose intermediary was a mystery man called Saul, who invited the Romans into Jerusalem to put down the uprising in 66 AD. The Pharisees, Josephus himself and Tiberius Alexander, Philo's nephew, supervised the destruction. Pharisees were pragmatists but did not endear themselves to the Essenes who were nationalists, nor most of the people who wanted shot of the invaders.

Yigael Yadin, thinks Jesus was an Essene who advocated revision of the *Manual of Discipline*. Here may be a distinction between the Essenes and the Nazarenes – the Nazarenes were less exclusive. They felt that all Jews should be warned that their time was nearly up, and that they should repent if they wanted to enter the kingdom. Barabbas does not regard any Jew as lost to Belial forever. His objective was to recruit Jews as soldiers of the Sons of Light for the imminent battle. Any Jew had the chance of repentance and a favourable outcome when the kingdom of God arrived no matter what sins they had committed. In this belief he was the successor of John the Baptist. His message was addressed to Jews and only Jews were included in the enemies you should love, not foreigners. The Jews were God's Chosen People. The New Covenant made with the Elect was a Covenant to guard the Old Covenant. In short the duty of the Elect was to try to carry as many of the Chosen as possible into the coming battle. The Essenes, Barabbas believed were the vanguard which had to mobilise the rank and file.

Paul took this extension of the Elect of God further still. He wanted to give *everyone* the chance to join God's Elect and enter God's kingdom, even if they were gentiles. Paul identified with the Essenes because they had split from the Jerusalem Temple. The Essenes contrasted themselves with the Temple hierarchy in the *Damascus Document*. Quoting *Proverbs* (15:8) it says:

> *The sacrifice of the wicked is an abomination to the Lord but the prayer of the righteous is his delight,*

which reminds us of Jesus's discussion with the Pharisee. For the Essenes the split with the Temple was of no further consequence. They were God's Elect and the dawn of the kingdom was nigh when all the wicked and their polluted Temple would be destroyed. The kingdom never came but the Temple was destroyed by the Romans leaving the two traditions: the Pharisaic and thc Essene. The one became Judaism and the other became Christianity.

Essene Revolutionary Activity

The evidence from coins found during the excavations of the ruins at Qumran are revealing. It gives us a good idea of when the buildings were occupied and to what degree people were coming and going. The camp seems to have been hyperactive during periods of insurrection!

If the community were self contained, it would have had little use for coins. But a degree of commerce with the world beyond the wilderness, particularly the village Essenes, occurred and, since wealth was held in common, new coins would be added to the exchequer as new converts arrived. Father de Vaux who excavated the site at Qumran discovered some 486 coins datable between 135 BC and 136 AD. The incidence of lost coins must conflate occupation of the site, level of commercial activity and number of proselytes arriving – in short the degree of activity. When the community was active, the incidence of coins would be high.

But coins are also found corresponding to known periods of abandonment. These must have been dropped by those seeking temporary shelter or casual passers by – or they were coins still in circulation when they were dropped at a later period of activity. From this a crude analysis can be made of the periods when the site was active and inactive.

The Qumran site seems to have been destroyed by fire near the beginning of the reign of Herod the Great (37 AD) and was not re-occupied until after the end of Herod's reign in 4 BC. De Vaux attributes this to an earthquake but it could suggest that the Community was unpopular with Herod and was suppressed by him, possibly violently. Yet ten coins were found which were minted in that period.

As a crude guide we can take the ten coins in the reign of Herod as the average coinage incidence corresponding to unoccupation. This is an incidence of 0.3 coins per year. So if the annual incidence of coins for any period falls below 0.3, assume the site is effectively abandoned. Then allocate the coins found in the abandoned period to the next occupied period on the assumption that the coins are likely to be old currency lost in a period when the Community was occupied. Thus in inactive periods the Coin Index is reduced to zero.

This method reveals that before 104 BC the site was unoccupied or inactive. The Community might have been based on booths in the nearby wilderness. Thereafter we find:

- Coin Index 5.4 – The initial period of activity corresponding to the founding of the permanent site between 104 and 76 BC.
- Inactivity 76-40 BC.
- Coin Index 3.3 – A short spurt of activity is apparent around 40 to 37 BC corresponding to the time when the Romans were establishing Herod as their puppet ruler.
- Inactivity in the reign of Herod 37-4 BC.
- Coin Index 2.6 in 4 BC rising to 11.1 around 44 AD. A long period of activity (embracing the lifetime of Jesus) from 4 BC to 44 AD and peaking around 37 to 41 AD. This is the period of Roman rule under the Prefects and Agrippa's short reign.
- Inactivity 44 AD to 67 AD.
- Coin index 54.5 – apparently frenetic activity occurring in 67 and 68 AD when the Jewish war was in progress.
- Inactivity 68 AD to 132 AD.
- Coin activity 4.3 – a final short bust of activity in 132-136AD during the revolt of Bar Kosiba.

The correspondence with periods of rebel activity in Palestine is remarkable. The Community by the Dead Sea became particularly active at times of trouble. They seem not to be simply pacifist monks but actively engaging in the rebellions. If the coins of Qumran are anything to go by, the longest period of occupation from 4 BC to 44 AD, the very period of the gospels, was a period of constant agitation falling only just short of perpetual insurrection.

From the Hasmonaean period to the intertestamental period two powerful tendencies sundered Judaism; one was Hellenisation and the other was Apocalypticism. In a way they were opposites because the Hellenisers saw a future in the Greco-Roman world whereas the Apocalypticists saw no future at all without a divine intervention. The pursuit of Hellenisation was loosening the ties of the Laws of Moses to permit Jews more freedom within the Empire whereas the pursuit of Apocalyticism was cleaving rigidly to the Jewish Law, separating from the gentiles and preparing for the coming kingdom of God on earth.

The outcome was paradoxical. The victory of the Hasmonaeans supported by the pragmatism of the Pharisees kept Hellenisation within bounds ultimately leading to modern Rabbinic Judaism. The Apocalyptic trend led to repeated rebellions and eventually to the destruction of the Temple and with it the priestly parties. But one apocalyptic sect – the Essenes – was to divide, break loose from the bounds of Judaism, become thoroughly Hellenised and eventually form a new world religion based on Jewish tradition and using the Jewish Holy Books.

Essenes as Proto-Christians

Nazarene?

Whenever as many as ten members of the Community gathered for a meal they took their seats in the order of their rank, and the Priest presided. No one could touch the bread or new wine until the Priest had blessed them and taken his. But in the *Rule of the Congregation* at a meeting of ten or more "Men of Renown" (Essene leaders – the Council of the Community) the Messiah is also present and takes bread and wine after the priest but before the others did, according to their seniority. Qumran scholars consider the sacred meal to anticipate the banquet in Heaven at the End of Days. They assume the participation of the Messiah to be symbolic – he was present only in spirit. But, from the description, It sounds as if the Messiah were really there. Maybe he was!

In the Qumran literature the Hebrew word Nasi, meaning "leader" or "prince" is used frequently to mean a messianic leader – not the Messiah as such but the "Prince of the Many". Did the Nasi play the role of the Messiah at the sacred meal of the Council of the Community? If so Nasi could be the real origin of the gospel term Nazarene. Nazarene certainly did not mean "of Nazareth" because Nazareth at the time was a milestone saying "Sepphoris 4 miles". Even if it existed it was so insignificant that it could never have been used as a helpful description. People would have said: "Jesus of where?" Nazarene was obviously a word which people understood. The Nazarenes were those who followed Barabbas, the messianic leader, the Nasi. The Semitic root NS relates to lifting or carrying and metaphorically translates as forgiving as in lifting and carrying away sins. Jesus was reputed to blaspheme by forgiving sins. It is possible that the Nasi had this power.

There are several other fascinating word links between the names of Jesus and his followers, and the Essenes. The Semitic root NSR means "protector" or "saviour". The Arabs still call Christians the Nasrani. Jesus is the Greek form of the Hebrew word Joshua which means the Salvation of God. Hosea, meaning Salvation, is the original name of Joshua. It is properly written Osee. The Aramaic for "save us" is "osanna" the cry of the multitude when Jesus entered Jerusalem as a king. Epiphanius speaks of the Ossenes, a Jewish sect by the Dead Sea obviously identifiable with the Essenes. Essene is properly rendered Osim, the Saviours. Thus the Osim were also the followers of the Saviour, Jesus. The Koran's name for Jesus is Essa from the same word, Osee.

Epiphanius also tells us that besides Nazarenes the early Christians were known as Jessaeans. David, the great king of the Jews, the model of the warrior Messiah, was the son of Jesse. So it seems that the Jessaeans were simply followers of Jesus because he was the heir of David (before he became the son of a virgin!). The truth is slightly more extended. The identification Jessaeans comes from *Isaiah* which records:

> *And there shall come forth a rod out of the stem of Jesse, and a branch shall grow out of its roots and bear fruit,*

(Isa 11:1 explained further in 10), a quotation much revered by the writers of the scrolls and by Christians – Isaiah also means the Salvation of God! The branch is an alternative name for the Messiah. The word NSR, vocalised as netzer, means a branch – it is equivalent to the word Nazarene. This is surely what was spoken by the prophets when we read in *Matthew* 2:23:

> *and came and dwelt in a city named Nazareth: that it might be fulfilled what is spoken by the prophets, that he should be called a Nazarene.*

Matthew's reference to the prophets has puzzled scholars because there is no explicit mention of "a Nazarene" in the *Old Testament*. In the sense given it by Christians it would be surprising if there were since it is a moot point whether Nazareth existed even at the time of Jesus let alone in more ancient days. The *Old Testament* reference is to Isaiah's branch out of the roots of the rod of the stem of Jesse, which gives us both Nazarene and Jessaeans.

Baigent and Leigh tell us the Hebrew for Keepers of the Covenant, one of the names the Essenes chose for themselves, is Nozrei haBrit, whence Nosrim – Nazarene! Finally we know from *Luke* that John the Baptist was a Nazirite, one who wore his hair uncut and did not drink wine, and so also was Jesus's brother, James, who became leader after the crucifixion. The Essenes also might have been Nazirites because the wine of the messianic meal seems to have been "new" wine or unfermented grape juice. Essene references to wine should be read as new wine and the same is probably true of the gospels. Jesus was not a wine bibber.

We have several words with relevant meanings all apparently serving as the origin of the word "Nazarene". Curious? Not at all. Jews at that time loved punning, and their language lent itself to it, especially in writing where vowels were not expressed. The Nazarenes and Essenes would have loved the multiple meanings God had associated with their name.

Nazarenes appear to be a type of Essene. It seems to translate "those belonging to the Congregation of the Messianic Prince". Within twenty years of the crucifixion they were being called Christians.

Jesus and the Righteous One

Jesus was a highly repected man whose prophecy that the kingdom of God was nigh kept his followers agog and expectant for many years after his death. As the immediacy of the kingdom receded, a corpus of teaching and narrative lore was needed to retain the interest of those who were still loyal and to attract new converts. Where did this all come from? Jesus the Nazarene has remarkable similarities with the Essene Teacher of Righteousness. Did some confusion arise between the two?

The Teacher of Righteousness is referred to in the *Manual of Discipline* and the *Damascus Document*. In the *Manual of Discipline* the Teacher is associated with "the time of the preparation of the Way in the wilderness" by "the teaching of the miraculous Mysteries" (cf. Isa 40:1-3 which is used in the description of John the Baptist). He is commanded to be "zealous for the Law and the day of vengeance" conjuring up explicit images of the Zealots. In *John* 2:27 Jesus has "zeal" and in *Acts* 21:20 James' followers are "zealous for the Law". In the *Damascus Document* the Teacher is to "walk in the Laws" until the "standing up of the Messiah of Aaron and Israel in the Last days" where standing up can be synonymous with coming, return, rising or even resurrection. In the *Damascus Document* the Messiah (singular) of Aaron and Israel will (or did) "atone for their sins" (cf. *Hebrews*).

There is a reference in a scroll fragment to the "putting to death of the Righteous One". Compare this with the passage in *James* (5:6) which says:

> *Ye condemned the Righteous One; ye put him to death though he doth not resist you.*

This fragment echoes other themes of, and the style of, James's epistle calling for patience and restraint. Even the language including the use of words like tongue and vipers are closely similar. Indeed the "tongue" imagery of *James* 3 is used to attack lying adversaries and the tongue is described by the identical, though common enough, expression, "the stumbling block", both in *James* and in the scroll fragment. This is beyond coincidence. In *James* 2:20-24 the "Man of Emptiness" knows not that "a man was justified by his works" and "faith without works is dead", a plain contradiction of Paul's message that faith alone brings salvation, now considered to be the essence of Christianity. *James* is an Essene document only slightly edited by a Christian.

Other fragments also suggest that the Nasi, the Prince, of the Community was put to death, though it could be interpreted that the Nasi put someone else to death. The context is that of that revered quotation from *Isaiah* – "a rod shall rise from the stem of Jesse and a branch shall grow from his roots" referring to the Messiah. Elsewhere a messianic figure will overthrow the evil generation. This fragment possibly refers to a crucifixion. Though the word is not complete the meaning seems to be confirmed by a subsequent command "Let not the nail touch him". If these fragments are not referring to Jesus but to a leader of the

Essenes who was crucified on an earlier occasion the whole of the gospel story is cast into doubt as a rehash of the earlier event.

The Scroll scholar, M.Dupont-Sommer, has summarised the remarkable similarities between the Teacher of Righteousness and Jesus Christ.

- Both were martyred prophets subsequently revered by their followers as the Suffering Servant.
- Both preached penitence, poverty, humility, love of one's neighbour and chastity.
- Both prescribed observance of the Law of Moses.
- Both were the Elect of God and the Messiah, the redeemer of the world.
- Both were opposed by the priests, the Sadducees; were condemned and murdered.
- Both seemed to found a church whose believers thought he would return in glory, whose central rite was a sacred meal presided over by priests and whose members held goods in common and believed in brotherhood.
- Both will be the supreme judge at the Last Judgement.
- Both apparently predicted the fall of Jerusalem.

Did the Essene Teacher of Righteousness who died over a hundred years earlier become the model for Jesus Christ after the crucifixion of Barabbas?

Dupont-Sommer examines the second part of *Isaiah*, often termed *Deutero-Isaiah*, which was long believed to have been written during the Babylonian exile 200 years after the first part. Here appears the account of the "Suffering Servant despised and rejected by men, a man of sorrows" who has "been wounded for our transgressions" yet by whose "stripes we are healed". Christians have taken this as prophesying Jesus, but Dupont-Sommer argues that it is a direct reference to the Teacher of Righteousness added to *Isaiah* as late as the intertestamental period. Dupont-Sommer urges a re-examination of other *Old Testament* passages in *Daniel*, *Zechariah*, *Psalms* and the *Songs of the Servant of Yahweh* in *Deutero-Isaiah* believing them to be all possibly inserted references to the Teacher of Righteousness.

If this is true it is easy to see how the followers of Barabbas transformed him into a reflection of the Teacher of Righteousness after his crucifixion.

Christian and Essene Common Features

Christianity and the Essenes sect have too many features in common for it to be chance.

- They both believe in baptism. Vermes tells us the *Manual of Discipline* ordained that the initiate "shall be made clean by the humble submission of his soul to all the precepts of God" but only after "his flesh is sprinkled with purifying water and sanctified by cleansing water".
- The earliest Christians "held all things common" – they were primitive communists. Yet the *Manual of Discipline* states that all shall bring their "knowledge, powers and possessions" into the Community, that they shall "eat in common and pray in common" and that a new member's property shall be "merged...to the Community".
- The early church in Jerusalem was led by the twelve Apostles (still twelve even after Judas had died showing that the Apostles were not particular persons but positions to be filled when vacant – fourteen or possibly fifteen Apostles are mentioned in the gospels) of whom Peter, James and John had special responsibility. The Community was led by a Council of 12 people, apparently with three priests having special responsibility.
- Both the Community and the first Christians were messianic: the Christians regarded Jesus as the Messiah; the Community had their "Teacher of Righteousness" with a similar history.
- Both communities also use the same phraseology. Jesus said: "blessed are the meek for they shall inherit the earth", an exact expression of the Community's beliefs about itself for they called themselves "the Poor" and "the Meek" and they were preparing themselves to inherit the earth when God's kingdom on Earth was created. Many other instances can be quoted especially from *Matthew* which was the one closest in language to the Aramaic.
- Both communities originally cleaved rigidly to the Law of Moses and so, evidently did Jesus because he says in the Sermon on the Mount that he has not come to destroy the Law but to fulfil it and that "one jot or one tittle shall in no wise pass away from the Law till all things be accomplished".
- If the confusion of the timing of the Last Supper in the *Bible* is anything to go by the calendar used by Jesus did not match the official Jewish one. The Community used a solar rather than the official lunar calendar which might have allowed Jesus and his disciples to have had their Passover meal a day earlier so that he was crucified before Passover started.

- Both communities had an identical ritual meal. The Christian one supposedly specially instituted by Jesus at the last supper, the Community one laid down in the *Manual of Discipline* in which the priest shall "bless the first fruits of the bread and new wine" after which the Messiah, who is present in spirit, or the Nasi, who is really present, extends his hand over the bread that they might begin.
- Both communities referred to their leader as "Master".
- Both communities held an important gathering at Pentecost.

New Testament scholars believed *John* was the last of the gospels written and was strongly influenced by Persian religion and Platonic philosophy. From the scrolls however some scholars now take a different view – *John* follows the tradition of the Essenes. *John* has the conflict of Light and Darkness and expressions like, "the light of life", "children of light", "walking in darkness", "the spirit of truth" and "eternal life" all of which occur in the *Manual of Discipline*. *John* has:

> *And all things were made through him, and without him was not anything made that was made.*

The *Manual of Discipline* has the following:

> *And by his knowledge everything has been brought into being. And everything that is, he established for his purpose; and apart from him nothing is done.*

The scroll fragments prove to be messianic, make use of the same frequent scriptural quotations used in the *New Testament* books, have similar concepts of Righteousness, Piety, Truth, Justification, Works, the Poor, the Meek and use similar vocabulary. The Hebrew word "hesed" in the Qumran fragments is translated by traditional Qumran scholars as "Piety" but it can also be rendered as "Grace" which is the translation used in Paul's epistles. Scroll words are Christian words.

Christian Language in the Scrolls

Some Scroll fragments are of hymns to the poor. The Qumran literature frequently refers to the Community as the Poor, the Meek and the Downtrodden, words all used frequently in the gospels. Like English, Hebrew has different words for them but in the scrolls they seem to be used interchangeably. One of the Community's names for itself was the "Poor Ones". The Star prophecy of the *War Scroll* reads that:

> *by the hand of the Poor Ones whom you have redeemed by Your Power and the peace of Your Mighty Wonders... by the hand of*

> *the Poor Ones and those bent in the dust, You will deliver the enemies of all the lands and humble the mighty of the peoples to bring upon their heads the reward of the Wicked and justify the Judgement of Your Truth on all the sons of men...*

Can it be coincidence that the Poor Ones was a name of the followers of James in the Jerusalem Church (Gal 2:10 and Jas 2:3-5)? Paul claims the only condition James imposed upon him in his missions to the gentiles was to remember the poor. It sounds patronising, as though James is reminding Paul that motherhood is a good thing. In fact he is reminding him to send money for the Poor Ones in Jerusalem, the Nazarenes who still had a lot of widows to support.

In his *Ecclesiastical History* written in the fourth century, Eusebius describes a deviant Christian sect, the Ebionites, who held the brother of Jesus, James the Just, in special regard. They refused to accept that Jesus was divine but thought of him as an ordinary man, naturally conceived and notable for his righteousness but having no divine aspects. They did not accept that faith was sufficient to save and were therefore careful to observe the Law in addition – "...they evinced great zeal to observe the literal sense of the Law". They had no regard at all for Paul. Eusebius thought their name came from their "low and mean opinions" of Christ – Ebionites comes from the word Ebionim meaning the Poor Ones. They could have been none other than the remnants of the Jerusalem Church of James the Just perpetuating the name used by the Nazarenes, the Essenes and James himself.

The Scrolls also use the same curious expression that Jesus the Nazarene uses in the Sermon on the Mount (Mt 5:3) but has never before been found in any ancient work and was long thought to have been a mistranslation – "the poor in spirit". It appears in the *War Scroll* and in the *Manual of Discipline*.

Other Scroll fragments are replete with Christian imagery. One focuses on the Righteous, the Pious, the Meek and the Faithful, all synonyms for those who follow the Way of the Community. Echoing the *Damascus Document*, it says God visits the Meek and calls the Righteous by name. God's spirit hovers over the Meek announcing to them "Glad tidings" and He makes the Root of Planting grow. The Messiah "shepherds the holy ones" and he commands the "heavens and the earth" including the "Heavenly Host". The fragments contain references to "making the blind see", "raising up the downtrodden" and "resurrecting the dead". The Pious (Hasidim) are glorified on the Throne of the Eternal Kingdom. In some of the fragments the bones passage of *Ezekiel* is used to promise resurrection for the Pious and the Righteous.

Jesus taught "love thy neighbour as thyself" (cf. James 2:8) and "love the Lord thy God". Josephus in *Antiquities* says John the Baptist taught "Righteousness toward men and Piety towards God" and also notes this as Essene practice. Scroll fragments tell us the Community's notion of Piety meant "loving God's name". Thus Essene teaching and the teaching of Jesus amount to the same thing. Both the *Epistle of James* and the Qumran texts associate piety with poorness and meekness and they and the gospels declare that wealth is not compatible with righteousness.

Isaiah 11.2 has:

> *The Spirit of the Lord would settle on him*

the origin of the imagery at Jesus's baptism. The scrolls have the same but expressed even more explicitly:

> *The Holy Spirit settled on His Messiah.*

Here the Spirit of the Lord becomes the Holy Spirit and the recipient of it, His Messiah, is explicit.

Other fragmentary texts convey to us that "Perfection" language is important to the Community. Thus the scrolls and fragments have "the Perfect of the Way", "Perfection of the Way", "walking in Perfection" and "perfect Holiness" (cf. 2 Cor 7:1). This may be compared with the Sermon on the Mount (Mt 5:48):

> *Be perfect as your Father in Heaven is perfect.*

"The Way" terminology also illustrated in these expressions and very common in the scrolls is similarly echoed in *Acts* (see 16:16, 18:24f, 24:22). The *Epistle of Barnabas* is a second century Christian but non-canonical work full of Qumran expressions such as The Way of Light, the Way of Darkness, the Way of Holiness, the Way of Death, keeping the Law, Righteousness, the Last Judgement, Uncircumcised Heart, Dark Lord and such.

Paul is very fond of Essene words. *2 Corinthians* 6:14-15 is purely Essene even to the use of the word Belial, the Essene word for Satan, the only place it ever appears in the *New Testament*.

The "many" or the "majority" are common *New Testament* expressions usually for groups of Christians. An equivalent expression occurs in the sectarian documents and is often translated "congregation". Equally the Essene documents refer to people in some sort of official role translated as "overseer" or "guardian". It is the word which was rendered into Greek as "bishop".

In *Daniel* 2:44 (possibly related to *Luke* 21:20) Daniel prophesies that God will set up a kingdom which will last forever. Qumran scroll fragments speak of an Eternal Kingdom ruled by a Messiah, the Son of God or the Son of the Most High, whose "rule will be an eternal rule". Compare this with *Luke* 1:32-35:

> *He will be great and will be called the son of the Most High;*
> *and the Lord God will give him the Throne of his father David...*
> *for that reason the Holy offspring will be called the Son of God.*

We have seen that, in the *Bible*, Son of God is a designation of a great king like David (Ps 2:7, Ps 89:27 and 2 Sam 7:14 and also Heb 1:5 and 5:5). From some scroll fragments we find the Eternal Kingdom will be an earthly one and that the Son of God will judge the earth and bring peace by subjugating all other kingdom's and peoples. The people of God will make "everyone to rest from the sword" so there will be peace on earth. The "sword of God" is a phrase met in the *War Scroll*. This imagery recalls that of *Matthew*,

> *I come not to send peace but a sword.*

Besides the sword of war there is also the sword of judgement but here its contrast with peace makes the meaning clear. The sword of war is necessary to initiate the kingdom which then brings the sword of judgement and finally peace.

In parts of another document there is a set of beatitudes like those of the Sermon on the Mount. Indeed the Sermon on the Mount is remarkably reminiscent of Qumran. Some similarities have been noted. Another is that Jesus teaches that oaths are unnecessary because no one should ever tell lies (Mt 5:33-37). We have seen the concern of the community for truth. The *Manual of Discipline* calls the group "the community of Truth"; they rail against "The Lie"; Josephus says they refused to swear on oath and were excused from taking the oath of loyalty to Herod. The Sermon on the Mount includes the duty to turn the other cheek towards an aggressor and this too is an Essene precept, as we have noted.

Remarkable also is the set of assertions in the Sermon on the Mount introduced by "You have heard it was said..." and linked to their rebuttal by "...but I say to you..." One Qumran document, apparently a letter, lays out a set of 22 false interpretations of Law and their rebuttal. The interesting thing about it is that it uses almost the same language as the Sermon on the Mount in *Matthew*. A series of assertions are prefaced "You say..." and are answered by arguments preceded by "But we think..." in essence the same as Jesus does on the Mount.

Scroll Language in Early Christian Documents

We noted above that Jewish scholar, Geza Vermes, finds no parallels in traditional Jewish literature with the Qumran *Rules* but several with early Christian literature. The *Testaments of the Twelve Patriarchs* is a non-canonical work which in its philosophy and expression seems to be a bridge between Christianity and the community of Qumran. Dr R.H.Charles, who translated the *Testaments* and dated them as early as 100 BC, thought there were many echoes of the *Testaments* in the gospels and even more in the *Epistles of Paul* – over 70 words are common to Paul's writings and the *Testaments* which do not appear anywhere else in the *New Testament*. The words "meekness" and "mercy" occur often.

At one point the *Testaments* speak of "a man who reneweth the Law in the power of the Most High" being called a deceiver and "not knowing his dignity" slain thereby "taking innocent blood through wickedness". It goes on to say...

> *...your holy places shall be laid waste even to the ground because of him. And ye shall have no place that is clean; but ye shall be among the gentiles a curse and a dispersion until he shall again visit you and in pity shall receive you through faith and water.*

These sound like references to Jesus, the destruction of Jerusalem and the dispersion of the Jews in 70 AD but it could perhaps refer to the Teacher of Righteousness and the capture of Jerusalem by Pompey in 63 BC. The *Testaments* repeatedly uses the Greek word Christos which of course could refer to Jesus but equally could simply mean Messiah. Particularly impressive is the similarity of *Matthew* 25:35-36 with a passage from the *Testament of Joseph*. The latter has lines like:

> *I was beset by hunger and the Lord himself nourished me. I was sick and the Lord visited me. I was alone and God comforted me...*

While *Matthew* has:

> *I was hungry and you gave me food. I was sick and you visited me. I was a stranger and you welcomed me...*

Passages of the Sermon on the Mount are also anticipated. It promises that the poor shall be made rich. The reader is urged to love God and "to love your neighbour as thyself". This doctrine seems to have become popular around that time. It appears in the *Book of Jubilees* and in the Zadokite documents – The *Damascus Document* has:

> *They shall love each man his brother as himself; they shall succour the poor, the sick and the needy.*

And it was was offered by Rabbi Hillel, when challenged to teach the Torah as succinctly as possible, in the form:

> *What is hateful to thee, do not unto thy fellow: this is the whole Law.*

Another early work was the *Two Ways* which also was not included in the canon and subsequently was lost. Later scholars found a Greek manuscript called the *Didache* or the *Teaching of the Twelve Apostles.* It began "There are two ways..." and appeared to be the missing document. It was manifestly a Christian work but portions of a Latin version were also found with scarcely any Christian references. Though Jesus is mentioned there is no indication of atonement indicating its very early date. Besides doctrines like the Way of Light and the Way of Darkness and the sacrament of baptism, it refers to the sacred meal of bread and wine and looks very much like a Christian adaptation of an early, presumably Essene, work.

Interestingly, a work that *was* regarded as canonical in the first few centuries of the Christian era is the *Shepherd of Hermas* where a Son of God features but is never referred to as Jesus or Christ. Furthermore the church spoken of by Hermas has a long history before the Son of God was sent to purify it and to recall it to God's commandments: it was not *founded* by the Son of God. Hermas also mentions the *Didache* and the *Two Ways* confirming our deduction above. Atonement was by baptism. This sounds very much like a Nazarene or an Essene text.

The conclusion from the body of evidence presented here must be that the Nazarenes and the Essenes had almost everything in common. Certainly there are differences, particularly those indicated in Christian documents. Some are differences that are phoney because they have been introduced by the gentile Church; the others are genuine differences because the Nazarenes were a branch of the Essenes. Mainly these all come to a relaxation of the exclusiveness of the Essenes. Yet even this might have been a part of the Essene philosophy in the sense that it allowed for the recruitment of the Simple of Ephraim to the Elect as described in the *Nahum Peshar*. When the diviners considered the time right a Nasi was sent out into the community to test the mettle of the Simple. This safeguarded the Essenes as a whole while allowing God to show whether the auguries were correct or not. John the Baptist was one such; Jesus was his heir. Jesus's success led him to think God was with him but then he failed in the north. He concluded he had not been positive enough and captured Zion itself. He was mistaken or forsaken – but his effort did not pass unnoticed.

The word Christianity was not used until about 50 AD in Antioch (*Acts* 11:26). Subsequent to then and during the earlier move from Palestine the original movement mutated into the Christianity we now know, but the foundations in the manuscripts of Qumran seem clear. The change was from a narrowly Jewish, nationalistic, xenophobic and apocalyptic sect attached to the Mosaic Law, to one which was cosmopolitan, free of legal obligations, dependent only on faith and pacifist. It was not a simple change and required the talents of an exceptional man to effect it. But in the wider Empire the soil was fertile and ready to yield to a vigorous plant. The Nazarene movement became Paulinised.

THE TRIUMPH OF PAULINISM

...the only early Christian who ought really to have been eaten by lions.

G K Chesterton

The Crucifixion

After only a short time on the cross Barabbas was given a drink and quickly expired. The others crucified with him had to have their legs broken to bring on a quick death. Joseph of Arimathaea asked Pilate's permission to take him from the cross. Pilate was astonished that he had so soon died and asked the centurion to confirm it, which he did, and permission was given. Joseph and Nicodemus, both behaving as if they had an interest in the body, wrapped it in linen and put it in a new tomb cut out of rock in a private garden. The tomb was sealed by a large rock pushed against the entrance.

After the Passover the two Mary's and others, or Mary Magdalene alone, came to the tomb early on the Sunday morning to wash and prepare the body. The stone had been rolled away and the tomb was empty. A young man (or two men) in pure white garments tells them that Jesus is risen and has gone to Galilee. At this point the earliest gospel ends (ignoring the final twelve verses which were added later). The significance of the pure white garments is not that these men are angels of God but that they are angels (messengers) of the Essenes. Jesus had an important position in the Essene order. His body was removed so that he could be given a proper burial in a place approved by the community. The messengers from the sect give orders to the disciples – they are to escape to Galilee, out of Roman jurisdiction. *Matthew* says soldiers had been placed on guard to prevent the disciples from stealing the body but no other gospel mentions this and it is transparently an editorial addition to overcome the criticism that the body had been stolen by Jesus's followers.

Immediately after the crucifixion the disciples had despaired and were incredulous to hear that the tomb was empty. This proves that Jesus cannot have taught his disciples to expect his bodily resurrection on the third day as the gospels maintain since otherwise they would have been expecting Jesus to rise, would not have despaired at his death and would have rejoiced to hear of the empty tomb. The five occasions Jesus spoke of his death and resurrection in the gospel stories look suspiciously like interpolations based on hindsight.

The Church's attempt at accounting for the inconsistency of the Apostles' behaviour was to accuse them of stupidity. Of course they were not stupid. If they were, Jesus must have been stupid to have chosen them. If they really did not understand when Jesus told them what to expect then his words must have been far more obscure than they are in the *New Testament*. The plausible explanation is that they were completely surprised by the news of the empty tomb. Jesus had made no prophecies about his personal resurrection. Their behaviour was therefore perfectly understandable. Their leader was dead, their rebellion had failed, God had not intervened – they despaired. Then someone had the temerity to steal the corpse! Tertullian, a Christian of about 160 AD, states that the body of Jesus was removed from the tomb by the man in charge of the garden wherein the sepulchre was situated so that his lettuces would not be spoiled by the crowds!

According to the verses added to *Mark,* it is Mary Magdalene who first sees the risen Jesus. As if to provide an explanation the author immediately tells us that Jesus had cast seven devils from her. It seems her madness was subject to relapses and further devils had then to be cast out. In short she was unreliable if not badly neurotic. Despite Jesus's apparent prophecies, the disciples did not believe her.

Christian belief depends mainly on Jesus's appearances rather than the empty tomb. Writing long before the gospels were written, in the earliest Christian works we have, the Apostle Paul never attempts to convince sceptics about the resurrection by quoting witnesses to the empty tomb. His evidence is Jesus's appearances: to the women, to two disciples on the way to Emmaus, to Peter and others in Jerusalem, to the Apostles on a Galilaean mountain. Paul was not interested in the living Jesus but only in the resurrection and, as the first Christian writer, having heard of a hysterical woman's reaction to Jesus's crucifixion and abduction, he could have invented additional appearances to confirm it. He adds a remarkable appearance to a throng of 500 which even the gospel writers must have found stretched credulity too far.

If, as some suggest, Jesus *did* survive the crucifixion he could hardly have been making appearances all over the place within days. He had been horribly wounded in arms, feet and side. He must have been kept in a safe house for months to recover, moved only if necessary and when sufficiently fit would have been taken out of the Roman Emperor's reach to Parthia.

Yet the disciples in the gospels are certain that Jesus was alive and not just a vision. The author of *Luke* is at pains to demonstrate that Jesus was truly alive. In *Acts* he tarries for as long as forty days. But he was not recognised by Mary Magdalene nor by two disciples on the road to Emmaus. In his final appearance in *John* by the Sea of Galilee, the disciples again do not recognise him. If all this were true and not elaborations of a Pauline invention then it implies that Jesus was heavily disguised – or being impersonated! These people knew him extremely well, so why otherwise couldn't they recognise him? If in disguise, he must have been hiding from the authorities! At his final appearance he behaves like a man about to depart quickly – to Parthia rather than Heaven – repeatedly urging his disciples to "take care of my sheep" – plainly meaning the lost sheep of the house of Israel.

The Quran says that Jesus survived because a substitute was crucified in his stead. According to the Basilidians, the substitute was Simon of Cyrene. Mark's and Matthew's gospels, from the point when Simon is mysteriously introduced into the account (Mt 27:32-44; Mk 15:21-32), are completely ambiguous about who was crucified. They could read that Simon was. Only at the point of death when they report that "Jesus" cries out is the doubt settled.

If these traditions hint at the truth, a lot could be explained. Simon had been substituted for Barabbas and had been crucified. But the Nazarenes did not want to risk the Romans finding out by leaving the wrong man hanging there. Most Romans would not have known Barabbas but collaborators would and the longer that Simon remained on the cross the more likely it was that the substitution would be noticed. So Simon was poisoned and whisked away by Joseph and Nicodemus after only a few hours on the cross when days would have been the norm. Of course, the problem was not solved because the Romans might want to inspect the corpse – so they disposed of it secretly! Jesus Barabbas was still alive but could only appear in disguise until such time as he could get away to the East. And so he does – there is a further tradition that Jesus eventually died in India.

Only *Luke* mentions the ascension into Heaven – in *Acts*. The words in *Mark* are simply that he was received up into Heaven and even these are in the last twelve verses now considered to be added. We are faced with an astonishing event, reputedly seen by many but recorded only by one. It simply is not credible that people seeing such an astonishing occurrence would not report it later. Plainly it is a fiction.

Crucifixion: a Pagan Rite

The odd thing about the crucifixion is that it re-enacts ancient pagan rites of human sacrifice. Eusebius tells us, quoting Philo of Byblus, the Jewish King traditionally gave his beloved son as a sacrificial offering for the nation as a ransom to avenging devils. Thus Abraham wanted to sacrifice his son Isaac; David attempted to stop a famine by sacrificing seven royal princes, hanging them before the Lord, at the beginning of the barley harvest, about the time of the Passover; Mesha of Moab sacrificed his eldest son; King Hiel sacrificed his sons when Jericho was founded; Kings Ahaz and Manassah burnt their children in sacrifice; Ishmael was nearly sacrificed by his father, like Isaac, according to Arab legend.

The king personified the tribal god and as such was the father of the people; the son therefore represented the people themselves. Thus the actual son of the king was sacrificed as the symbolic Son of the Father (bar Abbas) representing the unworthy tribe. With time this rite became more symbolic, a condemned criminal being substituted for the prince, as in the Babylonian Sacaea when the substitute was dressed in fine robes to represent the prince, a crown was put on his head, he was scourged and finally hanged or crucified – just as Jesus was!

Though human sacrifice was made illegal in the Roman republic in 196 BC, it seems to have continued till later, particularly associated with the military. In many places in Roman Britain for example human skulls or skeletons are found with the bones of sacrificed animals at the sites of temples or shrines. They might have been people who died naturally though it seems unlikely that a ready made corpse would be thought to propitiate the god rather than a sacrificial victim. More probably they were criminals who had been sentenced to capital punishment and so were used to double up as a human sacrifice. The mockery of Jesus by the Roman soldiers who dressed him in robes and crowned him with thorns prior to his crucifixion was plainly some such ritual – Jesus might well have been a human sacrifice in fact.

The sacrifice of a lamb or a kid at the Passover similarly was a symbolic human sacrifice. The substitution of a ram for Isaac in the story of Abraham probably represents the change over from human to animal sacrifice and provides the authority for it. The Laws of Moses make the change explicit. But when Jesus ben Pandira in the reign of Alexander Jannaeus was stoned and hanged from a tree on the eve of the Passover, was this an indication that tyrants in cruel mockery or even the people themselves sometimes revived the old custom?

Was the custom of the exchange of the criminal referred to in the gospel accounts a reference to the sacrifice of a condemned criminal at Passover alongside the lesser sacrifice of a lamb? In troubled times was a symbolic bar Abbas chosen from among the condemned, dressed as a king and sacrificed? Caiaphas said it was expedient for a man to be sacrificed for the good of the nation. Was it Pilate's joke that the king of the Jews should be sacrificed according to the defunct custom in mock piety? In 40 AD the mob at Alexandria, a town with a large expatriate Jewish population dressed up an old man with a crown, a sceptre and a purple robe and hailed him as Karabbas and Maris according to Philo Judaeus. Karabbas is plainly a misspelling of Barabbas and Maris signified a king. Was this another example of the old custom revived or was it a demonstration by orthodox Jews against the growing cult of the false god, Jesus Barabbas, The Christ?

The victims of the sacrifices were normally hanged on a tree until dusk as the *Old Testament* repeatedly indicates and in the Greek language hanging from a tree and crucifixion are synonymous. The two others hanged with Barabbas would, on this hypothesis, represent the king's attendants, one being on his right hand and one on his left. Even if the crucifixion were not intended as a human sacrifice, anyone who knew of the old custom must have seen it as just that.

Barabbas's attendants on the cross had their legs broken to shorten their lives but Barabbas was already dead. The object of crucifixion was to provide a slow death. The victims were usually tied to the cross or branches, sometimes with nailing also. Their feet rested on a support on the upright or trunk enabling them to press upward from time to time to relieve the strain on the chest and lungs. Once the legs were broken, the strain would soon lead to death, there being no relief. Since Barabbas was already dead without any broken bones and, according to *John*, on the eve of the Passover, he became the perfect sacrifice – the Paschal lamb had to be perfect; it could have none of its bones broken!

The piercing of Barabbas's side by the lance of the soldier testing whether he was still alive also ties in with ancient sacrificial custom. Strabo records that the early Albanians offered a human sacrifice to the moon goddess by piercing his side with a sacred spear. Similarly the sacrifices at Salamis, Odin where the victim was hung on a tree before being pierced, and in the worship of Mithra where the bull as Mithra incarnate was pierced in the side by a spear.

Thus, following ancient and largely superseded traditions, early Christians thought of Barabbas's crucifixion as sacrificial (1 Cor 15:3: "Christ died for our sins"). Paul's teaching of Christ crucified was central to the success of the evangelist. The followers of Barabbas were able to convince themselves that their hero had died as a human sacrifice. He had become the Paschal Lamb: it was God's will. Thus the dead Christ became more important than the live one almost as soon as the death occurred and certainly by the time Paul had taken it to the gentiles.

All the eastern religions of the Roman Empire had an incarnate god who died as a divine sacrifice and returned to life. It was a sine qua non of a decent religion! But here was something really novel – this one actually happened! And similarly most gods of the time ascended into Heaven. Adonis, Dionysus, Hercules, Hyacinth, Krishna and Mithras were among those who so ascended usually in full view for the benefit of their followers. And so did the epitome of *Old Testament* prophets, Elijah. The Christian God could do no less!

The cross was significant in itself. For Christians it is a mighty talisman giving cosmic insurance against evil or danger, or, as a gesture, expressing gratitude to higher powers for deliverance. The Apostle Paul said he would glory in naught "save in the cross of our Lord" (Gal 6:14). Yet the cross was an object of worship in its own right long before the Christian era. A Christians hymn to the praise to the cross goes:

> *Hail, O Cross, triumphal tree, true salvation of the world;*
> *among trees there is none like thee, In leaf, flower and bud.*

A tree had been sacred to various gods. An image of the god Attis was hung upon the sacred pine tree at the commemoration of his death. The faithful also worshipped the tree itself. The tree sacred to Osiris was similarly treated, the god's body being placed in its branches. Cyrus, called by Isaiah the Messiah, was crucified in some versions of his myth; Prometheus who suffered eternal torment for mankind was crucified according to Lucan. Crucifixion was understood as the pious bearing of suffering. The Druids worshipped a cross made from a large tree denuded of leaves and stems save for its two main horizontal branches. Buddhists also symbolise life with a cross sprouting leaves and branches.

The mark made on the foreheads of the righteous in Ezekiah (9:4-6) is in Old Hebrew TAU – "t" to us – the mark of the cross. It signified that they should be saved at the coming visitation. Thus it was the sign of life and so was associated with salvation, and paganism (it stood for the god Tammuz), centuries before Christianity. The mark of TAU was made on the foreheads of those initiated into the Mithraic mysteries just as Christian initiates were marked at their baptism. Ancient religions identified god with the sun and so the TAU symbol is often associated with the solar disk. One such is the Egyptian Ankh or Crux Ansata carried by Osiris. Another is the cross inscribed within a disk common as a halo in Christian art. The vestal virgins, devoted to the goddess Vesta of Roman religion, who took an absolute vow of chastity punishable, if broken, by burial alive, always wore a cross as a pendant round their necks just as nuns do today!

Paul was being typically opportunist when he spoke of the "cross of Christ", the "preaching of the cross" and the "blood of the cross" because he knew pagans would understand him fully. The worship of the crucifix carried on where pagan cross worship left off and that in turn was a continuation of tree worship.

The Jerusalem Church

Immediately after Barabbas had been crucified his followers had fled. Many had been killed in Jerusalem and more had been crucified by Pilate – they did not want to stay around to find out whether there would be more arrests. Peter, the gospels admit, cut off a man's ear, the merest indication Barabbas's gang used force resisting arrest. He was too scared to admit that he was a disciple and denied it three times.

Yet in *Acts*, Peter and the Apostles are active again in Jerusalem shortly afterwards. *Matthew* however says they fled to Galilee, out of direct Roman rule, a safer and more sensible option. *John* makes it clear they were in hiding, meeting only in secrecy, because doors were shut when they assembled. The apocryphal *Gospel of Peter* says explicitly that the Apostles were sought by the authorities as malefactors who wanted to set fire to the Temple. How then were they able to continue to proclaim their Messiah, only half-heartedly hindered by the civic authorities, as *Acts* maintains, so soon after an uprising?

The answer lies in events in the Roman administration. Pilate was withdrawn to Rome in 36 AD and the executive of the Empire changed with the death of Tiberius in 37 AD. After an interregnum the new administrators would have taken office with new concerns. The remnants of Barabbas's band then felt able to return from Galilee and tentatively to resume activity. The activity now was not revolution but persuading people that the Messiah was Barabbas and that he was soon to return on a cloud with a heavenly host as in *Daniel*. The disciples still expected a miracle and Israel to be liberated as *Luke-Acts* proves. And Peter continued to preach that God had promised to King David to put one of his descendants on the throne of Israel.

Considering the apparent failure of their Messiah they were surprised to find themselves enjoying much success in winning Jewish proselytes. The number of disciples in Jerusalem greatly increased and even priests adopted the new faith (*Acts* 6:1; 6:7). Few, perhaps none, of these new proselytes would have been gentiles though many may have been Hellenised Jews. The orthodox Jews feared that the whole population would be converted. A century later Tacitus writes that the death of Jesus was a blow "which, for a time, checked the growth of a dangerous superstition; but it broke out again, and spread with increasing vigour, not only in Judaea...but even in the city of Rome". The *Recognitions of Clementine*, a third century work possibly based on Nazarene tradition, confirms this success.

What was the reason for this astonishing success? It still seems surprising that a failed Messiah should posthumously become so successful. Jesus had spread the word that the day of judgement was at hand, indeed twice in *Matthew* (Mt 16:28 and Mt 24:34) Jesus promised to his disciples the kingdom within a generation. Ordinary Jews were superstitious and demoralised. With each hope dashed they sought another to cling to. Perhaps the message of Jesus's life remained valid though the messenger was dead – the kingdom was at hand, still! Most Jews believed in life after death, only the Sadducees did not, and talk of the recently deceased Nasi returning on a cloud with a heavenly host to realise God's will in fulfilment of the prophecy of *Daniel* renewed their faith in the Messiah just when it had apparently been frustrated.

Thus the disciples' initial disappointment at Barabbas's failure turned into a new hope and the Apostles benefited from a sort of apocalyptic hysteria. They convinced themselves that the late earthly Barabbas was not a warrior Messiah but represented Israel as the suffering servant of *Isaiah*. This spavined, sinful, ugly and despised man was sentenced to a dishonourable death, remained silent in his defence and was unhesitatingly dispatched but was rewarded with victory after death. Accounts of Barabbas's trials were written with this model in mind.

So Peter, John, the son of Zebedee, and James, the brother of Jesus, founded the Jerusalem Church.

The epistles of Paul confirm that James was a pillar of the church along with Peter and John. Peter and John were already Apostles but James was not (unless it could be shown he was James the son of Alphaeus). Why should he have been a founder of the Church? He was not one of the Twelve but he was Jesus's successor as head of the Church. The reason must have been that he was his brother and next in line. Perhaps this is the royal line of David, the Sang Real, especially since on James' death the son of another brother of Jesus, Jude, became leader. It was the norm for dynasties to head sects in Judaea at that time. The leaders of the Maccabaean revolt constituted a dynasty. The High Priesthood was a dynasty. The Zealots were led by the dynasty of Judas of Galilee. The clear succession of leadership which obviously existed is possibly evidence that the sect was not newly founded after Jesus's death.

Now Jesus's family are depicted in the gospels as doubting him so it is again mysterious that a brother should assume leadership on Jesus's death. *Acts* fails to mention that James is Jesus's brother, though Paul in a letter written much earlier openly admits it. Nor does *Acts* say anything about the martyrdom of James. Indeed *Acts* wrongly says Peter succeeded Jesus as the leader of the Jerusalem Church when all other evidence shows it was James. The lie was inserted later by the Church of Rome, traditionally founded by Peter, to give it greater authority.

The *New Testament* treatment of the family of Jesus is a further attempt by Christian editors to dissociate their god from his origins. After the quarrel reported in the gospels when Jesus leaves his family in disgust they are scarcely heard of again until the crucifixion. Jesus apparently rejected his family in the gospels because they had no faith in him. For a church desperately trying to be gentile, that served to prove that even Jesus's family connections with Jewishness had been severed.

The Church led by James, the brother of Jesus, was a Jewish sect, orthodox in all respects except for their belief that the Messiah had appeared in the person of Barabbas who had died a felon's death, hanging from a tree, but had been resurrected and would *soon* (within their own lifetime) return with the hosts of Heaven to free the Jews from persecution. They knew Barabbas as a devout Jew, who had not repudiated the Torah, indeed who was zealous for the Law. His Sabbath cures were not against the Law. They believed they were living in the End Time, the days just before the inauguration of the kingdom of God on earth when the pure would be selected to rule the world as the passages from the *Psalms of Solomon* above makes clear.

Emphatically they did not regard Barabbas as divine. Not only would that have been blasphemous but James and his brothers and sisters would have regarded it as absurd. They had lived with Barabbas all their lives and would have been aware more than anyone of his humanity. Since a Jewish Messiah could not be divine, they regarded him as human even though God had revived him from the dead! In *Acts* 2:22 Peter does not describe Jesus as a god but as "a man accredited to you by God" – a special man, yes, but a man nonetheless. The evidence even of the gospels is that Jesus could not have contemplated the blasphemy of a man claiming to be a god.

A feel of the original Palestinian fount of Christianity, the Nazarene Church, is given by the *Epistle of James the Just* (or Righteous) which was regarded by

Christians as far removed as Eusebius and Luther as unsuitable for inclusion in the canon. Its language is much like that ascribed to Jesus in the synoptic gospels and its sentiments very much like those of the Qumran Community, for example in emphasising the spiritual benefits of poverty. It is a document of the style of a Qumran exhortation with no mention of a dead and resurrected redeemer and indeed scarcely a mention of Jesus at all, This also supports the idea that the Nazarenes were a sect which existed before the crucifixion of Jesus, and, indeed, that it was not originally a religion "of Jesus" but one of righteousness and correct living which Barabbas had served as an unusual leader.

Schism in the Jerusalem Church

Curiously after Barabbas's death, in many ways little was different for the Jews in the Jerusalem Church. They were Nazarenes, a variety of Essenes – not the monastic Essenes of Qumran but the village Essenes. As Nazarenes they had been Apocalyptic Jews – they still were, but now expected the Messiah who would return on a cloud to be their late leader Jesus Barabbas. Before they had been the Elect preparing themselves through purity for the End Time – now the End Time had begun and the need for purity was absolutely pressing. Before they had had a set of complex Rules designed to ensure righteousness – the same rules applied. Before they had been certain they were the Chosen Ones of the New Covenant – now they were ecstatic with the certainty and wanted every Jew to join before Jesus returned to start the kingdom of God.

Nazarenes practised circumcision and accepted food prohibitions. They were accepted by other Jews as a Jewish sect and taught in the synagogues just as Jesus had. They were not persecuted by orthodox Jews, quite the opposite, the Nazarenes were considered as defenders of Jewish religious and patriotic ideas. None of this would have been possible if they thought that Barabbas was a god. And even in *Acts* (5:34-40) the Sanhedrin continues to accept the activities of the Apostles.

Unlike the Essenes of the Qumran monastery they worshipped at the Temple as village Essenes did. Their attitude to the Sadducees had not changed but Barabbas had symbolically purified the Temple anyway and would soon return to finish the job. Astonishingly James is reported to have been permitted to enter the Sanctuary. This can hardly have been true. The confusion possibly arises because James was a High Priest in waiting, trained at the Essene alternative Temple at Qumran and ready to serve when Barabbas established God's kingdom on earth. Eusebius, the Father of Church History, confirms that the Jerusalem Church continued to sacrifice in the Temple and to keep the Law even after the gentile churches had split away.

Like the monastic Essenes and unlike the village Essenes, the Nazarenes held goods in common as *Acts* makes clear. They were expecting the present world to end – and soon! So there was little point in keeping individual wealth. Converts had to turn over their belongings to the community when they joined. Josephus tells us Essenes who held anything back were severely punished. According to the *New Testament*, Nazarenes were also severely punished – God murdered them! *Acts* tells us God murders two such people, a man and his wife, Ananias and Sapphira, after Peter had demanded to know why they were holding goods back. It sounds harsh for a god of love. If Ananias and his wife were killed by God, for the trivial sin of withholding some of their possessions, one wonders why God is so lenient when much worse crimes are committed. No good god could have such warped standards. The *New Testament* avenger was Peter – not God.

After these deaths "a great fear came upon the whole Church". But why? Had they all been holding something back and thought God might finish them too? No, the incident can better be understood if it happened in the period when the Nazarenes were still underground and Peter's wrath was because the two had received money from elsewhere. They were informers! The members of the Church would then be naturally fearful for their lives, not knowing whether they had been betrayed or whether others were also ready to inform. Naturally the true story could not be told in the gospels without revealing that the band were outlaws so it was appropriately disguised.

Peter and John, the son of Zebedee, are twice arrested. Twice they are released. On the first occasion for fear of the people and on the second occasion because Gamaliel, the leading Pharisee and rabbi of the cautious and liberal school of Hillel, argued that the Sanhedrin should exercise restraint in case these men truly had the support of God – if they had not it would be evident soon enough. In his speech to the Sanhedrin Gamaliel compares the actions of Jesus's supporters with the uprisings led by Judas of Galilee and Theudas, the leader of another gang of 400 rebels. In this context the *New Testament* itself clearly identifies the disciples of Jesus with revolutionary gangs.

Two hundred years before, the Greek king, Antiochus IV Epiphanes, believing himself to be Zeus, had his statue erected in the Temple of Jerusalem. The Jews were appalled and outraged, calling the incident the Abomination of Desolation. It began the long period of Jewish resistance to foreign oppression. Another Abomination of Desolation occurred when Caligula insisted on erecting his statue in the Temple in about 40 AD. Tacitus says disturbances erupted in Judaea and food producers went on strike. Josephus, who would have been expected to give a full account of these events as important factors in the build up to the Jewish War, surprisingly mentions only protests when riots would have been expected. Was this the work of Christian censors? Had rioting actually occurred?

To the Nazarenes, for whom Barabbas had started the purification of the Temple and who expected him to return on a cloud, this second abomination would have been seen as a signal that the return was imminent. Were the Nazarenes the fomenters of the new tumults? Perhaps the tumults were of ecstasy or were strikes of workers seeing no point in labouring when the world was about to end. Though not violently revolutionary such actions would be disturbing enough to the authorities. But no mention is made of any of this in *Acts*, though the mini-apocalypse in *Mark* 13 possibly records it indirectly as Jesus's prophecy of hardship and tribulations to come.

By the time of the trial of Stephen, the Nazarenes had already split into two factions. Mainstream Nazarenes were Jews admitted to the Temple and subject to the Laws of Moses contrary to the impression given in the *New Testament*. Stephen was one of the Hellenised members of the community of Nazarenes, Jews who spoke Greek rather than Aramaic and used the version of the *Old Testament* called the Septuagint. Many were Jews of the dispersion, like Paul, and had a more liberal outlook than the Jews of Palestine, having integrated much more into the Greek culture that from the time of Alexander had dominated the region.

Closer contacts with gentiles made some of them more willing to consider changes to the Mosaic taboos. Gentiles had long been accepted into association with Judaism as "godfearers" who accepted the Jewish God, and indeed many Jews were not averse to having them as associates since they added to the Temple contributions. But actually to become a Jew, to convert, they had to undergo circumcision and accept the food taboos. Gentile women were willing to be converted but the idea of circumcision scared off many men. Stephen's blasphemy was to decry the Laws of Moses as outdated, outraging orthodox Jews. Stephen claimed Jesus had abolished the tedious Mosaic Laws so godfearers could become converts. Jews who remained orthodox objected to the message he was preaching and Stephen was called to account before the Sanhedrin.

Stephen put his liberal views at his trial. In his oration he refers to Jesus as The Righteous or Just One who they betrayed and murdered. In the Dead Sea Scrolls the expressions The Righteous One (Zaddik) and The Teacher of Righteousness occur frequently. Josephus speaks of a man called Sadduc who instigates revolt with Judas of Galilee at the time of the census of Quirinius in 6 AD. Sadduc (Zadok or Zaddik) might also be rendered The Righteous One.

The speech incenses the Sanhedrin and they order his stoning, and apparently the suppression of the church – *Acts* reporting: "they were scattered... except the Apostles". The new religion is hounded by the stubborn and malicious Jews – but not its leaders? Not the Apostles? Surely the leaders would be the first to be persecuted. The explanation is that the Apostles and their followers were not advocating a split with the Laws of Moses – they had done nothing wrong and could not be punished for anything. Only the Hellenist faction was persecuted. One of its oppressors was a young man called Saul. Saul later has a vision of the Christ, is converted to Christianity and adopts the name Paul.

In an interlude between Roman governors, the puppet king, Agrippa, murders James, the son of Zebedee, one of Jesus's chosen Apostles and far more important than Stephen, yet nothing is said in *Acts* except that it "pleased the Jews". Peter is again imprisoned but again escapes by a miracle, though it seems more likely that Agrippa had to release him because the people were so outraged by the murder of James that he was obliged to release Peter. It is at this point that Peter disappears and the narrative passes on to Paul. The *Acts of the Apostles* completely ignores the remainder of Peter's career, the fate of the Jerusalem Church and the rest of the original Apostles! They pass into total oblivion. Why do we know so little about them?

It is natural, of course, to write history from your own viewpoint and the truth is that the stories the other Apostles had to tell have not survived. Some died, some did not have their personal experiences transcribed, perhaps some who *did* failed to have them accepted into the canon. And, if our reconstruction is true, it is likely that most of Barabbas's chief lieutenants died with him. Many evidently died in action. We know of the two crucified at the same time but we don't know who they were except that they were in the same condemnation. The Romans would have rounded up and crucified as many of the conspirators as they could. The surviving Nazarenes, we have noted, had a lot of widows to provide for. The truth is probably that neither Peter nor the other Apostles who founded the Jerusalem Church were Jesus's chief confidants. They might have owed their survival to the fact that they were not at the top of the hierarchy. We only have their accounts of what happened and, since they were not of the inner circle, they were not in the best position to know.

This would, of course, explain why, in the gospels, they were so often in the dark about what was going on; why they often appeared so stupid – they were not privy to plans at the highest level. Thus they seemed not to know about the foal on the entry to Jerusalem. Jesus had had it already arranged – but by whom? It seems odd that these people did not know if they were really his chief confidants. They also did not know about the secret room in Jerusalem where the last supper was held or the man with the pitcher who led them there. The senior but not top ranking lieutenants of Barabbas who survived told the tale as if they were more senior than they were – human nature! In any event the momentum of the plot moves out of the hands of any of the original survivors because the story in *Acts* is now switching from Peter to the self-appointed Apostle, Paul.

Paul of Tarsus

Barabbas had no thoughts about founding a church. Paul, who never knew Barabbas in person, actually founded Christianity. He considered his visions of the resurrected Christ to be superior to direct experience of the living Barabbas.

The main sources of information about Paul are his epistles and the *New Testament* book, attributed to Luke, the *Acts of the Apostles*. The epistles naturally are partially autobiographical and liable to show him in the best light, and the author of the *Acts of the Apostles*, which was written later than the epistles, was partisan: he was a fervent supporter of Paul. In reading these sources we therefore have to guard against the bias for Paul there naturally is within them. The *Acts of the Apostles* has many faults. It is a sorry mixture of several sources, compiled selectively and heavily edited. The sequence of events in it is confused. It is not historical. It was written in Greek for a Greek audience offering the Pauline view of the origin of Christianity. The only independent source we have about Paul is an extract from the writings of the Ebionites which gives quite a different picture. No unexpurgated memoirs have survived of the men who actually knew Barabbas. The Christianity which came down to us is Paul's version – the version of a man who knew nothing about the life or work of Barabbas, had never met him and was not interested in him except as a divine sacrifice.

Acts indicates that Paul was a Jew of the dispersion born in Tarsus in Cilicia, Asia Minor (modern Turkey). He was originally called Saul, or more probably Solon because Tarsus was a Greek city, and was brought up in Jerusalem. Paul does not tell us his birthplace in his epistles but he does claim he was an Israelite of the tribe of Benjamin, a Hebrew and a Pharisee.

Acts says he left Tarsus to go to Israel to study with the leading Pharisee, Gamaliel. Paul however does not make this claim himself and it is likely to be false because the starting place for a student of Gamaliel was a profound knowledge of the Hebrew *Scriptures* and, though Paul is well versed in the *Scriptures*, most scholars cannot see sufficient depth in Paul's writings for him to have been taught in the best school. *Acts* claims that Paul was born a Roman citizen – his father must have been a Roman. Yet *Acts* also clearly implies that Paul was a member of the Sanhedrin (*Acts* 26:10 "my vote was cast against them" suggesting that he had a vote in the Sanhedrin). Both statements could not be true. *Acts* and Paul's own letters show that he was willing to distort the truth ("be all things to all men"). A blunt person would say he was a liar – he would say whatever was expedient.

Paul seems desperate to be seen as an orthodox Jew of a respected party, for despite the impression given in the *New Testament*, the Pharisees were seen throughout the Roman and the Parthian Empires as a serious and respectable religious group. Yet material relating to Paul seems uniformly anti-Pharisee. Thus he says he was flogged five times by "the Jews", *New Testament* code for the Pharisees. Why then did he claim to be a Pharisee? Biblical scholar, Hans Maccoby, argues that by so doing he strengthened his argument that Pauline Christianity was the successor to the Jewish religion. Paul, the devout Jew, who persecuted the original followers of Barabbas, the Nazarenes, by the grace of God was converted and then saw in the new religion the successor to Judaism. There must be something in a religion that means more to a devoutly orthodox Jew than his own!

Saul's family had had to flee from Gischala in Galilee, a breeding ground for revolutionaries, during some messianic disturbances – quite probably those involving Barabbas. Thereafter he disliked messianic movements, whence his persecution of the Nazarenes. Saul was the "young man" in The *Acts of the Apostles* who looked after the coats of the persecutors of the Nazarenes who were stoning the martyr, Stephen.

Saul went to the High Priest for letters to the synagogues in Damascus giving permission to extradite Nazarenes and bring them back to Jerusalem. In a vision on the way to Damascus Saul is confronted by Jesus who asks "why are you persecuting me?" and Paul becomes convinced that it is the heretics who preach Jesus's message, not the appointed Apostles. He becomes a convert to the Hellenist sect taking the name Paul and appoints himself as Apostle to the gentiles.

Such is the story, but could "a Pharisee of the Pharisees" work for the collaborating High Priest? It seems unlikely, even if the traditional enemies, the Pharisees and the Sadducees, were united in wanting to punish the Hellenistic branch of the Nazarenes opposing the Laws of Moses. Maccoby poses the following questions.

- Is it not odd that Saul should go to Damascus when he evidently had plenty of work harrying the Nazarenes in Judaea?
- Is it not also odd that an apparently private citizen should apply for permission to pursue the Nazarenes abroad – surely it was a job for the authorities if it had to be done at all?
- What authority would the High Priest of Judaea have over people living in Damascus, a Syrian city?
- What authority would the High Priest have over synagogues, teaching establishments run by rabbis and supported by local Jewish communities, wherever they were?

If Nazarenes had to be pursued, it is difficult to see why the High Priest would not have sent one of his own Temple Guard. Indeed all of this persecution by Paul would be better explained if he *were* a member of the Temple Guard, implying that Paul was a paid agent of the High Priest and therefore directly or indirectly an agent of the Romans. If Paul worked for the High Priest, it suggests that his claim to be a Pharisee is a lie.

These conclusions depend upon our understanding Damascus to be the famous Arab city in Syria. The reference in *Acts* to the street called Straight seems to confirm that it is. But if there were another Damascus in Judaea it could have fallen under the jurisdiction of the High Priest who could therefore have legally sent his policeman. If "Damascus" were a code word for the Essene community at Qumran then Paul would not have been going outside of Judaea to get to "Damascus". Acceptance of this idea would directly link Paul, the early Christians and the Qumran Community. Now in *Galatians*, Paul says after his conversion: "I went away into Arabia; and again I returned unto Damascus. Then after three years I went up to Jerusalem". This confounded scholars until the Essene headquarters was recognised as Damascus but now it is clear. After becoming a follower of Jesus, Paul went to Qumran to be initiated as an Essene, a procedure which takes three years. This is further demonstrated in his writings which use more Essene words than any other books of the *New Testament*. The references to the street named Straight and to Arabia evidently are editors' additions inserted through ignorance or deceit. And in *Acts* Paul's sojourn in Damascus is turned in typical fashion into a dispute with Jews not the period of initiation it really was – the disputes came later.

Back in Jerusalem, according to *Acts,* Paul became allied with the Hellenists led originally by Stephen and Philip. He appeared to switch from being ultra-orthodox to being ultra-radical. Paul's idea now was to let all those who believed in Jesus to become full members of the Church and blow the Mosaic Law. The author of *Acts* makes it appear that Paul upheld Jesus's idea that there was now a superior Law while the Jerusalem Church of Barabbas's original followers were too stupid to understand this and upheld the old Law. In fact, of course, Barabbas was as orthodox as his brethren and he is depicted thus in the gospels. But Paul wanted to substitute the new Law of the redemption of mankind from original sin through the sacrifice of the quasi-divine being. To this the Law of Moses was a hindrance.

James the Just and the Palestinian followers of Barabbas would hear nothing of it!

Since the Nazarenes were still a part of Judaism, the original Apostles did not trust Paul and eventually he incensed orthodox Jews of the Diaspora so much that the they threatened to kill him and he had to be sent to Tarsus. Thankful to be rid of him the leaders of the Jerusalem Church allowed him to go on his self appointed mission to convert gentiles. The Nazarenes were still expecting Barabbas to return on a cloud and if Paul could be gotten rid of converting gentiles in foreign parts then fine. But he returned in 49 AD again to seek to persuade the Apostolic Council of Jerusalem to abrogate the Mosaic Law for gentiles.

According to *Acts* Paul succeeded but Paul's own letters make no reference to this victory even though it would plainly have been a triumph for him. In fact the opposite is true – James reasserted the status quo: "godfearers" could only be associates of the Church; circumcision was necessary for conversion. The Nazarene authorities, who had known Barabbas during his lifetime, were adamant that the Elect would consist of Jews or full converts to Judaism. Paul proves it himself, for off he went writing letters illustrating his contempt for the associates of Jesus. (Gal 2:6, Gal 2:16, Phil 3:9). He writes of "false Apostles" and "reputed" pillars sent to counter his teaching, confirming that the Apostles opposed him. He berates the Galatians for accepting this "different gospel"; he refers to "another Christ whom I have not preached" showing clearly that there were two quite different and antagonistic interpretations of Jesus's purpose. Paul acknowledged to the gentile proselytes that the Jesus of the Jerusalem Church was "another Jesus" (2 Cor 11: 3-4). Later, representatives from Jerusalem visit him in Antioch apparently to accuse Paul of backsliding in his adherence to the Law. Paul and Barnabas are ordered back to Jerusalem. The first schism in the Church had been recognised.

If the *New Testament* is to be believed in respect of Peter, he is unsure which of the two factions, Paul's or James's, to follow. Paul writes that he opposed Peter's orthodox view at Antioch but persuades Peter of the correctness of the liberal interpretation and Peter then eats with gentiles. Faced with members of the Jerusalem Church, Peter reverts to the orthodox view. The *Recognitions of Clementine* speaks of a tradition that Peter tells followers at Tripolis to believe only those who bring the testimonial of Jesus's brother, James, from Jerusalem. He warns of: "false prophets, and false Apostles and false teachers, who indeed speak in the name of Christ but do the work of the devil". Peter was therefore opposed to Paul and Paul's influence on him sounds like more Pauline fantasy aimed at boosting his prestige.

So in 58 AD Paul was summoned to Jerusalem by James and the Elders for propagating views contrary to the Church. Paul's friends asked him not to go but he determined to do so. James and the other "Zealots of the Law" accused Paul of abrogating the Law of Moses. No reply was recorded but Paul agreed to undergo a solemn purification proving that the Nazarene Church again imposed its will upon Paul and that it had not abrogated the Law. James might have arranged this knowing that Paul had been teaching false doctrine and that he could not refuse a request to undergo purification without damning himself.

Paul was known by some orthodox Jews of the diaspora and hated by them as an apostate. This is illustrated in *Acts* when a furious mob gave chase to Paul. They felt Paul had violated the Temple by undergoing ritual purification, as James had ordered, though he was a hypocrite who deliberately and habitually preached violation of the Law. Only the Roman soldiers saved him and escorted him to safety in the Antonia fortress. The Romans intended to give Paul a whipping, presumably for causing a public disturbance, but Paul pulled another rabbit out of the bag. He revealed that he was a Roman by birth and could not be punished without trial. Some forty Jews then plotted to kill him but the Roman commander found out, supposedly from Paul's young nephew, and Paul was taken to Caesarea protected by a substantial body of troops! From Caesarea he is, after some time, taken to Rome for trial (on what charges nobody knows) and there he disappears from history after apparently living under house arrest for two years. The narrative ends suddenly.

There is much in this that is odd. Paul:

- turns out unexpectedly to be a Roman,
- has apparent wealth,
- began on good terms with the Temple officials,
- finished on good terms with the Roman officials.

In his *Epistle to the Romans* (16:11) he has a companion called "Herodion" and in *Acts* (13:1) a member of the Antioch Church is the foster brother of Herod the Tetrarch. The Herods were the family of the puppet kings of Palestine and the Herodians were the party of supporters of the Herods. Paul seemed well in with the Romans and the Jewish collaborators. Was Paul a Roman spy or agent provocateur? Was his mission to infiltrate the messianic movement in Judaea to undermine and betray it? We do not know what became of Paul – as we noted, *Acts* ends suddenly – although tradition has it that he was martyred. What though of another tradition that he went to Spain? Was he pensioned off by the Emperor in a Spanish villa?

There is one independent source about Paul. The Ebionites or poor men, were suppressed by the Church as heretical but fragments of their beliefs remain in *Heresies* by Epiphanius. They say that Paul was not a Pharisee, his parents were gentile converts to Judaism, he went to Jerusalem as an adult, became a henchman of the High Priest and eventually sought fame by creating a new religion. Ebionites did not accept Paul's view that Jesus was a divine sacrifice but saw him as a human sent to begin the new era, as prophesied. They accepted the *Torah*, obeyed the Law of Moses and regarded themselves still as Jews. They were the remnants of the Jerusalem Church! J.L.Teicher of Cambridge University, who identified the Qumran Community with the Ebionites, goes further – he believes the Teacher of Righteousness was Jesus and the Liar of the Qumran Scrolls was Paul.

Paul's letters were written before about 60 AD, only 30 years after the crucifixion of Barabbas yet already they speak of serious disagreements between himself and the Apostles in Jerusalem. As the true successors to the Nazarenes it was the Ebionites not Paul who transmitted the pure teaching of Jesus, for their founders, Peter and James, had known Jesus in life. Also by 30 years after the crucifixion, the Pauline gentile churches of Italy, Greece and Asia Minor and the Gnostic churches of Libya and Egypt had split from the Nazarene church in Jerusalem. The latter led by James the Just remained under the authority of the Sanhedrin and followed Judaic conventions.

The Fate of the Nazarenes

Paul's enemy, James, was the "brother" of Jesus. This seems to have been literally true but, even if brother was a form of address among the Nazarenes, it is plain that James knew Jesus intimately and would have known in detail the nature of his message. The Church maintains that James, a non-Apostle, suddenly appeared as head of the Church because he was miraculously converted by the resurrected Jesus. One would have thought that he would therefore, like Paul, have been in great demand as a preacher of the power of the new faith. But, apart from the one epistle which many Christians hate, sounding as it does very much like Jesus and very little like Paul, his testimony did not suit the Pauline church so he was virtually erased from history.

In the *Recognitions of Clementine* an attack on James in the Temple by an "enemy" and a mob is recorded. James is beaten with a club and thrown down a flight of stairs in the riot. James is rescued by friends and flees to Jericho to recover. Eisenman, quoted by Baigent and Leigh, claims that this event is the same as the attack on Stephen in *Acts*. Luke or later editors changed the name because the account could not record that Paul had assaulted the leader of the church, Jesus's brother. Jericho is quite close to Qumran, the headquarters of the Essenes. Later in the story in the *Recognitions* it transpires that the "enemy" has a commission from the High Priest to travel to Damascus with letters to arrest the followers of Jesus!

Clement of Alexandria (150-215 AD) called James Zaddik, the Righteous or the Just. According to Hegesippus, James drank no wine, ate no animal food, did not have his hair cut, took no baths and did not use oil. He wore priestly robes and was the only one allowed into the Holy of Holies. He must have been the High Priest. Epiphanius confirms that James wore the mitre of the High Priest. It seems odd that early church historians should not find it peculiar that a leader of the church was also a High Priest of the Jewish Temple. He must have been an opposition High Priest. That he "took no baths" is plainly an error: a scribe will have lost "never" in an expression like "never failed to bathe". He is obviously an Essene.

Now, if the reference to the stoning to death of James in Josephus is accurate, his death occurred between the terms of two procurators, around 62 AD, only a few years before the Jewish War began. The church historian, Eusebius tells us that following the death of James, Vespasian began to siege Jerusalem, a reference to Vespasian leading the Roman army of 66 AD. Using a technique of many early historians, he links by association the siege of Jerusalem with the death of James. Moreover in a passage in Josephus now lost there is also a reference to the war being a direct consequence of the death of James the Just: "who was the brother of Jesus known as Christ, for though he was the most righteous man the Jews put him to death". James seems to have been a more important person in first century Jerusalem than Christianity acknowledges.

Eusebius, says that the Nazarenes, like the Pharisee followers of Hillel, refused to join the rebels in the uprisings of 66 AD and 132 AD. In fact Pharisees like Josephus *did* fight in the Jewish War and it seems unlikely that Nazarenes would have remained aloof. They would have seen the War as a further act in the return of their Messiah to conquer the sons of Seth. In 132 AD it was a different matter. Bar Kosiba claimed a Messiahship which Nazarenes would have considered as false.

The contradiction might be explained if Eusebius spoke only of the Hellenised faction of the Nazarenes. In *Ecclesiastical History* Eusebius relates that the Nazarenes fled across the Jordan to Pella, a gentile city, at the start of the revolt in 66 AD. Yet if those escaping were gentile Christians opposed to the Jewish nationalist cause they cannot have survived long because Pella was sacked by the Jews early in the campaign. If, on the other hand, the orthodox Nazarenes, who had been involved in the rebellion, had fled to Pella when the cause seemed lost, they would have fled into the path of the advancing Roman armies.

Nazarenes escaping the victorious Romans would sensibly have fled south to Egypt alongside other Jewish militants and found refuge in the sprawling suburbs of Alexandria, a largely Jewish city. If they had remained pacifist during the war or participated but failed to escape to Egypt they would have taken to the hills and desert. Perhaps these are the ones Eusebius meant. They became the Ebionites or the Poor Men, and survived until the fifth century, revering Jesus as a man not as a God and rejecting the heresy of Paul. Their leader was chosen from among the heirs of Jesus, as the Jerusalem Church had done. The Ebionites accepted Jesus as their Messiah and expected him to return. They would not therefore have been willing to accept anyone else as the Messiah. The Ebionites refused to support Bar Kosiba and were persecuted for their stand.

Acts does not mention who founded eminent churches at Alexandria and Rome, though there are Christians at Rome when Paul arrives there and the Church of Alexandria was a major rival of Paul's churches. Nazarenes in Alexandria had established a church, with different views from Paul's. But as time passed with no heavenly hosts appearing, Jewish Christians came to accept Barabbas as a failed Messiah and reverted to Phariseeism or Rabbinic Judaism as it now was, while gentile believers accepted the Pauline heresy. *Matthew* illustrates this transition. It preserves much of the Palestine tradition, being the most overtly Semitic of the gospels but, like the others has as its hero a divine Son of God rather than a mortal Son of David.

Paul's teachings were heretical in that they opposed the leader of the Church at Jerusalem, James the Just. Paul only knew Jesus through his visions but arrogantly he claimed to know him better than Apostles that knew him in the flesh. He formulated his own eclectic theology and reflected it from the figure of Jesus crucified that he preached. The drift of the *New Testament* is strongly in favour of Jesus being the pre-existent Son of God, divine in his own right. This was Paul's intention though even Paul hesitated in claiming outright divinity for Jesus. To achieve his ambition Paul wanted the requirements of the Mosaic Law to be eased for his gentile converts. James refused. Non-Jews could already enter into the Jewish religion as "godfearers" but to become Jews they had to obey the Law. Paul had a vision of a universal religion but the Mosaic Law was an obstacle which had to be removed. He failed and was obliged to undergo an orthodox purification ritual proving to his own followers that he was subservient to the Jerusalem Church leaders.

Paul was probably not a Pharisee. Indeed he was only a first generation Jew, the son of godfearer parents who had become Jewish proselytes. But he realised the advantages of being thought a Pharisee and he adjusted his biography accordingly. He didn't miss a trick, pursuing whatever he thought might be useful to him, and always having something up his sleeve. He was all things to all men. He was a combination of mountebank and genuine evangelist. The era was noted for them – men like Simon Magus and Apollonius of Tyana. He taught that the *Torah* had been superseded by the death on the cross of Jesus, the Son of God, in atonement of men's sins. Faith in this was the only way to be saved. Paul reached these ideas from a synthesis of Essenism (with its dependence on the Jewish *Scriptures)* and mystery religions, convinced himself that they were true and propagated them with gusto.

Asia Minor, Paul's birthplace, was the source of several of the mystery religions that had entered the Empire and Paul could hardly have avoided their influence. Having heard from the Nazarenes about the death and resurrection of Barabbas and been impressed by their conviction, Paul equated Barabbas with the dying and resurrected Gods of the East. The theme of these religions were immensely popular and Paul realised that the idea of Barabbas had the added advantage of having occurred in real life in apparent fulfilment of the age old prophesies of the Jewish *Scriptures*. Paul could usurp the history of the Jews to use its long tradition as prophetic of his concept of Christianity with its dying and resurrected god of the mystery religions and its Heaven descended redeemer of the Gnostics.

The apparently simple message of Barabbas began being distorted by his image as the Paschal lamb, tortured to appease God. Pagan converts brought in their expectations of sacramental suffering, death and resurrection introducing aspects of the mysteries of Adonis, Hyacinth, Attis, Osiris, Orpheus, Mithras, etc., the gods who died for the sins of mankind. Since the women in the Christian story were unimportant or were introduced later, they began to attribute to the mother of Christ the characteristics of many of the great pagan goddesses, Isis, Cybele, Demeter, Diana. For their sacraments they took the Essene baptism by water and the Persian – Mithraic and Essene – communion by bread and cup. No Nazarene would have believed Paul's synthesis. Barabbas's message, acceptable to a Jew but seditious to a gentile, was twisted into Paul's message, blasphemous to a Jew but acceptable to a gentile. Through Paul, the strict apocalyptic Jew, Barabbas, was rejected by his own people and became Jesus Christ, a heathen god.

HEATHEN RELIGIONS

Lord, I ascribe it to Thy grace,

And not to chance as others do,

That I was born of Christian race,

And not a heathen, or a Jew.

Isaac Watts

Searching for Spirituality

Roman Religion

The Roman Empire comprised an agglomeration of disparate peoples bound by the cement of Romano-Hellenic culture and this was reflected in the religions of the Empire. Rome, like the modern USA, wanted to be a melting pot. Conquered people became provinces of the Empire and their religions melted into the Hellenic matrix.

The first religions in the culture that was to dominate the Mediterranean began as separate urban religions of the Greek city states. These Greek myths as we now call them became more family and individually oriented as the city states declined. Though we sophisticates find them amusing and little more than a source of fantasy, they constituted a serious religion practised for over 1000 years which was creedless, flexible, non-dogmatic and this worldly. It was a religion of everyday life, to seek blessings, good crops, health, peace, and so on – comfort in facing the problems of day to day living. The various gods each had their principle attributes and would be sought out by devotees wanting to enhance the quality of their lives in that respect just like the Christian saints. Athena was the goddess of wisdom; Apollo was the "pure one" concerned with morality and became the "divine physician"; Artemis evolved from being a Mother Goddess to being the embodiment of chastity; Tyche was the goddess of chance or fortune, and so on.

Like the Christian communion, worship was an orderly ritual, a procession involving hymns and short prayers often composed by famous poets, the revealing of sacred objects, and sacrifices of different types of animals often then eaten in a ritual banquet. Proper ritual was essential if the worshipper wanted to receive divine favour and this carried over to the Romans – and thence to Christians.

Roman nature was not to build extensive mythologies like the Greeks. They had a simpler basic idea – spirits – everything had its spirit or numen, a power for good or ill. Particularly important ones were those of the home and the hearth. The Genius of a man or the Juno of a woman was a divine spirit, an intuitive essence of the person which translated into the Christian Guardian Angel. On a birthday the Romans would celebrate the Genius of the person whose anniversary it was. The spirits of real men or women of power and influence became strongly favoured by Greeks and later by Romans in the cult of heroes. They believed Hercules to have been a real man, and he might indeed have been, but a complex of myths and legends grew and were attributed to his spirit after he died and ultimately he became a fully fledged god.

Though the Romans themselves did not build mythologies, they were great copiers, and were open minded about religion in a way which we cannot understand. They adopted first the Greek gods then later on Oriental ones. These foreign gods interested the Romans because their spirits were powerful – more powerful than those of everyday things. The worshipper's object was to get the gods to use them for his benefit. This could only be achieved by addressing the gods with their proper names and titles, and practising meticulously correct rites and liturgy. Indeed Roman religion evolved – degenerated might be a better word – into courses of complicated liturgical formulae, meticulously followed, in services for different purposes. This was all good business for the priests, the pontiffs. They elaborated the ritual further by introducing many lesser gods or "di minuti" akin to angels and demons who could be called upon to help – provided that the ritual was correct! A complex priestly hierarchy evolved, the head of which was the Pontifex Maximus, the model for The Pope.

Roman temples were all built on the pattern of an enclosure with a raised structure containing the alter and statue or image of the god. Some religions preferred simpler shrines. The highlight of their ritual was an animal sacrifice, though gifts were also acceptable. Priests had to be skilled butchers like Jewish priests, and for the same reason – the animal had to be sacrificed "willingly". Its dispatch had to be quick and unexpected. The best parts of the animal were then eaten while the rest was burnt for the god.

The Roman administration was usually tolerant of the religions of foreign immigrants but, for long under the republic, Roman citizens were forbidden to adopt them. As a consequence cults introduced into Republican Rome were not absorbed without struggle. But from the first century BC religious tolerance for all improved. Suppression did occur spasmodically but usually not for religious reasons but because some scandal outraged the Romans.

Under the Emperors, religious tolerance became policy. To effect greater political stability and to unite a disparate people, the Emperors of Rome attempted to reduce the potential for discord by a policy of syncretism – encouraging the merging of religions – and a policy of religious tolerance. In the tolerant atmosphere syncretism occurred quite naturally amongst the cults proliferating in the Empire through the adoption of rites and doctrine by one religion from another. It was also actively pursued to cement and unite the Empire.

It began when Rome became the dominant city in Italy and allowance had to be made for the absorption of the gods of neighbouring tribes and cities as the Roman sphere of influence spread. Later it benefited from the tendency towards monotheism. One god would subsume a lesser god. The lesser god became an aspect of the superior god but could still initially be worshipped independently by his followers. In later generations the hope was that allegiance would be transferred to the superior god and one god would replace two, uniting two sects who might have been, or become, rivals.

One way in which the policy was put into effect was by deification of the Emperor. Everyone had their Genius or Juno but kings and emperors were special because theirs were gods! This led to the Emperors being regarded themselves as gods. Initially it was not the mortal Emperor who was the object of worship, it was his Genius, the god residing within him. Even Nero did not call himself a god but, tongue in cheek, merely a universal Genius. But gods are immortal. When a king is the home of a divinity, what happens to the god when the king dies? The answer had to be that the king did not die – he must also be a god. And so the Emperors eventually claimed to be gods incarnate. But it was not until Domitian (81-96 AD) that an Emperor claimed the title "Lord and God" while he was still alive, and not until Aurelian (270-275 AD) that the title "Lord and God" was adopted officially.

Even today the followers of the Dalai Lamas of Tibet consider them to be gods as well as temporal leaders. The Japanese also considered their Emperor to be a god. Christians are happy to concur: they claim Jesus to be a god.

The Roman Emperors' purpose in declaring themselves gods was secular rather than some sort of religious egomania (though in some cases egomania played a part). Just as the sun was Lord of the Heavens so the Roman Emperor was Lord of the Earth. As long as everyone could accept this, imperial temporal authority was strengthened, but everyone could continue to revere their own celestial or spiritual god. Most did! The notable exceptions were Jews and Christians.

The Romans were tolerant of religious differences partly because they were indifferent to blasphemy. To a Roman it was absurd for a mortal to take up cudgels to defend a god. Romans sincerely believed that the gods were sensitive, petulant, and ready to intervene in the lives of mortals. If a god were offended by a mortal then the poor fellow had better watch out – at the very least he'd find his luck was out. Romans thought Christians courted disaster by deriding pagan gods as devils but they did not take personal offence. What *did* worry them was that vengeful gods might not be too discriminating, and innocent bystanders might suffer. It was this generalised fear of divine anger rather than intolerance of blasphemy that invited Roman displeasure.

So Imperial policy was that, subject to the requirement to honour the Genius of the Emperor, Romans could worship whoever or whatever they liked and how they liked as long as they respected and did not interfere with others and the ceremonies were respectable. However clandestine meetings were not allowed since they could be a cover for subversive plots. The priests and priestesses of the gods of the Empire were generally celibate and even Bacchanialian "orgies", by the intertestamental period, were merely drunken, not licentious.

Native Roman religion was worthy and pious but totally this worldly. It paid no attention to an after life. Romans originally had no thoughts of survival of the person in any way. On death a Roman simply joined the "Good People" (no singular). As the power of Rome grew and the population became more cosmopolitan, the religion became less attuned to the needs of the worshippers. By the end of the republic Roman religion had ceased to be a religion. Its festivals had become occasions of state ceremony. From the reign of Augustus, astrology became increasingly popular but ultimately failed because knowledge of the stars could not change destinies, particularly death. Only the gods could do that, but they lived beyond the stars and were not therefore subject to their influence. If only there were ways of compelling the gods to help. Theurgy, a type of magic aimed at forcing the gods to do the will of the practitioner, briefly became fashionable but also proved spiritually unsatisfactory.

Before Barabbas became deified Roman religion had ceased to provide any way of satisfying individual spiritual needs. Towards the beginning of Empire Romans began to seek a personal religion which would guarantee them immortality. Worshippers sought direct communion with a suitable god to procure his help in changing their personal destinies. The desire for individual rather than state gods led first the Greeks then the Romans to look to the East and import oriental religions. They filled their spiritual void via the mystery religions, whereby the initiate aimed to join with the god to share his immortality.

Eastern religions began to be introduced into the Roman sphere during the first Punic war (264 – 241 BC) when the cult of Astarte-Atargatis from Phoenicia became popular. From 204 BC, when Cybele was introduced, a succession of eastern religions arrived. In 186 BC the cult of Dionysus, then Isis worship (about 100 BC), Judaism, Mithraism and finally Christianity followed. Most ideas of the destiny of the soul existed in the Empire amongst this plethora of religions – damnation, oblivion, transmigration, reincarnation and divinity. In the early centuries of this era each of the various mystery religions of Rome were favoured first by one Emperor then by another, until all religions except Christianity were banned at the end of the fourth century AD. Syncretism had triumphed!

Mystery Religions

Because the old Roman religion lacked charisma, by the intertestamental years the people of the Empire had already begun seeking alternatives. The Roman pantheon of Jupiter, Mars, Janus, Quirinus and Vesta, with the addition of Sol Indiges provided the principles of decent living and brotherly duty to the citizens of Rome, and opportunities for worship but provided no satisfactory concept of life after death, or of the Absolute. Nor did it offer a satisfactory mother goddess. It neglected the mystical and spiritual needs of human nature. Death brought only Hades where the shadows of worn out souls wandered mechanically, unconsciously, like zombies, forever. Something was needed to fulfil the spiritual needs of the Roman people. It was provided by the mystery religions.

These mystery religions were no less spiritually satisfying than modern ones – they offered just as much in ceremonial, indeed more, than modern religions and sought equally to influence people's lives. Devotees of Dionysus would have been just as intense in their beliefs as pious Christians today. The initiation into one of the mysteries was possibly the highlight of a believer's life. The mystery religions were personal.

People of different psychological dispositions require different routes to religious enlightenment, according to Jocelyn Godwyn, who classifies religion into the five types War, Denial, Magic, Love and Knowledge. In practice few people are dominated by one aspect of their psychology and practical religions have mixed characteristics as we can see from Christianity. The eastern religions of Asia Minor, the Near East and Egypt provided one or more of these and ultimately had millions of devotees.

- ***War.***

Followers of this route believe the universe is in perpetual warfare between Good and Evil. The Persian religion placed emphasis on this duality and naturally passed it on to those influenced by it like the Essenes and followers of Mithras. War gods besides Mithras were: Mars, Hercules, Sol Invictus and Jupiter Dolichenus. Soldiers in the early period of Christianity preferred Mithraism to Christianity since it postulated a supreme Lord of Light opposed by a Supreme Lord of Darkness, Ahriman. The creator, Ormuzd, sent Mithras into our cosmos to rally the side of the Good in the battle against Evil. He is therefore the god of battles on earth. But the battle continues even after death. Mithraism and other mystery religions had a hierarchy of ranks of initiation like the Essenes and modern Freemasons. Christianity has taken much imagery from Mithraism and has its own salvation armies.

- ***Denial.***

Besides the dualism of the fight between Good and Evil preferred by those of a military disposition, there is the dualism between spirit and matter preferred by the ascetic. Religion's objective is to free the soul or spirit from the material world which restricts it. The Orphics and Pythagoreans believed we were incarnated on earth to expiate our sins. We are on the lowest plain of the cosmos, the sphere beneath the Moon, which, being imperfect, permits pain, suffering, decay and death. At higher levels, the spheres of the planets are successively purer states leading to perfection in the stars and the realm of the gods.

Though man's spirit is trapped in the material prison of the body, its natural home is the utmost level of the stars and the ascetic seeks to release it by mortifying the body. Non-spiritual people indulge their bodies spoiling it with food, drink, cosmetics and rich clothing. They pamper the prison of the spirit whereas the ascetic seeks to neglect it. Denial substantiates the idea that the spirit is being released by causing feelings of exuberance and hallucination known as mystical experiences. Sometimes, as in the Essenes and the Cathars of Montaillou, the aged would starve themselves to death.

The ascetics' attitude to their bodies is the same irrespective of the religion they profess. But sometimes the self-denial was only for a short time. Believers in Isis walked to her shrines on their hands and knees as do some Christians today. According to Appuleius the initiates to the mysteries of Osiris had to do without food and sexual intercourse for ten days before the ceremony. Chastity is especially valued by ascetics because the untapped sexual energy can give insights into higher spiritual plains, though it also can lead to tyranny through sexual frustration. Religious ascetics have been known to go so far as to attempt castration, as did the Church father, Origen. The priests of Cybele and Attis were self-castrated Eunuchs, and even circumcision is a form of symbolic castration suggestive of a denial of sexuality.

- ***Magic.***

Followers of this path are those who try to solve the duality of spirit and flesh by trying to unite them. The hierarchies of the universe have influences on each other. Thus man at a low level is made in the image of God; the movements of the planets affect the earth and the human spirit. The Magician attempts to exercise his influence at higher levels. Having offered a sacrifice to the gods, the gods had to return the favour. In the Taurobolium of the rites of Attis and Cybele and other mysteries, the blood of the slaughtered bull soaked the devotee who became "eternally born again". The animal's genitals were buried. Blood and sexual energy are the two key elements of magic. The fully evolved Taurobolium lasted from the second century AD to the fourth century AD but vestiges linger until today in the bullfighting and bull running of Spain and France.

Magic also made use of images of the gods to draw them down to the earthly level. The Christian sacraments of Baptism and the Eucharist use respectively water, and bread and wine – the image of the flesh and blood of the god – to draw down the spirit of the god, Christ, into the souls of the devotees. The demons who acted as messengers from the gods responded only to meticulously correct ritual. Thus in the Christian magical rites of the seven sacraments, the bread, oil, etc. are treated with a fixed spoken formula that in magic is intended to influence higher planes to the advantage of the communicants.

- ***Seekers after Love.***

The fourth path was that of love through which the devotee became part of god. The mystery religions are distinguished by the desire of their adherents to achieve a closer personal relationship with God. The mystery gods had suffered pain, loss or death as mortals do and had compassion for us. Love was thus an element common to the mystery religions. Osiris, Orpheus, Hercules, Christ, Dionysus, Attis and Adonis were all slain and resurrected; they all descended into the underworld to redeem the souls there also.

Ritual also helped especially in the form of a holy communion in which the blood and flesh of the god is consumed, albeit symbolically. Followers of Cybele and Attis had such a ritual and Dionysus was considered to be really present in the wine and flesh consumed by his worshippers. Godwin quotes a Persian Mithraic text that sounds remarkably Christian:

> *He who will not eat of my body and drink of my blood,*
> *so that he will be made one with me and I with him,*
> *the same shall not know salvation.*

Adherents of the path of love often conclude that the human condition is unworthy of God's love and become ascetics – a blend of adoration and self-denial is a characteristic of Christian saints.

- ***Seekers after Knowledge.***

The last route to God is through knowledge. Seeking truth about the god, according to Plutarch, is seeking the god. Aspirants meditated and studied the works of higher adepts or masters who had received a higher knowledge inaccessible to reason. For these, studying and seeking truth is more pious than abstinence or service in the church. Jesus was often depicted as a master, a teacher inspiring his followers, rather than the more popular image of suffering Messiah. Isis was also a lover of wisdom, according to Plutarch.

The mystery religions gave knowledge about life after death and instructions for the journey. The soul can eventually leave the visible universe and avoid any further need to be reborn, or it can remain in the visible universe, the Circle of Necessity of the Orphics and the Wheel of Existence of the Buddhists. All creatures eventually become divine. The mystery novitiate knows it and is purposefully stepping on the road to obtain it.

The Eleusinian Mysteries

A Mystery is a rite, secret from all save the initiated. Initiates were required not to describe what they had experienced and many kept silent. If anything *was* written down, it was subsequently destroyed by the triumphant Christians. Consequently modern researchers know amazingly little about them, whence their name. What knowledge we have comes largely from interpreting pictures of the initiations and festivals, and we cannot always be sure we are right.

The proceedings had to be secret to ensure ritual purity. If they were disturbed they would have been invalidated by the contamination of those who were not ritually pure. The god would be angered and disaster and ill-fortune would be the outcome. Note however that, though the proceedings were secret, they were held openly – that is at known times and places and the rules of membership were known to all. In Rome clandestine meetings were illegal.

Mystery religions had a hierarchy of levels of initiation just as the Freemasons do. The initiates or mystae were prepared under the guidance of a hierophant or "revealer of holy things". Only the hierophant could enter the inner sanctum where the holy objects were kept. Earthly life was considered a trial in which human souls were subjected to various tests. The object of initiation into the mysteries was to assist the soul in passing its tests so that it could proceed to a higher level of existence and, ultimately, to immortality.

Initiation normally involved at least four steps:

- purification;
- acceptance of mystic knowledge via teachings or exhortations;
- revelation of holy things where the initiate has to perform certain acts – the central feature of the rites – often some form of sacred drama;
- crowning or garlanding and concluding festivities.

Greece was the fount of the earliest mysteries. The Mysteries of Eleusis near Athens were the oldest and most famous in Greece. The Eleusinian Mysteries took place in September suggesting they had evolved from a harvest ceremony. But the original reasons were not known to the later initiates who saw the rites as pertaining to the soul not to barleycorn.

There were two grades of membership, the higher one requiring at least a year's fellowship at the lower level. The schedule of events was quite elaborate.

- 13 September – An opening parade from Athens to Eleusis.
- 14 September – The parade returned to Eleusis with the holy objects.
- 16 September – The novitiates heard the proclamation of the hierophant, who told each that if he was unready for or unworthy

of the initiation he should withdraw. They had to be Greek (or later Roman), above a minimum but young age, ritually pure and "pure of hand", and later pure of soul. The mystae then purified themselves with pigs blood and washed themselves clean in the sea. Finally a sacrifice was made to the goddess.

- 19 September – A splendid procession moved along the sacred way with the mystae and acolytes carrying an effigy of the god Iacchus (Dionysus). Each of many shrines along the route had to be attended so the procession did not end until after sunset. Then followed reveling of the mystae with their god. These mysteries were entirely seemly, even Christian critics not suggesting otherwise.

- 22 September – a mystic ceremony of initiation which took the form of a holy pageant or drama with the Hierophant, the Hierophantis (High priestess) and the Torchbearer playing the central roles of the gods. The daughter Kore (Persephone) is abducted, the Great Mother, Demeter, searches and sorrows and the daughter is at last returned. The setting was simple, there being no evidence of elaborate stages or scenery but a magical effect was secured through costume and lighting. The votaries were probably shown cult objects probably consisting of ancient statues of the goddesses and possibly an ear of corn symbolising resurrection of the soul after death, a relic of the earlier stage when the Great Mother was a corn goddess.

Some form of communion was also involved. The goddess in the mystery play drinks at one stage from a cup. The votaries would have had to do the same. The drink originally would have been beer. The corn or barley from which it was made represented the body of the goddess and the mystae would therefore have united with her. (In the nearby Samothracian mysteries the priest broke bread and poured a cup of wine for the initiates – just as the Christians do – but the meaning of the body and blood of the god is less obscured than in the Christian communion through its clearer link with the vegetative god of the vine and the vegetative goddess of the corn.) Next the mystae are given a pass word. They raise their heads to the sky calling "rain" then address the earth calling "conceive" – again demonstrating the agrarian origins of the ritual. Finally the Hierophant gives a closing address. It was called the "Logos" – the "Word"!

Now that the mystae have entered into a contract with the goddess: they promise her lives of exemplary morality while she promises them immortality after the death of their earthly bodies.

The Eleusinian mysteries attracted many initiates in Athens from about 600 BC. Later mystery religions followed a similar pattern, each with its own exotic god or goddess offering votaries personal favours, guaranteeing to watch over them after death and even offering them a form of divinity – immortality. Each of the eastern religions had a god who suffered, died and finally triumphed. In each the initiate was invited to partake of the body of the god and thereby gain spiritual immortality. Christianity was one of these Eastern Mysteries – the last one and the only survivor.

Gods who Die

Attis and the Great Mother Goddess, Cybele

Cybele was worshipped for over 500 years. She was the Great Mother of All Things: the Mater Deum Magna – Great Mother of the Gods, and of men, animals and plants. She was a mother of nature and a Mountain Mother – her shrines were often on mountains and in caves. She was identified with several other mother goddesses including Demeter and Gaia. She was, in her loving and comforting aspect, the equivalent of Isis, Hera, Juno and the Christians' Mary. But she also had a destructive aspect in which she signified the unknown, the unconscious and mysterious, the magical and intuitive qualities women in particular are considered to have. She is then Astarte, Luna, Hecate, Kali. Cybele was represented by a black meteorite set in the face of a silver statue.

Worship of Cybele arose in the prehistoric Phrygian Empire of Asia Minor. The main centre of the cult came to be Pessinus in Galatia. In 204 BC the Sibylline Oracle prophesied that enemies of Rome would be defeated if the Great Mother were taken from Pessinus to Rome. The cult and her symbol, the small black meteorite, were duly moved to Rome and established in 191 BC on the Palatine Hill in the heart of the city. Later the cult incorporated that of Attis who probably never had any following independent of her. The High Priest or Archigallus of Cybele was identified with Attis.

Her priests, the Galli, were eunuchs with hair perfumed and dressed with oils. Priests, priestesses, acolytes and initiates celebrated her rites with fast music and wild dancing until in a frenzy the participants exhausted and finally mutilated themselves by castration becoming candidates for the priesthood. Even the phlegmatic Romans were shocked at first by these rites and at first Roman citizens were banned from participating in them. The ban was not lifted until the beginning of the Empire but then Attis and Cybele worship became one of the three main religions along with those of Isis and Mithras. It made its last appearance under the pagan revival of Eugenius in AD 394.

These, to our mind, horrific rites came from the myth of Attis. Attis was a handsome Phrygian shepherd, the "Good Shepherd", the son of Cybele. Cybele loved her son intensely but Attis fell in love with a nymph and jealousy overcame the mother. In a rage she cast a spell of madness on Attis and he castrated himself at the foot of a pine tree. As his life blood dripped to the earth violets sprang up. Cybele, full of remorse took the body to a cave and wept. She first buried Attis at Pessinus but then used her power to restore him to life and they were reunited. She founded the cult with Attis the priest and made the pine tree sacred.

Just as Jesus acknowledged Yahweh as his senior, Cybele, the mother, is the senior of Attis. Like Yahweh, whose anger at mankind's disobedience could only be assuaged through the death of his son, Cybele's jealous anger could only be assuaged through the death of her son. Cybele's most solemn ritual was the Taurobolium, a sacrifice of a bull, like Mithras's. The blood flowed through the slats of the sacrificial platform. The initiate standing below thereby became "born again". People who could not afford a bull made do with a sheep and were described as "washed in the blood of the lamb".

The festival of Cybele and Attis was at the vernal equinox in the spring. During the reign of Claudius shortly after the crucifixion this was from 15 to 27 March. The calendar was:

- 15 March – The "reed bearers" enter and a six year old bull is sacrificed.

- 22 March – A pine is felled representing the death of the god. The acolytes and initiates proceed to the Temple of Cybele with the sacred pine bearing the effigy of the god in its branches. The tree is laid to rest at the Temple of Cybele.

- 24 March – The "day of blood". The effigy of Attis is buried in a tomb and a day of mourning, fasting, sexual abstinence and flagellation commemorating the Mother's sorrow follows. The High Priest playing the part of Attis draws blood from his arm and offers it as a substitute for a human sacrifice. That night the tomb is found brightly illuminated but empty, the god having risen on the third day. Initiates undertake the Mysteries and are baptised in bull's blood at the Taurobolium to wash away their sins whereupon they are "born again". They then become ecstatic and frenzied and sometimes castrate themselves in imitation of the god.

- 25 March – Hilaria: the resurrection of Attis and the onset of spring is celebrated with a sacramental meal and a day of joy and feasting. Those who castrated themselves become Galli – cocks – dress in women's clothes and wear perfumed oils.

- 26 March – A quiet day of rest and recovery;

- 27 March – The conclusion of the festival with a procession in which the statue of the goddess, meteorite embedded in her brow,

> is majestically carried to her temple and a series of religious dramas and entertainments follows.

Clay statues of the gods were made in ancient times just as tawdry statues of saints are sold today at Catholic shrines. Attis was depicted in his death throes drenched in blood, then serene after his resurrection, androgynous, released from his worldly sins and surrounded by solar rays. Or he was shown as a child, naked and dancing for joy. Cybele was depicted much like the virgin Mary with a baby or babies. An ancient figure of a Madonna and child in a church at Enna in Sicily was actually Cybele in her role of corn goddess (Demeter) and her daughter Persephone. The church was on a site formerly dedicated to the goddess. Pope Pius IX had the statues moved to a museum. The Black Madonnas of Italy are also on sites dedicated to Demeter, and the virgin of Chartres Cathedral was taken from a pagan alter.

Attis, the "Good Shepherd", was extremely popular in the Empire around the time of Christ. His death and resurrection were celebrated at the time of year we would call Easter. The "reed bearers" of Attis compare directly with the palm bearers of the entry into Jerusalem and the procession of the tree compares directly with the procession along the Via Dolorosa today when believing Christians enact the carrying of the cross, symbolically a tree. The effigy of the god Attis on the tree meant that ritually the god was hanged from a tree, like Jesus. The High Priest draws blood to symbolise the shedding of blood by the god for the good of men, just as Jesus is believed to have shed his blood for the salvation of believers. The brightly illuminated empty tomb directly parallels the Christian legend, the god having risen on the third day. The resurrection was celebrated with a sacramental meal and initiates baptised with blood to wash away their sins were "born again".

The site of a sanctuary to Attis on the Vatican Hill is where now stands the Church of St Peter! In countries where Attis was revered 25 March was adopted as the date of Jesus's passion and crucifixion rather than the moveable feast that was later adopted as Easter. Hilaria, 25 March is precisely nine months before the official birthday of Jesus on 25 December. It is therefore the day on which Jesus was considered to have been miraculously conceived of God. The Church celebrates it as Lady Day. One of the titles of Cybele was Domina – the Lady! It is difficult for any rational man to regard all of this as coincidence.

Adonis or Tammuz, and the Descent into Hell

Adonis or Tammuz, his Babylonian name, simply means, "the Lord". Adonis was the male vegetative principle. In Palestine the mysteries of Adonis seem to have taken place close to the Passover because Adonis denoted the revival of nature in the spring. Mortally wounded by the animal of winter, the boar, he died but was resurrected to be with his beloved mother Astarte. Attis and

Adonis are closely similar, and aspects of Attis and Cybele worship in many ways resemble that of Adonis and Astarte. Possibly Attis and Adonis began by being the same god, Attis being the Semitic version of Adonis, just as Astarte is the Semitic version of Aphrodite. Adonis's mainly female devotees would join with Astarte each year weeping for her lost son then would join in the rejoicing when he was restored to life. The attraction of this religion to women is acknowledged in the Jewish *Scriptures* by Ezekiel's need to scold the women of Jerusalem who wept for the dead Tammuz at the gate of the Temple. This cult spread from the Lebanon to Alexandria in Egypt and thence to Rome.

Antioch was early a centre of Christianity. It was also a centre for the worship of Adonis, who had been adopted as the god of Byblos, a few miles down the coast. According to Sir James Fraser, the festival to Adonis at Antioch coincided with the appearance of a star, the morning star – not the star of Bethlehem, but a curious link nonetheless. The whole tradition of Adonis closely resembles that of Jesus. The birthplace of Jesus identified by early Christians was in fact a shrine to Adonis!

Adonis suffered a cruel death, descended into Hell, was resurrected and ascended into Heaven. Each year his death was bewailed, an effigy was buried, the next day he arose to great rejoicing and his ascension to Heaven was enacted to end the festival. In Sicily an effigy of the dead Christ is prepared for burial amid wailing which continues from Good Friday until midnight on Saturday when the bishop announces that the Lord is risen and everyone greets the dawn with shouts of joy. A parallel tradition preserved by Christians in parts of Greece reflects pagan worship of the Spartan god, Hyacinth, whose three day festival was held each year in spring or early summer. On the first day his death was bewailed, on the second his resurrection was rejoiced and on the third his ascension was commemorated.

The Apostles Creed and the Athanasian Creed but not the Nicene Creed say that between the Friday night and the Sunday morning Jesus was in Hell. It did not appear as a tenet of Christianity until the fourth century AD, has no scriptural foundation save the vaguest implications in *1 Peter* yet is an ever present in the pagan religions of Hercules, Dionysus, Orpheus, Osiris, Hermes, Krishna, Balder, and so on. Indeed one of the most important aspect of the mystery religions seemed to have been the descent and ascent of the soul.

In the Eleusinian Mysteries, Pluto carried off Persephone in winter to the underworld but she returned in spring, an allegory of the vegetative cycle intended as fertility magic. The question is why should this rural allegory of nature's cycle appeal to city dwellers? Only by giving it a relevant reinterpretation as an allegory of the soul's journey to Heaven. Persephone descended from Heaven into the underworld – the level of earthly existence – but was restored to the freshness of her home (Heaven). Worshippers of Dionysus considered that the squeezing of the juice from the grape to make wine symbolised the soul leaving the body. Journeys like Odysseus's were allegories of the soul's journey home just as Bunyan's *Pilgrim's Progress* is. In the later Empire the cosmos, represented by the Zodiac, signifying the highest level of spirituality, in short Heaven, was used on graves to show what the dead person hoped would happen to his soul.

The story of Narcissus depicts the soul descending to the plant level where it is incarnated as a flower. Psyche is the Greek word for soul and the story of Cupid and Psyche is yet another allegory of the journey of the soul into Hell to be restored. Venus is jealous of Psyche's beauty and banishes her. Venus's son Cupid and Psyche fall in love but she disobeys him and he cannot prevent the punishment. Psyche desperately tries to find Cupid but suffers many tribulations before she descends to Hades. Cupid finds her overwhelmed by a magic sleep representing death and restores her to Olympus (Heaven). The soul is saved by divine love as it is in Christianity.

Osiris and Isis, the Heavenly Mother

Isis worship began in Egypt but she became Hellenised on the way to Rome adopting the Greek language and many non-Egyptian elements. Isis was worshipped in Greece in the fourth century BC and by the time of Julius Caesar there was a temple to Isis and Serapis on Capitoline Hill. The cult remained popular for another four centuries. By the first century BC she was regarded as a universal goddess, identified with Rhea, Demeter, Hestia, Hera, Aphrodite, Leto, Nanaia, Artemis and Astarte. She is the feminine principle, the Mother Goddess, like Cybele. Her advantage over Cybele was being Egyptian which gave her a history much longer than that of the Anatolian goddess. Isis and Osiris were sovereigns of prehistoric Egypt, quite possibly real people, but were thought of as incarnated gods who suffered in the world before ascending to Heaven.

Their worship was widespread and popular in the Roman Empire at the time of the foundation of Christianity. Though the worship of Isis began in Rome about 100 BC, by the start of the Christian era it was so widespread that a Christian writer said that some lands were full of the madness of Isis. There was a temple of Isis in Southwark, London. The last recorded festival of Isis was held in Rome in 394 AD but it was one of the last of the old faiths to die out, surviving less flamboyantly – it was illegal – against the Christian onslaught until the fifth century AD.

Osiris and Isis were brother and sister but, after the fashion of the Pharaohs they married. Osiris was murdered and thrown in a coffin into the Nile. The coffin was washed up on the coast of Syria and became lodged in the trunk of a tree which was cut down and used in the construction of the palace at Byblos where Isis eventually found it. She took the coffin and set the tree in a temple swathed in linen like the tree of Attis. Back in Egypt the evil powers found the body of Osiris and tore it into shreds. Finding him mutilated Isis reincarnated him from the pieces and Osiris was resurrected. But she could not find a penis and had to make a synthetic one to conceive their child Horus. Osiris then reigned as the king of the dead while Horus reigned on earth. Osiris, Isis and Horus are the Egyptian Trinity.

Serapis, the god of Alexandria, was the personification of Osiris through the Apis Bull, worshipped at Memphis. He was the equal of Isis with whom he ruled and eventually became an alternative aspect of the Sun-God.

The followers of Isis liked two of her aspects in particular, the bereaved wife weeping for her dead husband and the heavenly mother of the child Horus. Her first role likened her to Demeter who mourned Persephone in the Eleusinian mysteries, to Astarte who mourned her dead son Adonis and to Cybele who mourned her dead son Attis. In her second role Isis had a pronounced effect on the Christian perception of Mary, the mother of Jesus. Isis was endlessly depicted holding the divine child Horus, so there was no break in continuity when the Christian image of the Madonna and Child took over. Looking at old figurines It is often quite impossible to tell which was which.

Mary was first called the Mother of God in Alexandria, the Egyptian centre of Isis worship, in the third century. Just after 400 AD Epiphanius denounced women who worshipped Mary as a goddess. Yet by 430 AD Proclus hailed her as the Mother of God and an intermediary between God and man. Nestorius objected to this. But a decisive sermon was preached in 431 AD at Ephesus which led to Nestorius being discredited and Mary elevated to the Queen of Heaven. In another of those pointed coincidences, Diana or Artemis, whose day was 13 August, had been the goddess of the Ephesians and represented an aspect of Isis. In the sixth century a popular myth that Mary had been miraculously carried to Heaven by Jesus and his angels was officially recognised by the Church as The Assumption. Now it is a great Roman Catholic festival held on... 13 August!

There are several other strange coincidences.

- Many paintings of the Virgin Mary contain a crescent moon. Isis and Artemis were associated with Selene, the moon goddess.

- The pagan Queen of Heaven was Astarte, the Ashtaroth of the *Bible*. In Paphos in Cyprus women made offerings to the Virgin Mary as Queen of Heaven in the ruins of the ancient temple of Astarte!

- In many countries Mary is the Stella Maris, the Star of the Sea. Isis was the goddess of the sea, a role she had assumed from Venus (Astarte) who was born of the foam of the sea, mourned Adonis just as Isis mourned Osiris, and of course was the Morning Star.

- The festival of the Annunciation of the Blessed Virgin is held on 25 March because it is precisely nine moths before the official birth date of Jesus on 25 December. It is no coincidence that the birth of Jesus was set on the same day as the birth of the sun god who was identified with Horus (Ra), the son of Isis and Osiris. 25 March is thus also the date of the Annunciation of Isis.

The death of Osiris caused the Nile to flood and the land to become fertile. In one manifestation of the Osiris legend the man playing the god is wrapped in a shroud and is led back from Hell carrying a napkin by two priests, a tradition which seems to be echoed in the John's story (Jn 20:6-12) of the tomb empty save for two shining figures, a shroud and napkin.

The festival of Osiris was held in early November when lamps were lit and allowed to burn all night in honour of the god in particular and the deceased in general. This is reminiscent of the Christian festival of All Souls held at the beginning of November when candles are burnt all night in honour of the dead. Though the Church only recognised this ceremony in 998 AD, Sir James Fraser has shown that it was simply incorporating the ancient pagan custom. The festival of All Saints held one day earlier was recognised in 835 AD and undoubtedly has the same origin.

Dionysus and Orpheus

In 186 BC the cult of Dionysus was introduced into Rome. The republican senate took severe measures to suppress it but it survived and became a major religious institution. In Imperial Rome it consisted both of a serious religion and a conglomerate of supporters' clubs, a variety of eating and drinking societies held under the auspices of the god.

Dionysus seems to mean Son of God from Dio – god, and Nyos – son or child. Dionysus was a god of the lower regions including the earth and the regions below. Thus he was in charge of the fate of men and of their souls and was considered an important god to stay on good terms with.

The Mysteries of Dionysus rivaled those of Demeter at Eleusis but were more active. Dionysus was the son of Zeus and Persephone and was called "Zagreus" as their heir. But the Titans tore him to pieces and completely devoured him except for his heart which Athena saved. Zeus punished the Titans by firing a thunderbolt to turn them to ashes. From the ashes he made mankind. A mortal woman, Semele, took a love potion made from the heart and mated with Zeus. But she forced Zeus to reveal himself and shriveled up, as mortals who see the face of a god do. Her baby however was saved and, sewn into Zeus's thigh, was protected until he was reborn – another interpretation of the name Dionysus is "twice born". The god Dionysus then saved his mother from Hades and elevated her to Olympus.

The rest of his career he spent wandering the world giving mankind arts, crafts and agriculture, particularly cultivation of the vine and wine making. His disciple, Acoetes, was, like Peter, a boatman and in one adventure, like Peter, he was freed from jail when the doors miraculously flew open. Dionysus is the intelligence of the world. Because he is part of everyone he provides us with perception, understanding and creativity – he was the god of poets.

Dionysian initiation is to awaken the higher mind, to comprehend its participation in the whole. Nightly celebrations were held in which the votaries ate animal flesh symbolic of the Titans' eating the body of Dionysus. Since the flesh represented the god the worshippers absorbed part of the god giving them communion with him. Having temporarily received his powers they abandoned themselves to frenzied dancing becoming ecstatic. Because Dionysus was the god of the vine, worshippers practised ritual intoxication and, because he was the god of fertility and the regenerative power of sex, they practised ritual intercourse. The cult survived well into the Christian era despite persecution by the Christians. His life and death cycle however was unusual in being celebrated in alternate years, one for his death then the next for his resurrection as "the Light of the East".

Dionysus was the product of a God's union with a mortal woman – he was a Son of God – and was represented as a bearded young man of distinguished appearance. He taught men laws, gave them happiness and peace as well as the vine, and taught them how to be civilised. He suffered a violent death, descended into Hell, was resurrected and ascended into Heaven. Communion with the god was by a meal.

There was also a story that he had ridden on two asses which he then placed in the heavens as constellations. In the Babylonian calendar the zodiacal sign cancer was the foal and the ass and marked the zenith of the sun's power before it began to decline to winter. Barabbas, of course, triumphantly entered Jerusalem on "an ass and a colt, the foal of an ass" curiously matching the Dionysian legend rather than *Old Testament* prophecy which meant only one animal. A Gnostic jewel shows a foal and an ass together with a crab and is inscribed: "Our Lord Jesus Christ, the Son of God".

In mythology a god becomes identified with the animal sacred to him. There is an image from the wall of the Domus Gelotiana on the Palatine showing Jesus on the cross but with the head of an ass. The ass is associated with the vine – Justin Martyr speaks of the ass tied to the vine – and Jesus is also associated with the vine. He says, "I am the true vine." To the people of the time he might as well have said "I am Dionysus". Furthermore, the Eucharist cup in the early Christian text, the *Didache,* is described as "the holy vine of David" so the wine was Jesus and Jesus the wine.

The cult of Orpheus remodelled the Dionysian cult. Orpheus was probably a real person, an early reformer of the Dionysian religion just as Jesus is supposed to have transformed Judaism, Zoroaster the Persian religion and Buddha Hinduism. Orpheus became the name of Thracian Priest-Kings who were thought of as the god Dionysus incarnate and originally might have been ritually slain.

In myth Orpheus married Eurydice who was bitten by a snake and died. Orpheus was heartbroken and determined to find her, eventually descending to Hell to recover her. He charmed the nether gods with his music and got them to promise that Eurydice could return with him on condition that he did not look back as she followed him on the journey back to life. But, fearing that she was not behind him, he looked back and Euridice fell back to the underworld. Orpheus was totally distraught and rejected the ministrations of the Thracian women who tried to console him. Enraged they tore him to pieces.

Orphism was an ascetic, more intellectual form of Dionysianism. From the myth of Dionysus the Orphics believed their god died and rose again. They also believed in a form of original sin. Zeus had killed, with a thunderbolt, the Titans who had eaten Zagreus, and mankind sprang from their ashes. Mankind is therefore partially good, from Zagreus, and partially bad, from the Titans. Orpheus worshippers had to rid themselves of the bad and this they did through living lives of ritual and moral purity through a series of incarnations. If they succeeded through all the levels they became free of the "circle of birth" or "cycles of becoming" gaining immortality through divinity. The rules of purity included absence from any kinds of animal foods, avoiding the pollution of death and birth, wearing white raiment and other ascetic practices.

Orphic mysteries re-enacted the death of Zagreus, and its ritual involved the sacrifice of the calf or kid of Dionysus. Small portions were eaten raw (omophagia) as a sacramental meal. When the initiates had fulfilled the "solemn rite of the banquet of raw flesh" they became permanent vegetarians, dressed in pure white garments and avoided the taint of childbirth and funerals. The votary adopted the name Bacchus (the Roman name of the god) to symbolise that he had become at one with his Lord. When Orphics died they were buried with small gold tablets inscribed with instructions for their conduct in the underworld.

Orpheus is a missionary for civilisation: a musician, polymath, mystic, astrologer, he travelled the world doing good works. Orphics actually made use of missionaries which was unusual among Western religions. Hitherto there had been no concerted attempts by them to recruit believers but thenceforth missionary zeal began to spread, culminating in the dominance of Christianity. Some scholars consider Saul of Tarsus to have been an initiate of Orpheus, and Orphism and Christianity seem to have coalesced in some places.

Orpheus and Jesus both performed miracles, descended to Hell, suffered cruel deaths and were raised to Heaven by divine fathers. But they offered their adepts different routes to salvation: Orpheus appealed to those who sought salvation through self-effort and knowledge; Jesus appealed to those who favoured divine love. Otherwise they were much the same type of religion. Orphism greatly influenced the philosophy of Pythagoras so that Pythagorean philosophy is essentially that of the Orphic religion. The Orphics and Pythagoreans had an ethical approach at least equal to that of Christianity and in Orpheus's ability to charm the beasts extended spirituality to them too, an aspect not seen in Christianity until St Francis of Assisi, more than a thousand years after Christ.

At Delphi Dionysus was received into the priesthood of Apollo, and he also has the title "Dendriticus" meaning "He of the Tree". Sabazius is another name for Dionysus and some old writings suggest that the Jews at one time worshipped him. Orpheus was clearly connected with Jesus in the minds of the early Christians from his frequent depiction in the Roman Catacombs. Orphic figures represented King David or Jesus himself.

Mithras

Mithraism entered the Empire from Persia spread by slaves in the middle of the first century BC. But it took until the first century of this era before it began to take off in popularity and was not officially recognised in the Empire until the end of the second century AD. It was one of the last of the Eastern Mystery cults to reach the West and one of the most vigorous. For a long time it was the chief rival to Christianity.

In the original Persian pantheon Mithras was a very minor god, too unimportant for Zoroaster to include in the *Gathas*. He was ranked lower than Ormuzd, the Supreme Being, but higher than the Sun. Later he became more important than his creator, Ormuzd, because he acted as mediator between men and those on the divine level. Eventually Strabo could write:

> *[The Persians] honour the Sun, whom they call Mithras,*
> *and the Moon and Aphrodite, and Fire and Earth, and*
> *Winds and Water.*

Mithras became omniscient, the god of light, the Heavenly Light, a spiritual Sun, the enemy of darkness and therefore of evil and hence the god of battles and of military victory. Mithras was the god of contracts and oaths, he embodied the seven divine spirits of goodness, he protected the righteous in this world and helped them into the next. He sent rain from Heaven and light from the sun and helped mankind by slaying the primaeval bull fertilising the earth. He is the Logos (the Word). His enemy was the Demiurge, Ahriman, a minor god with power over mankind's level of the cosmos, and therefore over men. The Magi identified Ahriman with the Evil Spirit, yielding a trinity of Mithras, Ormuzd and Ahriman, comparable to the Vedic trinity of Varuna, Mitra and Aryaman. Ormuzd and Ahriman seem to be mirror images of some complex power and Mithras is the link. Mithras only takes the side of Ormuzd at the earthly level, otherwise he is neutral between the two principles.

The Mithraism that entered the Roman Empire was a combination of Persian Mithraic belief, Babylonian astrology and Greek Mysteries. Like other Oriental religions, Mithraism had a long history and a reputation for wisdom. Mithras was a redeemer but also offered a role model as an epitome of morality. Mithraism began to spread because it appealed to three main groups of people; the merchant classes who valued its demand for high moral standards and therefore honesty, to the lowly and humble such as the slaves and particularly to the military. Adherents were all male and were sworn to secrecy. It had strong elements akin to Freemasonry in its organisation. Females worshipped Cybele, Isis and later, Jesus. Mithraism had no extensive priestly caste. Each small group of worshippers had a "father". Major centres of worship had a "father of fathers", equivalent to a Christian bishop. It always remained a private religion, never receiving huge state patronage, so the shrines and churches of Mithras remained humble and the worshippers pious and egalitarian. In Mithraic churches noble, freedman and slave met as equals. Mithraism had its male celibates and expected its initiates to repudiate worldly offerings expecting instead heavenly wealth.

The story of Mithras begins with the Demiurge oppressing mankind. Mithras is incarnated from a rock on 25 December, the old date of the midwinter solstice. He enters the world, observed by lowly shepherds, on the darkest day of the year – he is the Light of the World. During his incarnation he carries out miracles just as Jesus did. And just as Jesus did he dies for the good of mankind. He kills the sacred bull, but the bull is an aspect of himself so he kills himself, just as God, the Father, kills himself by offering himself as a victim in his aspect as God, the Son, and is resurrected. His mission done he holds a last supper with his disciples and returns to Heaven in the solar chariot. He will be victorious over evil at the last battle and will sit in judgement on mankind. He finally leads the Chosen Ones over a river of fire to immortality.

Mithras worship took place in churches called "grottoes" which often actually were caves or catacombs. Devotees sought communion with Mithras to prepare for the final judgement. They knelt along a narrow aisle at the end of which was a symbolic mural or tapestry of Mithras slaying a bull. Though Mithras was often depicted as Sol, he was more commonly shown as slaying the cosmic bull created by Ormuzd, the God of Light, to prevent Ahriman from slaying it. The bull is the Sun's gift of fertility to the crops and animals, the grotto mural showing the bull's blood re-entering the earth representing vitality, peace and plenty, symbolised by ears of corn. Since the bull is an aspect of the god himself as the source of life in the original fertility myth, in its developed form it represents the self-sacrifice of the god for the redemption of believers.

The Sun and the Moon observe the sacrifice. Two torch bearers are in attendance, one with an upturned torch and one with a downturned torch, signifying light and dark, summer and winter, life and death, spirit and matter, the extinction of the soul's light in the material body and its rekindling after death. A serpent drinks the bull's blood. The setting is a cave encircled by the chariot of the sun and the signs of the zodiac. Other symbolic objects present include a tree.

A lion headed figure in the coils of a snake represents Ahriman, the "Prince of Darkness" and therefore evil. The Christian expression for the devil, "Prince of Darkness", used for example by Milton, matches Mithraic as well as Essene use – Mithras was Light and Darkness was Evil. The force of Good necessarily was opposed by a force of Evil in the old religions. Ormuzd was opposed by Ahriman in the Persian religion; Osiris was opposed by Set in the Egyptian religion. Other names for Satan trace him to earlier pastoral gods Pan and Zeus Myiagros, respectively Mephistopheles and Beelzebub, the Protector of Flocks, the Lord of the Flies as the Jews mockingly called him, Baal of the Philistines.

Initiates of the Mysteries of Mithras had to be ritually pure and were purified by baptism. There were seven levels of initiation, one for each of the seven levels of the planets, the highest level being that of the Father, Pater. On achieving the level of initiation called Miles or soldier, the mystae of Mithras were symbolically branded, the priest making the sign of the cross upon their foreheads to redeem their sins and to mark them as soldiers of Mithras ready to "fight the Good Fight". Tertullian, a third century Christian from North Africa, complains that the Devil was imitating the Christians' "divine mysteries" because initiates of the Mithraic religion were baptised in this way. Christians use the expressions "soldiers of Christ" and "put on the armour of light", somewhat inappropriate metaphors for a religion of love, one might think, but entirely appropriate to their Mithraic origins. Above the rank of Leo votaries were called participants because they participated in a sacred meal; below the rank of Leo they were called servants and served the higher levels – the similarity with Essenism is striking. The Mithraic sacred meal was essentially identical to the Christian Eucharist. Justin Martyr complained that Satan had copied the Christian Eucharist because the adherents of Mithras also partook of consecrated bread and water symbolic of the incarnate god's body. The bread consisted of wafers – each marked with a cross!

Mithraic language and symbolism are widespread in the *New Testament*. The Dayspring from on High, the Light, and the Sun of Righteousness are all Mithraic (or Essene) expressions used of Jesus. Mithras was born out of a rock – Theos ek Petras – and so caves were sacred to Mithras. Christian imagery shows the stable, in which Jesus was born, as a cave. (The infant Mithras was adored by shepherds who brought him gifts.) It was not originally oppression that led the early Christians to use catacombs for worship but simply a desire to copy the practice of the worshippers of Mithras. They decorated their catacombs with paintings, one of the most popular ones being of Moses striking the rock. Mithras, struck a rock to produce water for his followers to drink! The most popular picture of all however was Christ as the Good Shepherd. Mithras too was the Good Shepherd.

The Cilicians introduced Mithraism to Rome. The chief city of the Cilicians and one of the main centres of Mithraism was Tarsus, home of St Paul. When Paul writes (1 Cor 10:4)P:

They drank of that spiritual rock... and the rock was Christ,

he leans significantly toward the Mithraic idea of the God from the Rock, as does Jesus when he says (Mt 16:18):

Upon this rock I will build my church,

referring to Peter. Mithraic remains have been found beneath the Vatican Hill at Rome now sacred to Peter but formerly evidently sacred to Mithras. The throne of St Peter at Rome is older than the Church. From the carved motifs decorating it, it was probably Mithraic.

Both Mithraism and Christianity introduced symbolic sacrifice: Mithraists by depicting the sacrifice of the bull prominently in their churches and Christians by images of the crucifixion of Jesus and the symbolic drinking of his blood in the communion. The shedding of animal blood was originally a substitute for the shedding of human blood. The bull is interchangeable with a ram – the Ram in the Persian Zodiac is a lamb. So Mithras can also be sacrificed as a lamb just as Jesus is the Paschal Lamb. Remember Mithras is also the seven spirits of goodness just as the *Book of Revelation* has a slain lamb with seven horns and seven eyes representing the "seven spirits of God". Easter when the Paschal Lamb was eaten was the Mithraic festival. In the seventh century the church tried to suppress pictures of Jesus as a lamb precisely because of its pagan associations.

Mithras was referred to as "Dominus", the Lord, and his sacred day was Sunday. So Sunday was "The Lord's day" long before the Christians took it as their sacred day. The head of the Mithraic faith was the Pater Patrum, the Father of Fathers, who sat in Rome, just as the head of the Christian faith was the Papa or Father – the Pope – who also sat in Rome. Why is the Pope's crown called a tiara, a Persian headdress? A link with Mithraism?

Ernest Renan, a scholar who wrote a famous Life of Jesus, believed that if it were not for Christianity we should all today be worshippers of Mithras. The two religions had almost everything in common: a divine Lord who offered men salvation; a sacramental meal; baptism; the idea of the believers being crusaders against evil; an ultimate judgement of the soul; ideas of Heaven and Hell; a high moral code. The reasons for the success of Christianity were its overwhelmingly syncretic nature, the admission of women, the expropriation of the Jewish *Scriptures*, and the claim that the Christian incarnate god was a historic figure.

Mithraism eventually died out after its suppression by the Christians in 376-377 AD. By then its doctrines and ceremonies had been merged into Christianity so it had little basis for an independent existence. Mithras *was* Jesus.

CHRISTIANITY

Scratch a Christian and you find the pagan

Israel Zangwill

The State Religion

Judaism...Christianity

In the Roman Empire, gods were becoming saviours who died for mankind. The idea had begun beyond the Roman Empire in the countries of the Middle East. Marduk or Tammuz, the Babylonian God, was to come to earth as a saviour; Saoshyant was the similar saviour of the Persian religion; Khrishna had the same role; the Egyptians of 2200 BC expected a saviour described as the shepherd of his people who shall gather together his scattered flocks and in whom there is no sin. The dying god became common in the East of the Roman Empire then the need for the god to suffer to ensure redemption spread west to become popular throughout the Empire. Attis, Osiris, Tammuz, Adonis, Dionysus, Hercules and Prometheus all were worshipped as divine victims whose resurrection offered salvation for their mourning followers.

Devout Romans did not believe that their chosen god was the only one, even though for them it was the best – they respected other people's. There was little conflict between the religions of the Empire. Imperial policy used them to draw the Empire together in a spirit of tolerance. But one religion stood out, offering a marked contrast – the Jewish religion.

Jews were everywhere in the Empire. Though they came from a small country, their commercial and manufacturing skills had led to their dispersion over the Empire long before the Diaspora of 70 AD. The importance of Jews in the Roman Empire was akin to their importance in the USA today. But the Jews resolutely refused to worship any but their tribal God, Yahweh, who had chosen Israel as his people. Thus, the Jews of Alexandria arose in 38 AD in protest at the imposition of the cult of the Emperor, even though it allowed established religions, including Judaism, to practice as before. The Roman authorities considerately responded by considering it sufficient if Jews prayed to their own God for the Emperor rather than requiring them to pray to the Emperor or his Genius. Many Romans objected to this concession but some found the Jewish God strongly attractive, just as others were attracted to different eastern religions.

The attractions of the Jewish religion were several. One was its long and well documented history written down in the *Scriptures*. The Judaic proselytes were hugely impressed by the sense of purpose through time shown by Yahweh in choosing his people then attempting to effect his will through them. This pageant in time started in antiquity and was not yet consummated so the future beckoned, offering fulfilment of God's purpose. The will of God would be done when evil was conquered and the kingdom of God on earth would be instituted with the Chosen People the leaders. That was a third attraction – to be at the top of the pile at Judgement Day.

Thus Romans attached themselves to the congregations of Jews as associate members known as godfearers. Many would have become full converts were it not for the stringent requirements made by the Laws of Moses. In particular Roman males were highly reluctant to undergo circumcision. If this requirement had been relaxed Judaism might well have grown into a mass religion like the other Oriental religions. But it did not – a few adjustments were necessary first and Christianity provided them and in so doing became Judaism for gentiles.

The ravishing of Judaea in 70 AD left the followers of Paul able to recover the ground lost when Paul had been humiliated by the leaders of the Church in Jerusalem barely ten years before in 58 AD. With the dispersion of the Jerusalem Nazarenes and the Jewish Christians of the Empire becoming apostates, the heresies of Paul had no one to oppose them and they became the mainstream. The propagators of Christian beliefs became those who followed Paul and not those who had known Barabbas and his original claims. Christianity was now centred on Rome where it developed as a gentile religion. Paul assured gentile men that circumcision was no longer necessary, and so the male godfearers of Judaism converted to Christianity. The many women proselytes of Judaism, like ripe fruits, dropped into the Christian basket.

Jewish religion, influenced by Persian religion after the Exile, had adopted some of the beliefs of the mystery religions. The Wisdom literature of the *Old Testament* and the *Apocrypha – Job*, *Proverbs*, *Ecclesiastes*, *Ecclesiasticus* and the *Wisdom of Solomon* – show their influence. Yahweh is the Lord of the whole earth not merely the Jews, mankind is divided into the Wise and the Foolish rather than Jews and gentiles, and piety is valued more than obedience of the Laws of Moses. The absolute god was Ain Soph – literally "The Absolute" – who was reflected in ranks of angels who represented various aspects of him. The topmost level was the Divine Wisdom or the Logos representing reason and order. The Jewish seven branched candlestick or Menorah represents the sun and the six planets, the higher planes to which the soul aspires. The "Spirit of the Lord" or the "Holy Spirit" is the guiding spirit.

Religious sects, like the Essenes, found views like these acceptable and formed secret brotherhoods to conduct mystical rites assuring initiates of eternal life. The Essenes revered a Messiah who apparently had taken the role of the pagan gods who suffered and died. But the Jewish Messiah was expected to come in the future in glory. Thus the Messiah must have descended to earth to suffer and die in the past but in the future would rise again and return in triumph. The Essenes' leader in the first century BC, the Teacher of Righteousness, a messianic figure, had been persecuted and had been put to death around 63 BC but was expected to return at the end of time, which they felt was imminent. Barabbas, the leader of the Nazarenes, called by Paul Jesus Christ, was regarded in just the same way by gentile converts to Christianity. With their pagan background they saw Jesus as one of the dying and resurrected gods with which they were familiar.

The final victory over the angels was expected at the god's imminent second coming. In these early days details of Jesus's life or indeed of his death were unimportant to converts because his return was the more important business. In one of the earliest *New Testament* books, *Revelations*, there is only the slightest hint at the manner of the Messiah's death and that is likely to have been a later interpolation. That the sacrifice of the god had occurred was sufficient knowledge of the past. Full of anticipation of the return, they waited joyful day by day – but nothing happened! When it failed to happen year after year Jewish Christians reverted to Judaism – the second letter attributed to Peter addresses this problem. The gentile faithful, accepting that the time of the second coming depended upon God, began to think less about the prospects of an immediate return of the Christ and more about the god's tribulations on earth at his earlier incarnation. If their god was not to return soon they wanted to know more about him.

Moreover critics of Christianity denied that Christ had ever lived in the flesh. To answer criticisms and persuade believers, more needed to be known about the god's earthly sojourn, his suffering and the manner of his death. The mystery religions had their stories complete but what was known about the Christian god? Before long enough to fill several books!

- To start there were the letters of Paul.
- Oral tradition about Barabbas was uncovered.
- Biblical messianic prophecies were used to add details to his life and death.
- Essene writings provided a wealth of wise sayings, hymns, testimonia and parallels between Barabbas and The Teacher of Righteousness.
- Later wholesale importations from the pagan gods were used.

The identification of a wise and humble god who died and was resurrected with an unsuccessful messianic pretender in Pilate's prefecture was almost complete.

With Israel a hotbed of revolution and anti-Roman feeling, these gentile Christians in the wider Empire sought to distance themselves from the Jews and to prove that they had always been a peace loving order. They rewrote history, the oral tradition of the Nazarenes, as gospels to persuade the doubtful, to absolve Romans of the crime of murdering the Son of God and to blame instead Barabbas's own countrymen, the Jews. The betrayal by Judas was invented to put more guilt on the Jews. It makes no sense at all in the context of a loving God unravelling his plan unless he were part of God's plan, in which case he should be a saint not the eponymous traitor. The story is clearly allegorical. Judas is the Greek for Judah, the Jews, and he, like the Jews, betrayed the Christian God. Judas is the Christian's personification of Jewishness.

With the demise of the Jerusalem Church, Mark wrote the first and most factual gospel aimed at the godfearers to provide a new authority, And when it came to writing *Acts*, Paul's argument with James was depicted as Paul's victory not the defeat it was. No clear mention is made in the books of the *New Testament* to the Jewish War and its consequences, the destruction of the Temple and the destruction of the Jerusalem Church. That is deliberate. The gospel writers did not want to give away clues to the true circumstances in which Christianity was founded.

Mystery religions provided initiates with the prospects of salvation and immortality and Christianity was the latest and last of them. Christianity and Mithraism both accepted all ranks of society but Mithraism excluded women. Christianity, though it accepted both sexes, in practice mainly appealed to Hellenised housewives, especially those who were already Jewish proselytes. Right up to the fourth century when Christianity triumphed, it was primarily a religion of girls and housewives – perhaps 80 to 90 percent of congregations were women. The gospel writers and editors played up to this by inserting many incidental but flattering references to women such as the plea of Pilate's wife (Mt 27:19) and many instances in *Luke*.

The original Essene ideal of maintaining ritual purity ready for the impending day of judgement led to Christians being extremely puritanical about sex. Influenced by Paul, the idea that chastity was in itself godly remained even when the day of judgement receded into the future. No doubt this left Roman husbands happy that their wives were safe at church while they were out with the boys. It would not have been uncommon for the men of a third century Roman household to have been worshipping Mithras while the women worshipped Christ.

Christianity also appealed to poor freemen and slaves who had little or no stake in society. The Empire had displaced and unsettled millions of people who had to live in the slums of large cities. They sought the love of a god who promised riches in Heaven as a reward for enduring Hell on earth while punishing in Hell their oppressors who enjoyed riches on earth. If a god had been or become a man, had suffered and died and then been reborn and returned to Heaven, he would personally understand what suffering was.

But despite its egalitarianism Christians did not challenge the slave system, the corruption and privilege, or the harsh Roman notion of justice. Christians had no thoughts of challenging society. They were content with offering charity to the poor and ensuring a route to Heaven for their souls. For the lowest members of society, Christianity offered a sense of moral value and pie in the sky – but so did its main rivals!

Vilifying the Pharisees

The Christian editors of the gospels made changes to the stories of Jesus to suit the developing theology of the growing Church. Among the first distortions was the vilification of the Pharisees who were to go on to preserve Judaism, Christianity's rival, after the destruction of the Temple. But, because the changes were made piecemeal, they were not consistent and these inconsistencies offer scholars the chance to work out the truth. As usual use the rule that when events occur that go against the general message of the gospels or that contradict Christian doctrine, an editor has not been totally diligent – the inconsistent story is an old version that has escaped the editor's blue pen!

An example of inconsistency occurs in *Luke* 13:31 where Pharisees warn Jesus that Herod was intent on killing him. Pharisees warning Jesus? Christian scholars have had to try to explain this anomaly: they say the warning was a false one aimed at getting Jesus to leave Galilee to go to Judaea where they would have more chance of getting him themselves. But if the Pharisees were plainly Jesus's enemies, why should he trust them, and why did the editor not make their underhand intentions clear? The event was surely genuine and has escaped the notice of later editors.

Sometimes changes made in one gospel were not made in others. For example, compare *Mark* 12:28-34 with *Matthew* 22:34-40 where a lawyer, a student of the Jewish Law of Moses, a Pharisee, asks Jesus what the greatest commandment was. In *Mark*, the earliest gospel, the exchange is friendly; the lawyer commends Jesus on his wise answer, based on *Deuteronomy*, while Jesus tells the lawyer he is not far from the kingdom of God. This expression, used here by Jesus, was in common use at a time of messianic expectation: "Repent, for the kingdom of God is nigh". The Pharisees would have been quite familiar with it. In *Matthew* the exchange is much more gladiatorial with the lawyers seemingly trying to catch Jesus out and being routed by his counter-question to them. Since the anti-Pharisee bent increases in successively written gospels, one assumes that pro-Pharisee passages are early.

A clue to the distortion of the truth in the gospel of *Mark* is that the Pharisees allegedly plotted with the "partisans of Herod". Now since Herod was the collaborationist ruler imposed by the Romans and hated by ordinary Jews and their teachers, the Pharisees, it seems unlikely that the rabbis in the gospel story would ally with such a hated enemy. The real allies of the Herodians were the

Sadducees whose leader, the High Priest, was also appointed by Rome. It was the Sadducees not the Pharisees who, being fundamentalists, were stricter on the observance of the Sabbath than the Pharisees, allowing no exception. Nor did Sadducees accept resurrection though the Pharisees did, as was well known even among non-Jews at the time. In *Mark* 12:18-27 Jesus answers the Sadducees just as a Pharisee would, sounding as if he were a Pharisee. Essenes also hated Sadducees. Clearly an editor has replaced Sadducee in many places in the original by Pharisee in the amended version expecting that none of his gentile readership would know the difference – nor, in general, would they. Even when the gospels were written the Sadducees had disappeared from history so it was easy to make the substitution.

The story of the adulterous woman in *John* 8:1-11, charming not just for its denouement but for the way it depicts Jesus's embarrassment, is another example of gospel deception intended to blacken the Pharisees. Pharisees bring to Jesus in the Temple a woman found committing adultery, the punishment for which is death by stoning, and ask his guidance. Jesus averts his face to hide his embarrassment by doodling in the dust with his finger, but then replies: "Let the one among you who is free of sin throw the first stone". None feeling able to, the Pharisees disperse muttering. When they had gone Jesus asks the woman, "Has no one condemned you?" Since none had, Jesus commands her to go her way and to never sin again.

The story is a blatant interpolation. It cannot be a genuine story about Jesus because, in fact, by that time the Sanhedrin had abolished stoning as a punishment for an adulterous woman. Even before then stoning was not common because of the strict requirements of the Sanhedrin and Jesus's answer expressed the Pharisaic view handed down by Hillel. If the basic story is genuine it must have occurred beyond the administration of the Sanhedrin, possibly Samaria, not in Jerusalem or it must have been a mob not a group of Pharisees. Otherwise it shows that Jesus had given the answer the Pharisees expected – he had passed their test!. Pharisees undoubtedly disliked Jesus's religious nonconformity and might well have enjoyed trying to embarrass him. In principle they would have allied with him against the Sadducees and the foreigner and, though in practice they would have stood back, there is no convincing evidence of a Pharisaic plot against him. As an Essene Jesus would have had contempt for the ultra-cautious political stance of the Pharisees but many of the theological differences between them would to us have seemed like nitpicking. Certainly much of it in the gospels is unconvincing.

The motives for some of the first changes made to the gospel stories were to discredit the chief religious authorities of the Jews, the Pharisees, and to retain the credibility of the Sadducees, the allies of the Romans. If Christianity was to spread in the wider Roman Empire, the feathers of the Roman ruling class could not be ruffled lest they decided to repress the new religion – not for religious reasons, the Romans were generally tolerant of religious differences, but political ones, as opponents of Rome's political allies. After the fall of the Temple there could be only one Jewish enemy – the Pharisees.

Syncretism Rules OK

The Emperors saw monotheism as a way of implementing their syncretist ideas. Different emperors favoured different gods. Augustus picked Apollo as Sol Indiges; Claudius preferred Cybele; Vespasian and Hadrian favoured Serapis; Domitian chose Isis. The Emperor Commodus (180-192 AD) was an initiate of Mithras, indeed he had the "Caesarian delusion" that he was Mithras incarnated. The Syrian priest, Elagabalus (218-222 AD), tried to introduce monotheism in the form of the Sun-God, Baal (Lord), but it did not catch on until Aurelian toward the end of the third century AD. He incorporated all other gods as aspects of the universal god, a revived Sol Indiges under the new guise of Deus Sol Invictus, the Unconquered Sun God, encompassing Helios, Apollo, Mithras and Baal. The Sun-God was seen as the all powerful spirit pervading all the rest of the pantheon. Many of the gods had some solar aspect and could be absorbed fairly easily. In 303 AD an inscription of the Emperor Diocletian acclaims Mithras as "Sol Invictus, Protector of the Empire".

Christianity did not defy this stage of syncretism. Indeed it adopted many of the features of its rival religions and even finally identified with Sol Invictus through the idea of Jesus being the Sun of Righteousness (Mal 4:2). Constantine was a supporter of the universal Sun-God until he wanted the help of the Christians and declared that the Sun-God had been created by the Christian God. In return the Christian bishops announced that, though Constantine was not a god himself, he was in particularly close touch with God – he was a "Man of God". Constantine only finally espoused Christianity on his death bed in 337 AD but by then he had united the worship of Sol Invictus and Christianity to strengthen his own hand. Christian iconography used the solar disc in the form of a halo to denote a holy person ever after.

It was Constantine who called the Council of Nicaea in 325 AD that officially recognised Jesus as god. Even in the epistles of Paul a clear distinction is maintained between Jesus and God. No Jew could accept more than one god and Paul said he was a Jew. Jews could accept a Son of God but could not make the identity of the Son with God. In *Revelations*, chronologically the earliest book of the *New Testament* other than the epistles of Paul, Jesus is still not god, nor in *Acts*. In the synoptics the same and indeed he is depicted as refuting the idea as in *Matthew* 19:17 and 20:23, as well as the cry from the cross. *John* shows some development in calling Jesus the Word ("and the Word was God"), allowing Thomas to say "My Lord and my God", though elsewhere more conservative phraseology is used.

In the fourth century BC Aristotle had pronounced "all things are three, and thrice is all". The ancient Egyptians arranged their gods in trinities, Osiris, Isis and Horus, for example. The Hindu Trinity of Brahman, Siva and Vishnu is another example. Jesus never mentioned the Trinity. He could not because a Jew can recognise no god other than God. Nowhere in the *Bible* does the word Trinity appear. It was adopted by the Church 300 years after the death of Barabbas and its origins are pagan. Before that, Christians had a God and his son, who was partly divine, and the Holy Spirit, an emanation of god known to the Jews, but all three had to become equal to form the Trinity. The Hebrew word for the Holy Spirit meant wind or breath and in *Genesis* this spirit moved upon the face of the waters and was the breath of life of Adam – an idea stemming from the Egypt of the time of Akhenaton in 1370 BC. Thus The Holy Spirit existed at the Creation. The Logos, the Word, discussed by Philo, a Hellenised Jew of Egypt, was pagan but it had entered Judaic thought as the means by which God revealed himself. It was therefore also co-eternal with God and, as used by John in the introduction to his gospel, helped Christianity toward the deification of Jesus.

Paul speaks of "the grace of the Lord Jesus Christ, the love of God and the communion of the Holy Ghost" thus expressing the Christian Trinity at an early date (2 Cor xiii 14) without explicitly making Jesus a god. Early Christian baptisms seem to have been done in the name of the Trinity though the *Apostles Creed* makes no mention of it nor does it state that Jesus is god. The *Nicene Creed* does. At the Council of Nicaea in 325 AD the Church decided that the Trinity, which of course included Jesus, was present at the creation. Jesus will also be present at the Judgement Day, the Council of Constantinople of 381 AD adding a full description of the Holy Ghost. The Christian Trinity had arrived. The pagan gods of Old Egypt had asserted their influence. Despite the manifestly pagan origins of the Trinity, a Christian's salvation was made to depend upon belief in it on pain of everlasting death. The Church persecuted heretics who denied the divinity of Jesus into extinction.

Though Christians had allegedly been persecuted under Nero (64 AD), Marcus Aurelius (166 and 177 AD), Decius (250 and 251 AD)and Diocletian (303 AD), now that they were in a position of power under their trinity of gods they persecuted other faiths mercilessly until there was a counter attack by Julian the Apostate (361 to 363 AD). But Christianity was on the rise and in 391 AD the Emperor Theodosius banned all non-Christian cults. Apart from a brief revival of the "heathen" cults under Eugenius (392-394) the Christian victory was complete.

Anyone worshipping the Old Gods was a witch. Ergo, they had been casting spells on people. Casting spells on people merited the death penalty in the Roman Empire as did many other crimes. The pagan Romans did not like witches but they were never thought of as anything other than individual sorcerers. With the triumph of Christianity witchcraft became a mass conspiracy of Satan to be expunged en mass. Christians were told witchcraft could only be effective by invoking demons since the Absolute God would not be used in this way. And there were a lot of powerful demons about – they were the pagan gods the Christians had banned! Christian horror of the power of witchcraft really depended on the Church's success in painting the Old Religions as the work of the devil. People had, until Theodosius, believed in the effectiveness of the gods of the mystery religions as strongly as the Christians believed in their god. Pagan parents had told their children about their faith in their god but the Christian deacons then told the children that they were devils. So the idea of black magic as being the powerful enemy of the Good God became firmly fixed in people's minds.

Yet before triumphant Christianity had banned other religions, many Christians tolerated other gods to the extent of being willing to attend their temples, just as Romans did generally. They might have sought some favour that was a speciality of the pagan god, or wanted to worship in a family group though different members of the family favoured different gods. After the edict of Theodosius banning paganism in 391 AD the Old Religions unquestionably continued either underground or tolerated in some regions by the local authorities for another 200 years at least. Their fate was sealed, though. The Christians had all the power of the state behind them and determined to destroy all unofficial religions. Most pagan shrines and temples were destroyed. Our lack of knowledge of pagan ceremonial and ritual is partly, if not largely, because Christians destroyed pagan records of their liturgies and hymns when they prohibited heathen religions. Meanwhile Christians pinched the charismatic practices and festivals of the old religions to help those reluctant to convert to the new order.

The sayings of Jesus purveyed simple truths appropriate to the apocalyptic circumstances he saw. In none of them does Jesus speak of a Queen of Heaven, advocate endlessly complex ritual or grand clothes, nor does he claim to be founding a church, the statement to Peter being obviously interpolated. Yet within a few decades of his death his church had been founded and its theology and ceremonial were developing apace. Mary by the fifth century had become the Queen of Heaven replacing Isis in that role and by the seventh century the Moslems thought the Christians worshipped a goddess and two gods. Between the sixth and ninth centuries the originally simple clothes of the clergy got grander and grander. Dressing up for divine worship goes back to the stone age but does not seem to fit in with the teachings of humility attributed to Jesus nor the simple white vestments of the Essenes.

From pagan mythology Christianity adapted many useful ideas: from Adonis worship the tale of the star in the East, building upon the Star prophecy of Judaism; from Osiris and Dionysus worship the tale of turning water into wine; from Mithraism the birth in the cave, the adoration of the shepherds, the idea of being washed in the blood of the lamb and the expression "born again" (common in pagan religions); the use of bell, candle and Holy Water, the use of catacombs for worship, the Vatican Hill as a holy site; the ceremonious court paid to God. For Romans gods were potentates and required their acolytes to behave like a commoner in the court of an unpredictable king, with flattery and blandishments. Today any intelligent man will see that the supreme God must be far above such nonsense.

Heathen gods were admitted to the church as saints: Castor and Pollux as St Cosmo and St Damien; Dionysus as St Denis of Paris; Diana Illythia as St Illis of Dole, etc. Places sacred to the old gods became Christian churches and chapels; the holy springs and wells of the heathen became the holy wells of the church; the statues of Jupiter and Apollo became statues of St Peter and St Paul; shrines to nymphs and goddesses became chapels to the Madonna and figures of Isis and Cybele became figures of the Madonna – Madonna lilies are the sacred lotus flowers of Isis and Astarte.

Christianity began with three elements, the figure of their god dying for the redemption of mankind, the Essene code of brotherly love taught by Jesus and recorded in the gospels, and the God of the Jews with its long history of trying to achieve an objective on earth through a Chosen People – no longer the Jews, but the community of Christians. With the fall of the Nazarene Church and the destruction of the Essenes, they had no ritual other than possibly baptism, some prayers and the messianic meal. To become a religion to rival those of Imperial Rome they had to take their ritual entirely from other sources, all pagan. Pagan religions gave to Christianity the form of their churches, their use of candles, incense, alters, liturgies and hymns, vestments, choral music and sermons.

The Eucharist

The faithful of the newly founded Christian religion met to eat a meal together in anticipation of the return of their god. This was the messianic meal of the apocalyptic Essenes transferred into the wider Empire by the apocalyptic Christians. The *Didache* or *Teaching of the Apostles* written before 90 AD and based on an Essene original gives instructions for the meal which was held, it says, on Sundays. A cup of "the holy wine of David" was passed round, no reference being made to Christ's blood. Then the bread described as "the life and knowledge made known to us by Jesus" was handed out. Then the group ate heartily, giving thanks at the end.

But Paul, in *1 Corinthians*, complains that some regarded it as a free meal and an opportunity to get drunk. Even so early it had degenerated into an unruly occasion – you could not expect Romans to stick to "new" wine. Urging decorum, Paul tells them it is a sacred meal involving the body of Christ and explains its origins at the Last Supper when, he maintains, Jesus instructed his disciples to break bread and pass a cup in remembrance of him. He uses the word "communion" of the blood and the body of Christ and warns against similar ceremonies for pagan gods whom he calls devils.

This passage shows Paul knew that pagans as well as Essenes had ritual meals, and he calls it a communion. Initiates of the mystery religions sought communion with their god to achieve immortality. That was the purpose of the pagan meal – a communion – food symbolising the body of the god was eaten to unite the god and the worshipper. Primitive societies believe that cannibalism can be used to confer the qualities of the person eaten to the person eating. It is a slight step to eating a person assumed to be a god incarnate to get the qualities of the god himself. If cannibalism had died out in the Roman Empire by the time of Christ, rites that imitated it were very common. In the mysteries of Dionysus the baked image of a child was eaten. The first Christians must have been quite familiar with such cannibalistic rituals. Words like as "Except ye eat the flesh of the Son of Man and drink his blood, ye have not life in yourselves. He that eateth my flesh and drinketh my blood shall have eternal life..." (Jn 6:53) were written by someone who regarded eating human flesh as normal, at least symbolically – an initiate into the mysteries of Dionysus?

The original messianic meal of the Nazarene tradition was altered by Paul into a communion after pagan models. The aspect of a rehearsal for a messianic banquet shortly to be held diminished when the end of the world did not come, and the idea of mystic communion gained importance as Christianity developed in its pagan environment. As a mystic communion it did not need to be a full meal, it needed only to symbolise the sacrifice of the dead god, and so the bread and new wine of the original meal came to symbolise the body and blood of the god as Paul had instructed.

From this the idea of transubstantiation developed so that real bread and wine became actual flesh and blood. Loaves were even made in the image of a man and the faithful had different parts depending on their social rank, a practice eventually forbidden. Of course the reason why the bread always looked and tasted like bread was because God realised how awful it would be for humans to eat human flesh so he successfully hid its real nature from the communicants. This whole nonsense is because of the adoption by Christianity of pagan sacraments.

Paul's instructions were later written into the gospels as if they had come from Jesus. And the legend grows with time. The references to Jesus's blood are slight in *Mark* and *Luke*, have "for the remission of sins" added in *Matthew*, and are extensive in *John*. Somewhere around 100 AD the meal of remembrance became a sacramental rite and water was substituted for wine. Pliny speaks of the meal in 112 AD saying that it was quite innocent. In 140 AD Justin Martyr describes how the faithful receive bread and water representing the body and blood of Christ from the deacons. But at the suppression of paganism at the end of the fourth century, water was forbidden because of its pagan associations.

Holy Days

The *Christian Bible* has no calendar of holy days and at first Christianity had no festivals, holy days or Sabbaths. When the Saviour might arrive on a cloud at any moment, one has little interest in constructing calendars. To gentile Christians all days were the Lord's day so there was no basis for separating out just some of them. As hopes of an early return faded, the traditional festivals of Passover and Pentecost, the latter from the Essenes, were remembered as commemorating the crucifixion and the events of *Acts*. But, once Christianity became a state institution, principles gave way totally to pragmatism and Holy Days were introduced to front pagan festivals which people had become accustomed to celebrating and could not easily be suppressed. The great festivals at Easter in honour of Attis and other gods were popular and had to be given a Christian raison d'etre. The church was quite open about this as a letter of Pope Gregory in 601 AD shows, but it might come as a shock to many Christians to know that Christmas, Easter, the Assumption, the feast of John the Baptist, the feast of St George and the fast of Lent are all pagan.

The Christian Sabbath is also pagan. The Babylonians adopted a seven day week based on the cycles of the moon and directed that certain types of work should not occur on certain days called Sabbaths. The seven days of the week were early identified with the seven known planets beginning with the sun. The first day was therefore dedicated to the sun and the last day to Saturn. But the god Saturn was considered unlucky so no work was risked on his day. The Jews were exiled in Babylonia and adopted the local habit of not working on a Saturday. The story of the Jewish Sabbath, the day when God in the creation myth rested from his labours, was devised to offer an explanation for the custom they had adopted.

On their return from Babylonia, the Jews imposed such a strict interpretation on the day of rest that a man could be executed for lighting a fire on the Sabbath and indeed the *Old Testament* records that, in the time of Moses, a man was executed for gathering fire wood on the Sabbath (Num 15:32-36). It was, of course, an exemplary tale written after the Babylonian exile and not by Moses himself as legend has it.

Early Christians believed that Jesus had repealed laws on the Sabbath and did not include observance of it in his ordinances. Even Paul attacked the *Galatians* for observing a special day as holy and he repeated his view in *Colossians*. In the second century Irenaeus confirmed that Jesus had cancelled observance of a Sabbath. Tertullian added in the third century that Sabbaths were unknown to Christians. The church fathers, Victorinus, Justin, Clement, Origen, Eusebius, Epiphanius, Cyril, Jerome and others were all emphatic that Christians knew no Sabbath!

Now obviously Sunday was a special holy day for sun worshippers which included the worshippers of Mithras who also called it the Lord's Day. Thus there was a whole tradition in the Roman world of having Sunday as a sacred holiday and the early gentile Christians found it convenient to match it. Because of the remnants of Nazarene/Essene tradition associating Jesus with the sun, justified by Malachi, and backed up by the tradition that Jesus had risen from the dead on a Sunday, it became customary even in the first century for Christians to meet on a Sunday. For Christians Sunday also became the Lord's Day. Irenaeus and Tertullian both thought the Lord's Day should be a day of rest but plainly there was no adoption of any strict observance of it, though it was regarded as a special day.

In 321 AD Constantine, still not yet a Christian, ordered that the "venerable day of the Sun" should be a compulsory day of rest. And so it became, gradually taking on a stricter religious purity so that, despite the protestations of Luther that people should dance and feast on that day, the puritans took it over and turned it into a day to rival that of the Mosaic Law of the post-exilic Jewish priesthood!

The birth date of Jesus is unknown. Poor and illiterate parents in undeveloped societies do not remember the dates when their children were born and often do not even remember the year – simple people are not ruled by clocks and calendars as we are. If, as *Acts* claims, Mary, Jesus's mother, lived with the disciples after the crucifixion, evidently she had forgotten when her son was born. This would be surprising even for a poor person considering the interest shown by kings, shepherds and angels at the time. Mary could not have experienced any of this because the gospels indicate that she had no recollection of it.

Nor had the first Christians ever heard of it. They believed that Jesus's birth date was irrelevant – only his divine life was relevant and that began at his baptism. Sadly they did not know the date of the baptism either and arbitrarily chose 6 January. Why? Because that date had long been associated with people bathing in blessed water. Followers of the god Osiris, the deity of the Nile, had held a festival, the "Festival of the Immersion", on the river on 6 January from time immemorial. Christian Copts celebrate it still. The Hierophant poured holy water into the river and blessed it, then people bathed in it. The Greeks identified Dionysus with Osiris and so on 6 January the sacred waters were blessed in both the religions of Osiris and Dionysus! Epiphany is a continuation of these pagan rites.

The Egyptian Gnostics known as Basilidians, seeing the immersion ceremonies as a symbol of the baptism of Jesus, celebrated it on 6 January and gradually Christians elsewhere adopted this date as the anniversary of the Jesus's baptism. By 386 AD the two great Christian festivals were Easter, the festival of the crucifixion, and Epiphany when rivers and springs were blessed and water was drawn and saved for baptisms throughout the year. Aristides Rhetor in about 160 AD tells us that water drawn from the Nile at the "Festival of the Immersion" is at its purest. Stored in wine jars, he says, it improves with time just like wine. And so does the myth! Two centuries later Epiphanius writes that the stored water actually changes into wine! In Dionysus worship water turns to wine on 6 January. The miracle at Cana when Jesus turned water into wine is celebrated in the Christian calendar on 6 January!

Today the Epiphany celebration is most closely associated with the visit of the Magi at Jesus's birth and has been since the fourth century AD. The Magi were Persian priests so it seems likely that the legend was introduced from Mithras worship, originally a Persian religion. The babe Mithras was adored by shepherds who brought gifts as in the *Luke* version of Jesus's birth. The editor who inserted the birth narrative into *Matthew* took a different tack. He aimed to show the superiority of Christianity over the other eastern religions: the divine baby Jesus is superior to the divine baby Mithras whose priests bring gifts to the new god.

Cassian at about the beginning of the fifth century says the Egyptian provinces regarded Epiphany as being the birth date of Jesus. This was because Jesus was thought to be exactly 30 years old on his baptism. Note also that the Persian law-giver Zoroaster was exactly thirty when the spirit of god descended on him, and the Egyptian Pharaohs held a celebration called Sed exactly 30 years after the day they had been chosen by their father as his successor, their spiritual birth day.

Toward the end of the fourth century, to counteract the Manichaean heresy – that Jesus was never born at all but was a phantasm – church leaders decided to move the date of Jesus's birth "after the flesh" from 6 January to 25 December, the birth date of the sun. During the third and fourth centuries Mithraism had become the most important solar religion in the Empire, Mithras being called, "the Unconquerable Sun". Thus 25 December was celebrated as the "Birthday of the Unconquerable Sun" in the calendar of Philocalus in 336 AD. The solar celebration was so widespread and popular that the church could neither stop it, nor stop it being identified in the popular mind with Jesus's birth anyway.

The Emperor Honorius (395 to 423) speaks of 25 December as being a new festival, and a text of about the same time says it is one of the three great Christian festivals so holy that theatres had to close by law. The churches of the Eastern Empire accused the Western Church of idolatry and sun worship. Jesus was identified with the sun by both Cyprian and Ambrose. Jesus and Mithras had become almost identical in the minds of the western populace. Saint Augustine was one who did not approve of this particular concession to paganism.

Midsummer Day is the Feast of St John the Baptist and is dedicated also to Saints Philip and James. Saints Peter, James, Andrew and Paul were given unimportant days even though they were Christ's Apostles.

Pagan Traces

Some scholars claim that Christianity did not copy rituals of the mystery religions but developed them separately. Christianity...

- had an initiation rite,
- had a redeeming saviour figure who died and was resurrected,
- indulged in a symbolic sacrificial ritual, the sacrifice of the god having rendered lesser sacrifices superfluous,
- had an assurance of salvation of the soul.

It revered its saints, in the same role as the lesser gods of the mystery religions, as guardians, intermediaries, patrons and protectors; it revered cult objects and relics of the saints particularly if they were bits of human body, a truly primitive adaptation; it assured its favourites victory in battle as it did Constantine at the Milvian Bridge, a cynical extention of the original Nazarene belief that God would help the Elect in the battle for the kingdom; just like the mystery religions, it provided centres of pilgrimage where votive offerings were made, often to effect healing; it replaced genii with guardian angels; it replaced divine rulers with the divine right of kings – a distinction of no practical importance; it depicted its holy people with the solar halo like solar deities and Roman Emperors.

Since the rituals of the mystery religions had been established by the time Christianity came along and the environment of the Christians was steeped in them, it is too far fetched to imagine that Christianity developed these same rituals, beliefs and practices independently or that long established religions had to pinch the rituals of Christianity, a newly invented one.

Manifestly pagan or magical customs survived into the Christian era. Animals or animal heads were cemented into the foundation of important buildings, often churches, just as the Romans used to. Holy places especially wells but also standing stones and hilltops were re-dedicated to Christian saints and the custom of making votive offerings (usually coins) to the spirit of the well continued as it always had under the old god. Churches or chapels would be built over wells or on top of hills, the latter usually dedicated to St Michael. Remember the Essenes identified the Archangel Michael with the Prince of Light and high places such as hills and tall structures such as the pyramids of Egypt and Mexico were always dedicated to the Sun. Tree spirits became “Gospel Oaks” beneath which Christian vicars spoke their sermons.

About 900 AD people fancied they took part in nocturnal processions led by the goddess Diana (Cybele), or, some say, Herodias, the wife of Herod Antipas. Some observers thought the people taking part were dreaming or deluded. The Church didn’t think so. It issued the *Canon Episcopi* saying demons were at work endangering souls. The Church considered these demons important and persistent enough to keep on issuing edicts like this until 1310 AD. Margaret Murray argued convincingly that a pagan religion continued underground until the Middle Ages. It seems unlikely that any widespread, popular and organised pagan movement could have survived so long. But remnants of one of the pagan religions that went underground in 391 could have persisted after organised resistance to Christianity had faded away. These daring and arcane customs of ancient and forbidden wisdom were normally practised by only a few "witches" but occasionally grew in popularity as a fad. When they did the Church got neurotic and issued an edict.

The Sheela-na-Gig in Irish tradition is considered to be lucky. It is the obscene figure of a grotesquely ugly woman, exposing her vulva, found carved on churches from about 1000 AD in countries on the Atlantic seaboard of Western Europe. Equivalent male figures are found in the Continental countries. In Egypt similar though less grotesque clay images of the Roman period are found. They were probably warnings of the sins of the flesh and often appear in that context with other carvings. Yet they were considered to be lucky rather than the opposite. How then did the idea of good luck come to be associated with a warning about sin? Could it be because they were associated with a folk memory of a mother or fertility goddess or, in the male examples, a god like Priapus? The Romans had a custom of giving a building strength and protection by carving somewhere on it a phallus. And the "green man", this time a grotesque male sprouting leaves and branches around his face or from his mouth, is another pre-Christian figure found on churches that seems to stem from the Roman period.

And yet more remains! There is a series of Christian Mysteries: Gnostic cults; Celtic Church; Cathars and Albigenses; the Fedeli d'Amor and Knights Templar; the Masons; the Rosicrucians and the Illuminati; the Hesychasts. Theosophists and Anthroposophists continue the tradition, believing Jesus was a man trained to a high level by the Essenes. At the age of thirty he donated his body to the Christ, one of the highest gods, third in the hierarchy of the Absolute, the Demiurge, the Christ – the Overseer of the Jewish People, Jesus. After working through Jesus for three years the Christ departed on Easter Day as Tibetan sages also did but returned on an astral plane to continue to teach his disciples. Arius held that before the creation the Absolute created a Logos, a divine spirit that entered Jesus replacing his own spirit. Jesus is therefore an avatar of this divine principle.

Christianity is largely a pagan faith.

MANIPULATING THE GOOD NEWS

...it is only Christian men

Guard even heathen things
G K Chesterton

Christian Censorship

The Missing Records

An alleged event in the past can be regarded as historical only when testimony of it is many, varied and essentially consistent. Otherwise we cannot be sure that something really happened. The same criteria apply to people. We cannot be sure that someone really existed if the evidence is sparse or inconsistent. We have seen that even obscure Jewish sects, some not mentioned in the Christian gospels, have been faithfully chronicled in their day. If a god were crucified by Pilate in about 30 AD surely we could expect more information about him from contemporary sources.

Few independent records survive from the time when Barabbas lived. From what little evidence there is, it is not easy to get the truth because most of the scholars researching it are Christian theologians or, at least, committed Christians who willfully or subconsciously do not want to come to conclusions which contradict their faith. How many Christians could accept that much in the *Bible* was not intended to illuminate the truth but to veil it. Christians suppressed anti-Christian and even non-Christian works. After the beginning of the fourth century AD when the church reached political power, reports hostile to Christianity were expurgated or destroyed.

No non-Christian or anti-Christian record of the events of the time of Jesus remains today unless J.L.Teicher's theories of the Dead Sea Scrolls are correct. Pliny the Younger, Suetonius and Tacitus are the nearest authors in time to Jesus's life but are later and much of their evidence scholars regard as doubtful. None of them refer to a "Jesus", only to someone called Christ which we have seen is merely Greek for Messiah. We cannot always be sure whether a reference to "Christ" implies Christians or messianic Jews generally.

A letter from Pliny the Younger to Trajan was written about 112 AD some eighty years after the presumed date of the crucifixion. Pliny had to punish the Christians as a subversive group but he wrote that he had found them to be harmless people who sang hymns at daybreak (just like the Essenes) to their Christ as to a god. The fact that Roman officials found Christians practising their "superstition" as Romans called it tells us nothing about its origins.

The apparent allusions to Christians in Suetonius (120 AD), one in the section on Claudius and one in the section on Nero, are ambiguous. Suetonius wrote of a Jewish revolt at Rome in the reign of the Emperor Claudius apparently instigated by "Chrestus". By 41 to 54 AD when Claudius was Emperor scholars doubt that Jesus's supporters could have spread to Rome in sufficient strength to cause a revolt. Chresto however is a proper name so common that it occurs over 80 times on Roman inscriptions. Suetonius might have been simply giving the name of a Roman rabble-rouser. Nonetheless he probably meant Christo, Messiah, but not specifically Jesus. The disturbance would have been caused by messianic Jews possibly responding to the messianic claims of a contemporary. If Chrestus meant Jesus, the riots were probably by orthodox Jews incensed by early Christian missionaries on Stephen's wing.

Tacitus says that the Christians were accused by Nero of setting fire to Rome in 64 AD. And in the *Annals* he accuses the Christians of hating the human race. He says that members of this mischievous sect which took its name from a Christ who suffered death under Pontius Pilate, were horribly tortured and their confessions led to many others being convicted. But what does this tell us of the origins of Christianity? By 120 AD the Christian tradition that Christ had died under Pilate had been established – Tacitus was not recording a historical event but the Christians own explanation of their origins. And Tacitus would have thought an action like this typical of Pilate. In any case, scholars maintain there could not have been many Christians in Rome even by 64 AD and that Tacitus, writing 60 years later, is confusing the Christians of his day with those instigated by Chrestos in Suetonius, messianic Jews. This would better explain the accusation of "hating the human race", a curious accusation to make of Christians but one which could apply to Jews, especially orthodox Essenes, who considered themselves as God's Elect, thought gentiles were inferior and hated the Romans.

Gibbon points out that, if Nero persecuted Christians, it was the only example of Roman intolerance up to the Jewish War. Even Origen, the early Christian apologist could declare that "the number of martyrs was very inconsiderable". The Christian fathers, *Acts*, Justin and Origen all say little or nothing about the Christian persecutions of Nero, because the victims were predominantly Jews. The only other reason for the silence would be if the passage in Tacitus was interpolated. Notice that *Acts* concludes by saying that Paul was not forbidden to teach in Rome, he did it with all boldness – and the year was around 64 AD.

Christians explain the lack of official records of the events of Jesus's life by claiming that they were totally unimportant at the time. For a vast empire, insignificant events occurred in a distant country of which Romans knew nothing and cared less. To children in Sunday school this sounds quite convincing. But it is not true and should not be repeated by honest adults.

Palestine was not a minor country of little importance to the Romans. The Jews were already widespread as merchants and artisans in the Empire and Judaea was strategically important astride the trade routes to Persia, Arabia and India, and the military corridor by land from Africa to Asia. The countries to the east had been serious rivals to Rome not long before and were still strong and independent. They remained a threat at the time of Barabbas though later the Romans briefly annexed them. Romans mistrusted Jewish links with these countries. Many Jews still lived in Parthia preferring to remain even though Cyrus the Persian had allowed them to return from Babylonian exile. And the Jews, though inhabiting only a tiny country, had a record of militancy that, combined with their strategic position, meant they could not be ignored. Thus events in Judaea were watched keenly by Roman observers at diplomatic and military levels if not by the hoi polloi, and statesmen demanded regular and accurate dispatches.

Jesus was proclaimed a king as even the gospels admit and as such he was a rival to Caesar and a threat to the Empire. That was no trivial crime and required detailed reports from the Roman governor to the Emperor. If, though, as Christians maintain, it was not worth recording and indeed was not recorded, it seems curious that early opponents and critics of Christianity failed to question the absence of independent evidence of Jesus's existence. The Christian apologists did not attempt to answer any such questions, so apparently they were not put. Only in modern times have critics argued that Jesus never existed at all.

In the early days of Christianity, its critics' main argument was a different one – Jesus was a bandit and a magician and, remarkably, that the records of the time proved it! A Jewish source says Jesus was crucified at Lydda as a false teacher and a beguiler. Celsus and Lucian early in the second century and Sossianus Hierocles late in the third tell us that Jesus was a sorcerer and a fomenter of rebellion who committed highway robbery at the head of a band of men. These documents existed because later scholars refer to them. But where are they now? Gone! Nothing of this remains now because Christians, when they came to power under Constantine, began to destroy anything contrary to their own view.

The death penalty was prescribed for anyone owning or trying to preserve any books describing Jesus as a magician or an agitator.

The writings of Arius and Porphyry were ordered to be burnt. *De Judaeis* by Antonius Julianus completely disappeared. We only know it existed because Josephus mentions it. Another book, vital because it was written at the end of the first century by Justus of Tiberias, who organised the revolt in Galilee, has also gone. But Photius, Bishop of Tyre in 448 AD, commenting on Justus's book which still existed then, expressed surprise that it made no mention of Jesus. Justus knew the events of that period from direct experience and could hardly have avoided mentioning the execution of a claimant to the Jewish throne. But the Christian censor had been at work for a century. Thus Photius tells us that when the writings of Eunapius, a critic of Christianity, were republished after the death of Julius the Apostate, all anti-Christian references had been expunged.

Passages were removed from Lucian. The works of Celsus and Sossianus Hierocles were suppressed and we now only have quotations made from them by Christian polemicists. Many old manuscripts in museums and archives are testimony to the Christian censors blotting out sentences or sometimes obscuring whole pages by spilt ink.

Besides official censorship, Christian editors and copyists, altered passages as they saw fit. Even Josephus which has managed to survive has been "improved". The paragraph in *Antiquities of the Jews* bearing witness to Jesus was not in its present form in 250 AD and is thought by many to be a Christian forgery.

The missing books of Tacitus possible owe their disappearance to their having references to Jesus. The books of Tacitus come to a halt at the siege of Jerusalem. The Romans considered both Christians and orthodox Jews to have participated in the Jewish War, and Sulpicius Severus, a Christian writer, does not demure. He asserts, in his *Chronicle* written in the fifth century, that the Romans destroyed the Jerusalem Temple to stop it from being an inspiration to the Jews *and to the Christians*. (These Christians could only be those of the Jerusalem Church, the Nazarenes or Ebionim.)

However this is not confirmed by the works of Josephus as they stand today and it is an amazing statement to be made by a Christian especially at such a late date. Because it is quite contrary to anything the Church would want to maintain, it could not be an invention of the time. Yet, if it is based on a contemporary source, it must have been a prestigious one to carry weight against Josephus. The only source with such prestige is Tacitus. Since it is just at this point that the works of Tacitus are lost, there is again a strong hint of Christian suppression.

Jews also had to alter their records if the Christian censor was not to burn them. Explicit references to Jesus were replaced by references to "a certain one". The version of the *Old Testament* written in Greek, the Septuagint, was also tampered with by the Christians who then accused the Jews of altering their own version. In the pogroms of the Middle Ages, Jewish *Scriptures* were burnt by the cartload. In 1263 AD King Jayme I of Aragon in Spain ordered that all Jewish books should be destroyed. The greatest act of Christian vandalism of all was the torching of the magnificent library of Alexandria in the fifth century. This wholesale destruction of accumulated wisdom in the name of God precipitated the dark ages from which we did not recover until the Renaissance.

What of the Roman archives? Josephus is believed to have had access to the Imperial Archives and to have found there a report by Pilate on the trial of Jesus. Christian writers Tertullian and Justin Martyr both firmly believed a record of Jesus's trial existed in the Roman archives. Other Christian writers at later dates made the same claim. A record of the trial is said by Eusebius to have circulated in 311 AD but he claimed it was a forgery. After the adoption of

Christianity by the Emperors nothing but forgeries existed... Christian ones! The records must have been destroyed when Christianity became the state religion after 325 AD.

Christian Censorship in Josephus

Flavius Josephus was the Roman name of Joseph ben Matthias. Josephus wrote long and detailed histories of the Jews and the events leading to the Roman victory in the Jewish Wars but has almost nothing to say about Jesus and even that is probably added by Christians to fill a prominant gap left by the censors.

He was born in Jerusalem only a few years after the crucifixion. He shows an interest in the Jewish religious groups of the time. He tells us about the Jewish religious parties, about John the Baptist who Christians say was the herald of the Messiah and about Jesus's brother, James, whose death he says was a reason for the start of the War in 66 AD. But he tells us nothing about the crucifixion or how it occurred. A man almost contemporaneous with Jesus and whose reputation was built on detailed histories of the Jewish people fails to mention him except in two brief passages, if they are genuine.

The precocious Josephus had studied all the Jewish religious sects before the age of 19 when he decided to become a Pharisee. He became a clerk to the Sanhedrin and at 26 went as an envoy to Rome to plead for some priests sent to Nero by Procurator Felix for trial. With the help of Poppaea, the Empress, who was possibly a Jewish proselyte or at least a godfearer, he succeeded. He was thus in Rome at much the same time as Paul, the Apostle to the gentiles.

Back in Jerusalem in 64 AD, revolt was simmering. Josephus was patriotic enough but had seen the power and extent of the Empire and knew that rebellion was futile. When the war broke out Josephus was made a general by the Sanhedrin and fought in Galilee with John of Gischala, the Zealot leader of the Galilaeans. Vespasian captured him after the town of Jotapata had been sieged for 47 days and decided to use him as an interpreter. Josephus got on well with Vespasian, predicting that he would become Emperor, which he did. Vespasian asked Josephus to write an account of the Jewish War for his campaign Triumph, a Roman victory parade. It was to be a warning to the people of the East not to try to defy Roman might.

Josephus wrote a draft in his native Aramaic which he called *On the Capture of Jerusalem*. This he polished into his book, the *Jewish War*. To gather his material, as the appointed historian of the Emperor, he was granted access to official archives, to the Reports of Roman Governors, the campaign diaries of Vespasian and Titus, the Emperor's commentaries and he also corresponded with Agrippa I, for a short while King of Judaea before the war. His work had the ultimate stamp of approval – that of the Emperors themselves.

When Josephus uses official sources it is usually evident. He often tells us who filed the report from which he is quoting and transcribes it verbatim with little effort to paraphrase. Thus even non-signalled passages from official sources can be identified by their style. When writing from experience he is more informal, sounds less official and is less impersonal in the information he imparts.

Our present versions of the *Jewish War* mention none of Jesus, John the Baptist or Menehem, who revolted in 66 AD, but they do tell us of Judas of Galilee and Theudas, both messianic nationalist leaders. He records that the Jews merely protested when the Romans erected a statue of Caligula in the Temple, an act grossly contemptuous of the Jewish religion. This is a curiously subdued response for the fanatically religious Jews. In their outrage, history suggests they must surely have rioted, if not revolted. Also strange is the omission of the fire in Rome in 64 AD which Nero attributed to the Christians. Such passages smack of censorship because Josephus usually fastidiously records the smallest detail of events relevant to his subject. It looks as though a whole chapter might have been erased by Christian censors because it depicted Jesus and his followers as fomenters of rebellion. Some manuscripts of the *Jewish War* contain a passage on Jesus extracted from Josephus's companion volume, the *Antiquities of the Jews*, proving that someone has tampered with the original text, presumably in an attempt to fill the obvious gap left by the initial excision.

The inserted passage is favourable towards Jesus even though he was viewed, rightly or wrongly, by the Roman hierarchy as a terrorist. Josephus would have been taking an unlikely risk by making such an assessment. Remember he was a captive who had been adopted by Vespasian and given certain privileges in return for certain duties – privileges which could easily have been withdrawn. Domitian, who was Emperor when the *Antiquities of the Jews* was published, could have been no lover of Jesus or his followers. He even ordered all descendants of King David to be rounded up for questioning in an attempt to detect potential rebels and he banished two members of his own family for wanting to be Christians.

Early Christian writers make no reference to Josephus's commendation of Jesus as they must surely have done had it existed. Origen, for example, writing in about 250 AD puzzled: "though he [Josephus] did not admit our Jesus to be the Christ he none the less gave witness to so much righteousness in James". Elsewhere he adds: "although [Josephus] disbelieved in Jesus as Christ". Plainly Origen's version of Josphus's works did not have the passage to which we are referring, but by 340 AD the version used by Eusebius did.

The passage in *Antiquities* sounds very much like Josephus in style. If it is a bald insertion it has been written in a style compatible with Josephus's, but it could be a skilful redaction of a genuine passage. After the Christians became supreme in the reign of Constantine they planted evidence on Josephus, turning the leading Jewish historian of his day into a witness for Jesus as Christ.

Josephus, in *Antiquities*, *does* mention both John the Baptist and James, the brother of Jesus. A reference to Jesus in the original version must have been excised to render it acceptable but Christian copyists, finding that their crudely censored versions contained no reference to Jesus felt obliged to insert one. As a result more space is devoted to John the Baptist in our editions of the *Antiquities* than to the master whose coming the gospels assure us he was proclaiming. A section covering the career of Jesus in considerably more detail than the short passage we now have must have been deleted.

The passage giving testimony to Jesus in *Antiquities* comes during a catalogue of calamities that the Jews experienced at the time of Pilate taking office. Josephus seems here to be drawing upon official sources and lists Pilate's raising of the standards in Jerusalem and his taking Temple funds to finance the construction of an aqueduct into the city. Then he mentions Jesus and concludes with two incidents in Rome that occurred, according to Tacitus, in 19 AD. This chronology implies that Pilate was governor and Jesus was active much earlier than Christians today believe. The next section of *Antiquities* has skipped almost two decades to a revolt led by "The Egyptian" (the one that Paul was mistaken for in *Acts*) in Samaria in 35 AD. So two tumults in Jerusalem and two incidents in Rome bracket a short paragraph praising Jesus, then there is a jump forward of 15 years to the next strand of the story. Something looks amiss.

Following the testimonial to Jesus, the first of the two incidents in Rome is introduced by: "About the same time also another sad calamity put the Jews into disorder..." but there follows a description of a woman tricked into intercourse with a man pretending to be a god in the Temple of Isis in Rome, a passage eight times longer than that allocated to Jesus and of no apparent relevance to the Jews, despite its introduction. Logic requires this introduction to be that of a passage about the tumult accompanying the arrest of Jesus and described in the gospels. This section was deleted in some copies of Josephus and strongly edited and put forward in others so that the ministry of Jesus would not be described as a calamity. The only relevance to the story of Jesus was that the conniving Priests of Isis were crucified by Tiberius, although it might have been included as a satirical commentary on the myth, new at the time, that Jesus was born of a virgin.

Provincial governors had to dispatch, to the Emperor, "acta", official reports of all that occurred under their jurisdiction. Important trials such as those requiring the death penalty had to be filed, particularly if the trial concerned an attempt at insurrection against Imperial rule. On the evidence of the gospels Pilate must have filed an account of the trial of Jesus, and one must have existed in the Roman archives. We know that Tiberius had an almost obsessive reverence for the legal and civic reforms introduced by his predecessor, Augustus, and paid meticulous attention to the governance of the provinces. Officials had to take care not to step outside of their powers and particularly not to oppress their inferiors. Taxation was light and the policy in frontier regions was to avoid conflict. It is inconceivable that Tiberius should not have been informed of the trial of a man charged with riotous assembly and treason.

Josephus had access to the *Acts of the Governors* and he would have needed it to get an accurate view of events between 6 AD when his earlier source, the books of Nicholas of Damascus, court historian to Herod the Great, ended and about 55 AD when his direct experience as a scribe to the Sanhedrin would have become relevant. So for the period of about 50 years, which covered the ministries of John the Baptist and Jesus, Josephus's main source would have been Roman and Herodian archives.

In his *History of the Church* in 325 AD, Eusebius informs us that the *Acta Pilati*, *the Acts of Pilate*, were published in 311 AD by the Emperor Maximinus Daia precisely to prove that the claims of the Christians were false and the verdict of Pilate was correct. Oddly these documents date Jesus's trial and crucifixion to 21 AD, apparently at odds with Josephus who says Pilate did not take up office until 26 AD. Eusebius concludes the *Acta Pilati* were forgeries. But it is stretching credulity to suggest that the Roman administration were so incompetent as to unnecessarily change the date when they were altering the record to discredit the Christians.

What reason could they possibly have to want to alter the date especially with Josephus so well known? It is more likely that the triumphant Christians only a few years later decided to alter Josephus to put Pilate's rule outside of the period when the *Acta* were dated. The Christians had control of the copying of books after the time of Constantine but their opponents could have hidden copies of the Roman records. By altering Josephus, any copy of the true record that emerged could be shown by reference to Josephus to have been a forgery. And altering the dates in Josephus needed only two simple numeric changes – to the Greek number for the length of Pilate's Prefecture (from 18 to 10 years) and the Greek number for the length of the Prefecture of Gratus, his predecessor (3 to 11 years).

Gratus had appointed four High Priests according to Josephus. Now John's gospel (11:49) describes Caiaphas as "High priest that year", implying that it was usual for High Priests to be changed each year. That is just what Gratus had been doing, confirming that three years was his term of office. Gratus had appointed a new High Priest for each year he was governor and had appointed the fourth one, Joseph Caiaphas, in the year he was recalled, Pilate arrived, found Caiaphas High Priest and kept him in place for his full term of office. When Pilate was recalled, Vitellius, Legate of Syria, Pilate's boss, sacked Caiaphas also. So there is good evidence that Pilate and Caiaphas ruled Judaea in tandem for eighteen years from 18 to 36 AD. The policy of Tiberius was not to change governors believing that, like leeches, they left the body alone when they were sated. Pilate's long period of office is testimony to the policy if not the theory,

To return to the *Acts of Pilate*: we are faced with the following chain of logic.

- Either the *Acta Pilati* existed or they did not.
- If they did not exist Pilate must have neglected his duty in not submitting them but Pilate was a conscientious bureaucrat and would not neglect such matters. It is difficult to believe that none were written or submitted.
- If they existed either they were favourable to the Christian story and so would be part of the Christian canon or they were unfavourable to the Christian story and so would have been destroyed or altered. They are not part of the canon and so they were unfavourable to the Christian cause. They were either destroyed or altered.
- If they once existed but had been destroyed someone must have known and therefore claims that they once existed would have been made. Claims that the *Acta* once existed have been made.
- If they once existed but had been altered someone must have known and therefore claims that they had been forged would have been made. Claims that the *Acta* have been forged have been made.

It looks very much as though the *Acta Pilati* once existed as would have been expected but have been destroyed by the Christians. The only reason they would have destroyed them is that they did not match the story the Church wanted to be believed.

There is a Slavonic text of Josephus's Jewish War which seems to be an early version. it is not free of Christian alterations but tells a different story from the usual. Jesus is not named as such but is called the "Wonder Worker" and led a band of 150 disciples into Jerusalem in a pathetic attempt at revolution. He was crucified around 21 AD. Christians tell us this is a mediaeval forgery!

Christian Mythology

The Making of a Myth

We find nothing explicit in Rabbinical literature, nothing in Philo of Alexandria, no mentions in Roman works until Tacitus writing about 120 AD. Pliny the Elder allegedly had read 2000 books, loved marvels and noted them assiduously in his *Historia Naturalis* compiled about 40 years after Jesus's death. But he made no mention of any of the miracles of Jesus. Justus of Tiberias, a Galilaean historian born only a few years after Jesus and whose works are now lost, made no reference to him that has been quoted by polemicists for or against. Photius, Patriarch of Constantinople in the ninth century, was surprised not to find any reference to Jesus in Justus's work. There are only two passages in all the work of Josephus (about 93 AD), one of which looks like a later addition and the other might also have been.

Even when contemporary writers are discussing matters to which the gospel accounts are relevant, they make no mention of them. Josephus does not mention the Christians when he discusses Jewish religious sects; Paul and Clement do not cite Jesus even though the teachings of Jesus that we know would strengthen their argument; Seneca and Pliny the Elder do not allude to the darkness at the crucifixion even though they are chronicling eclipses and earthquakes.

Neither Paul's nor any of the early epistles suggest any familiarity by the author with an historical person and they say little about Jesus's life. Paul's letters were all written well before the gospels but make no unequivocal reference to any of the material in them – not to Mary and Joseph, the virgin birth, John the Baptist, Judas, Jesus's miracles and his teachings, nor to the circumstances of his death other than that he was crucified. He simply speaks of a new Jewish sect which adored a leader called the Messiah who had died and been resurrected. He conveys to the faithful instructions that had been given to him by the Messiah in visions not in real life, though they later appear in the biographical works as if they were real. Nor do references to Jesus in these, the earliest Christian documents, imply that he lived in the immediate past.

The lack of references to Jesus embarrassed the later Christians and they were not above claiming they existed when they knew they did not, and forging them when necessary to give the authenticity they sought. One such was composed in Rome in the fourth century AD and purported to be a letter between Seneca and Paul but is now accepted by all to be a fraud. Justin and Tertullian both claimed that Pilate wrote a report to Tiberius telling him the full story, miracles, resurrection and all and that it could be found in the archives. Tiberius was said to be so impressed that he proposed to make Jesus a god but the Senate demurred. However, though Christians after Tertullian repeat this tale often, no one had mentioned it before. Gibbon makes it clear that Pontius Pilate would not have written a report incriminating himself against a god, that Tiberius who despised religion would not have wanted to create a new god, that the senate would not have dared to contradict his wishes if he did, and that the record of all this in the archives at Rome would not have escaped the attention of historians.

When later reports attribute some spectacular act to a person that on-the-spot accounts had not mentioned, we should doubt that the alleged event had occurred, for why otherwise would the earlier reports have omitted it? If some other famous person is known to have performed such acts we may begin to suspect a deliberate falsification, an exaggeration or an invention; a desire to put our hero on a par with some other. If we find that motives existed for stories to be made up to create or enhance a reputation, our suspicions should certainly be aroused.

Christian documents fit this sort of pattern. The later Christian works are, the more details of the life of the god they contain – his life seems to grow with time. For the gospel writers, the motive to exaggerate was that they wanted people to join the Christian movement rather than some other.

G.A.Wells compares it with the growth of the legend of Faust. Faust lived in the sixteenth century and gained a modest notoriety in his lifetime. He was an educated man, a doctor, who travelled widely, performed magical feats and then died mysteriously. His contemporaries wrote about him and related something of his unusual behaviour. But in the 50 years after his death, his life was hugely exaggerated, his accounts and deeds multiplied. Reality became so overlaid with layers of fancy it could not be distinguished from legend... Why?

To serve as a guide to Christian believers – a warning not to bargain with the devil!

To serve as a guide for Christian believers biographies of Jesus were written about 50 years after his supposed death but, unlike Faust, there is no unequivocal contemporary evidence of his life. Later Faust stories served the aims of their authors just as later versions of the gospels served the interests of their editors – those of the growing Church. Most of what we know of the life of Jesus has accreted like the legend of Faust. Like Faust there seems to have been a real person at the core of it but, unlike Faust, we know little about that person.

Jesus's reputation seems to have been fancifully embellished:

- previous heroes performed similar deeds;
- there was a visible motive for inventing the stories;
- contemporary documents were altered;
- once the historicity of Jesus was accepted, the references to him multiplied;
- later documents give more details than earlier ones;
- careful research by scholars to get at the truth is ignored or vilified by those committed to the myth.

Even the crucifixion was not original. Thousands died on the cross at that time. And even before! Jewish history records an uncannily similar event from the previous century. The *Talmud* tells of a Jesus ben Pandira who was slain and hanged from a tree on the eve of Passover about 100 BC when Alexander Jannaeus crucified 800 Pharisees. Furthermore ancient religions are replete with incarnate gods who suffered for mankind, died, were buried, descended into Hell and rose from the dead to save the faithful. Many incidents in Jesus's life have already happened to earlier gods or in earlier Jewish history.

In the first century AD people thought in terms of the miraculous and accepted the most unlikely assertions as being fact. The gods of Olympus manipulated nature for their own purposes and so too the divine Christ of the first century Christians had to show his supernatural power. He raises the dead, walks on water, turns water into wine, stills tempests and feeds multitudes with a few loaves and fishes. Angels sang at his birth and the dead walked at his death.

All of this is consistent with the story of Jesus being essentially mythical. It does not prove that it is, but the development of the gospel stories in the first century can be explained by unhistoric embellishment of an otherwise shadowy figure originally of little historical importance, a minor rebel who became a fantasy, a figment of Paul's obsession with the god who dies.

The Virgin Birth

Mankind will not emulate extraordinary leaders but instead fall to their knees, adore and worship them. Rather than follow a difficult example it is easier to deify the exemplar thus providing an excuse for not emulating him – "How can mere men do what gods can do?" This inclination to worship Jesus as a god rather than follow him as a man stems from the earliest days of Christianity.

Within 60 years of the crucifixion Jesus's adoring followers had created the myth of the conception of Jesus by the Holy Ghost making him at least half a god from the start. He thus became an impossible role model for merely mortal men. Yet even the half of him that was human passed on by his mother was too much for the adorers – they wanted a fully fledged god. After centuries as a tolerated heresy, in 1854 the doctrine of "The Immaculate Conception of the Mother of God" was adopted by the Roman Church rendering Jesus's mother a perfect being from her own birth, free of original sin, incapable of sin throughout her life – a sinless mate for God Almighty to conceive a divine son. Jesus as a fine example of loving manhood had been usurped by the adorers and worshippers.

No mention is made of the Virgin Birth in the epistles and in fact Paul could not be more explicit in recording that Jesus was "of the seed of David according to the flesh" as if he were refuting the suggestion. For Paul Jesus was the Son of God through the "Spirit of Holiness" which did not require a supernatural conception. Nor does the earliest gospel mention the virgin birth. The mystical *Book of the Revelation of John the Divine* does not mention it, though it would be perfect for inclusion in such an allegorical piece. None of the Jewish patriarchs were born of virgins and, though older women beyond the menopause had their wombs "opened" to conceive Isaac, Jacob and Samuel, no divine impregnation was suggested.

The virgin birth appears in *Luke* and *Matthew,* years after the event, to prove Jesus's divinity. The birth stories in the two gospels come from different sources and differ widely but both contradict their central thesis that Jesus's mother was a virgin by giving a genealogy to show that Joseph was descended from David, an irrelevancy if Joseph had not impregnated his wife. The original idea was obviously to trace Jesus's lineage through Joseph to David to fulfil messianic prophecy. Then the idea of making Jesus more divine through a virgin birth arose and was tacked on spoiling the object of the genealogy.

The editors of both gospels see a problem and try to avoid it: in *Luke* by inserting "as people thought" to show Jesus was not really Joseph's son and in *Matthew* by slyly separating Joseph from his son by inserting after "...Joseph" "the husband of Mary, of whom was begotten" Jesus. If the intention was to imply that Mary was begetting Jesus then the person inserting the story was either ignorant or depended on the ignorance of his readers for only men could beget according to Jewish convention.

Neither *Luke* nor *Matthew* refer to the birth story again and indeed it contradicts the main story. Presumably his family or at least his mother would have been aware of all that feting by kings and shepherds, and glory in the heavens, and the reason for it all. Yet later they are continually puzzled and disappointed by Jesus's behaviour. And why bother trying to establish a divine conception when both refer to Joseph in the main narrative as the father of Jesus. The Ebionites accepted Joseph as the natural father.

An attempt was made by the early Christians to justify the virgin birth story by referring to *Isaiah* 7:14 where is written, "Behold a virgin shall conceive and bear a son". The word employed in the Greek version of the *Old Testament* was parthenos. But a reference to the original Hebrew yields the word almah. Both parthenos and almah did not necessarily mean a virgin as we understand it, a woman who had never had intercourse. In Greek it could mean youth, the state of unmarriage, or even a person who is first married. In Hebrew it could mean beside the usual meaning, an immature girl who could not conceive because she had not yet started to menstruate.

The idea of a virgin as a premenstrual girl allows her to have children and still be a virgin. If she were to conceive from her very first ovulation, she would not have menstruated but would be a mother and still a virgin. If she conceived at the first ovulation after the birth, she could be a virgin mother of two children of different ages. Since Jewish girls often married before menstruation – in *Joel* 1:8 an almah's husband is mentioned – virgin mothers were not unusual. Now Mary was described as "betrothed" to Joseph implying that she was a minor under the age of twelve and a half. After that age she could become his wife. Thus the "virgin" Mary could have given birth. If she did, the truth was misunderstood in the gentile world of the Roman Empire, and indeed beyond, where it was de rigeur not only for gods but also great men to be born of virgins. Ra, Hatshepsut, Amenophis III, Cyrus the Great, Julius Caesar, Perseus, Plato, Apollonius of Tyana, Fohi, Lao Kium, Zoroaster and Attis all came of virgin births according to their followers.

Herodotus explained that such conceptions occurred by way of a ray of light and according to Plutarch's book on Isis and Osiris it entered through the ear. Tertullian confirms it was a ray of light. Thus medieval pictures of Mary at the moment of conception show a ray of light entering her ear. Furthermore it is common for gods and those akin to gods to have mothers called Mary or a cognate name. Adonis was born of Myrrha, Hermes of Maia, Cyrus of Mariana or Mandane, Joshua of Miriam, Buddha of Maya and Khrishna of Maritala. Since Moses, the first Messiah, was born of Miriam, Jesus the final one also had to be. As an Essene Jesus was quite likely to have been surrendered to the order as a babe. If he was not abandoned by his family as a child, the gospels maintain he was as an adult. It is likely that his mother had no role to play in the gospel events and that she and several other women were added in the earliest days of the gentile church as a sop to its female congregations.

The disciples of Barabbas knew nothing of him being born of a virgin. The story was tacked on to hype up the new god. Yet now most Christians arc outraged if its truth is questioned.

Early Life of Jesus

Nothing certain is known about Jesus's birth, childhood and early manhood. The earliest and latest gospels say nothing before his ministry begins. *Matthew* and *Luke* have something to say but each says something different. *Matthew* says Jesus's parents came from Bethlehem in Judaea but on returning from Egypt they settled in Nazareth in Galilee. *Luke* says they lived in Nazareth and go to Bethlehem to be taxed. *Mark* says Jesus is of Nazareth and does not mention Bethlehem.

That Jesus was associated with a place called Nazareth is wrong. In fact Nazareth seemed not to exist until the fourth century AD when, according to some critics, an obscure site in a suitable location was named Nazareth to fit the story. He was described in the *New Testament* as Jesus the Nazarene. The introduction of the village of Bethlehem looks like a further attempt to relate Jesus as Messiah with David whose home town this was.

No census in the reign of Augustus is known near the supposed year of Jesus's birth. Furthermore Roman custom was to register people for a census at their place of residence not at their place of birth which would impose absurd burdens. And Galilee was ruled by the puppet Herod Antipas not the Romans when Quirinius or Cyrenius taxed Judaea.

Matthew says Jesus was born in a house, *Luke* that he was born in a stable which is usually depicted as a cave. The cave at Bethlehem said to be the birthplace of Jesus was, the Christian father Jerome tells us, actually a rock shrine to the god Tammuz or Adonis whose symbol was a cross. The Christians took over a pagan sacred site as they did many times over and adopted a common symbol of the old religions. Apollo, Cybele, Demeter, Hercules, Hermes, Mithras and Poseidon were all adored in caves. Furthermore Hermes was wrapped in swaddling clothes and laid in a manger. So was Dionysus who bears many other similarities to Jesus. The mythical ancestor of the Ionians, Ion, was similarly born in a cave and was placed in a basket.

Matthew says Joseph learnt in a dream that Herod would kill the baby and so took off to Egypt just in time to miss the massacre of the innocents of Bethlehem by Herod. Herod died in 4 BC, apparently before Jesus was born and Josephus, who records all the crimes of Herod, does not mention this atrocity. The story is the same as that of Abraham who Nimrod attempted to murder by killing all the infants in the land, the Jewish first born in Egypt who were threatened by the Pharaoh to eliminate Moses, and Hadad, who fled to Egypt when Joab tried to account for him by killing all the men of Edom. Suetonius also relates that the Roman Senate attempted to dispose of the baby Octavius, later the Emperor Augustus, with such a massacre.

The earliest gospel disposes of the forty days in the wilderness, the wild animals, the temptation by the Devil and the ministrations by angels in one verse. *John* does not mention any of this. Yet *Luke* and *Matthew* give details of the fasting and the temptation with Jesus offered the world from the top of a mountain. By coincidence:

- Elijah fasted on Horeb in the wilderness for forty days;
- Moses did the same on Sinai.
- Zoroaster was tempted by the Devil in the wilderness;
- Buddha was also;
- Jupiter was led by Pan (the Devil) to the top of a mountain called the Pillar of Heaven whence he could see the countries of the world;

Forty is one of those mystical numbers that pop up in old religions: there were forty days of sacrifice in the Persian Salutation to Mithras; forty days of mourning in the mysteries of the goddess Persephone; the deluge lasted forty days, etc. The story is introduced to establish Jesus as a great leader, superior even to Moses. Furthermore the offer of the kingship of the world by the devil was intended by gentile Christians as a rebuttal of the idea that Jesus was a Messiah in the Jewish mould who would become a world ruler – that is what the Devil offered him and he refused it.

What Jesus Looked Like

What did Jesus look like? There are no descriptions of him in the gospels but descriptions must have been written of him – when the Sanhedrin issued its warrant for his arrest as *John* describes and when Pilate submitted his account of the trial. Each of these would contain the name, charge and description of the criminal.

The Christian image of Jesus is derived from a forgery issued to counter the publication of the *Acta Pilati*. This forgery is called the Letter of Lentulus, Lentulus being a Roman of higher rank than Pilate to discredit the latter. "Lentulus" describes Jesus as a man of classical European beauty. He has light, curly, shoulder-length hair, blue eyes, a ruddy complexion unblemished by spots or marks, a faultless nose and mouth, and a short divided beard; he has a grave demeanour. This letter describes Jesus as tall, but that is belied by the measure of his height which is given as 15 palms and a half, roughly 4 feet 6 inches. Both Tertullian and Celsus described Jesus as short and of mean appearance. The apocryphal *Acts of John* says Jesus was a man of small stature and Jesus's twin brother is described as small in the Syrian *Acts of Thomas*. In *Luke* 19:3 Zacchaeus

> *...sought to see Jesus who he was; and could not for the crowd, because he was little of stature.*

Christians interpret this ambiguity as meaning that Zacchaeus was little of stature when it really means that Jesus was. And indeed Jesus calls himself "but little in the kingdom of God" (Lk 7:28) apparently meaning the least significant but also punning on his small height.

The *Slavonic Text* of Josephus's the *Jewish War* pictures Jesus not as fair, handsome, tall and upright, and in the prime of life but as a bent, short, possibly hunchbacked, elderly man with beetling brows and a dark skin. Even *John* tells us indirectly that Jesus was middle aged. In *John* 8:57 the Jews say to him: "Thou art not yet fifty years old." The implication of these words is that Jesus was nearer fifty than forty. How would that tally with his being 30 at his baptism? Well, perhaps he looked older than he was. Or perhaps the baptism made him crown prince but he did not become leader until John was imprisoned. Or simply his ministry was longer than the gospels tell us.

Was Jesus unmarried? If Jesus was unmarried, it was unusual. Celibacy was unusual for a Jew at the time. But Moses had stopped living with his wife to undertake his prophetic role and the Rabbis deduced that prophecy and marriage were incompatible. However at the time of Jesus the age of prophecy was over and it was the duty of all Jews to procreate – some first century rabbis compared celibacy to murder. The Hasidim had mixed views. Some, like Honi and Hanina were married but others accepted that abstinence led to holiness and ultimately to the holy spirit, to "resurrection of the dead and the Elijah of blessed memory".

Soldiers in campaign and those taking part in worship had to abstain from intercourse. The Essenes, who regarded themselves as preparing for the terminal battle, did segregate themselves from the opposite sex in their pursuit of holiness. Jesus seems to have had little in common with Essene asceticism possibly because he was a village Essene or a member of a variant order, the Nazarenes, whose duty was to persuade Jewish sinners that they were needed by God in the coming battle. A village Essene was unlikely to have been unmarried but because Jesus considered himself a soldier in the coming battle he, and his companions, would have chosen chastity. The provision needed for widows in *Acts of the Apostles* shows that Nazarenes in general married like the village Essenes of the *Damascus Document*.

The Catholic Teacher

Many of Jesus's sayings have been distorted in recording them either deliberately to suit one faction or the other or, in many cases simply by faulty recollection, faulty translation or misplaced context including attributing to Jesus sayings that were originally those of the evangelists, the words of Essene catechisms or those of the Essene Teacher of Righteousness.

Jesus's method of teaching as expressed in the gospels was probably traditional. He appeared to teach in midrashim and pesharim, quotations from scripture with a commentary or interpretation. Christian editors however have often dropped the *Old Testament* quotation to make the interpretation or commentary stand alone and sound original when they often expressed the active principles of pious Jews of the time whether Pharisees or Essenes. Such passages can often be detected by the comment being introduced by "For" with no apparent purpose.

Most of the gospel sayings were reiterations of old truths. Thus the *Psalms* say that the meek shall inherit the land and *Jeremiah* says He giveth his cheek to him who smiteth him. Many seem to oppose barbaric Jewish practices. Yet from the *Old Testament* we find that *Jeremiah* rejects blood sacrifices, appealed to individual conscience and preached non-resistance to enemies and *Isaiah* prefers the concepts of justice, truth and love. The biblical Jesus was introducing little or nothing in these respects that Jews of one sect or another did not already accept with the provision that Jews only were considered.

Jesus urged his followers in *Matthew* (5:48):

> *Be ye perfect, even as your Father in Heaven is perfect,*

using characteristic Essene language, but even that, with minor change, comes from *Leviticus* (19:2) which records God's command;

> *Ye shall be holy, for I the Lord thy God am holy!*

Pharisees tried to obey these commands – though they realised they could not be achieved outside of Heaven – just as it appears Jesus did. Was the command of *Matthew* 5:44 to love your enemy? Not really! The practical side of it is expressed in *Proverbs* where people are urged to help their enemies and as far back as *Exodus* 23:4. Essenes believed in brotherly love as the *Damascus Document* makes clear but brotherly love could have extended no further than the Children of Israel, and even then probably only in the End Days. It did *not* extend to foreigners.

Jesus's most controversial innovation as a teacher seemed to be the rejection of the Jewish dietary laws expressed in *Mark* 7:19 as

> *Thus he declared all foods clean.*

This must have been so controversial that it could hardly have been forgotten if true. Yet both Peter in *Acts* 10:13-16 and Paul seem unaware of it. Peter is much troubled by his dream of eating things unclean before visiting the gentile, Cornelius; and Paul, though glad to get rid of such troublesome laws for his gentile converts, never once cites the teaching of Jesus as authority for it – unless it be in Romans 14:14:

> *I know and am persuaded in the Lord Jesus that*
> *nothing is unclean in itself,*

which sounds more as though he is expressing his own view, convinced in his faith that he is correct. In reality, he neither knew nor cared what Jesus had taught but, from his supernatural knowledge of Jesus, he justified himself in what he did. Later the gospel writers had to justify Paul's ruthless innovation through Jesus in their accounts of his life. Thus the immovably orthodox Jesus unknowingly became the author of a huge change to the Law of Moses.

Jesus respected the Law so highly that the gospels record his saying that no one who transgressed the least of its ordinances could enter the kingdom of God. *Mark*'s apparent refutation of it is an alteration to suit the later teachings of the Pauline church. In the original story the dietary laws were quoted to illustrate a spiritual point not to be rejected.

The Sermon on the Mount occurs in *Matthew* and *Luke* but not in the other two gospels where the sayings included in the sermon are scattered throughout the narrative. The sermon is a device to pull together groups of sayings. Possibly it was used in the common source of *Luke* and *Matthew* and the latter in particular used it to emphasise Jesus's authority and the novelty of his message. *Matthew* apparently gives Jesus great authority to change what the Jewish *Scriptures* had taught;

> *You have learned that our forefathers were told...but what I tell you is this...*

We saw that Matthew might have been an Essene and that a similar formulation has been found in polemics at Qumran. *Luke* does not make the words so assertive.

The historian, Arthur Weigall, apparently loyal to Christianity, says the authors of the gospels could not have collected all this wisdom and make it seem to fall from the lips of an imaginary figure, especially one so simple, tender and gallant, concluding "If ever there was an authentic personality in history, it is that of our Lord". But manifestly this is nonsense, the sayings could easily have been collected by others from a variety of Essene sources and the gospel writers simply used them. They could also have drawn upon some other simple, tender and gallant figure for their model of Jesus. The Essene origin of the Jesus myth could explain all this. No attempt had been made to create a romantic figure deliberately but a consistent personality emerges from the uniformly Essene origins of the sources. The emphasis in early Christian societies on purity of living in readiness for the coming kingdom would have given the incarnate life of their god the characteristics of a holy teacher. It proved convenient to attribute to the failed rebel the wisdom of the Essene Teacher of Righteousness. All of these stories were originally related in Aramaic. The very act of translation would have added a smoothing effect, and we know from *Luke* that there might well have been several renderings of the stories before they came to us in the gospels.

Not that Jesus Barabbas would have been a rough lout to be the leader of a rebel gang. He was a king and would have had to have had a king's wisdom and authority. The gospels tell us that he had. Furthermore Jesus was described as a carpenter and the son of a carpenter. In Jewish writing of the time the name for a carpenter (naggar) also means a craftsman in general and includes the meaning of "scholar". The only subject available to a "scholar" was to study the *Scriptures*. The real meaning of scholar was apparently rendered literally as carpenter at some stage, probably when the work was translated into Greek. And, in fairness, there is nothing absurd about the scholar being a carpenter! In those days there were no endowed professorships. Even rabbis had to earn a living in some practical way. Perhaps the scholar worked his passage as a carpenter.

The Wonder Worker

Taken literally it seems that Jesus's aim was to assist the physically, mentally and spiritually sick.

> *It is not the healthy that need a doctor, but the sick; I did not come to invite virtuous people but sinners.*
>
> Mk 2:17

> *Today and tomorrow I shall be casting out devils and working cures; on the third day I shall reach my goal.*
>
> Lk 13:32

According to Geza Vermes, these statements characterise Jesus as a charismatic healer. In fact the political and spiritual sickness of the people was being described in an esoteric language which represented it as physical sickness. This is clear in the above quotation from *Mark*. For Essenes the physically sick and infirm were already saved and under the protection of the Angels of Holiness – they did not need special attention. Jesus was intent on winning over people's hearts. But both spiritual and physical sickness were caused by demons and they had to be driven out to effect a cure.

The idea that demons were responsible for moral and physical evil, stemmed from Persian Zoroastrianism. It entered deeply into Jewish thought from the time of the Babylonian exile. The *Book of Enoch* (1 En 10:4-8) speaks of Azazel, the fallen angel that had corrupted the earth and was responsible for all sin. Mastery over these devils depended on mastery of an arcane art known only to a few. Noah and Solomon were two who had mastery over these secrets. The Essenes, for whom Noah and Solomon were counted among the Righteous, and the Therapeutae in Egypt were also adepts.

Josephus records the Essenes' interest in ancient books which provided for the well-being of the body and the soul, their searches for cures by "investigations into roots and stones" and their practise of exorcisms by invoking the name of a sage like Solomon, chanting his incantations and using drugs from plants. Thus Jesus's disciples, and one who was not, expelled spirits by invoking Jesus's name. Furthermore, the buildings at Qumran, on a recent interpretation were used for extracting essences from plants. The Pharisees might have frowned on these magical rituals but they had to tolerate them for fear of casting doubt on their own rituals of purity which no doubt seemed equally magical to ignorant people.

On the face of it Jesus carried out exorcisms without pronounced ritual. To cure people he seemed only to use his own spittle and to effect exorcism he simply gave a firm command. As an exorcist he was not unique either in Jewish history or at the time. A fragment from Qumran tells of Daniel curing the King, Nebuchadnezzar, who recalls, "I was afflicted with an evil ulcer for seven years. A "gazer" pardoned my sins". This story is interesting because healing is effected without scandal or blasphemy by forgiveness of sins. When curing the paralytic, Jesus says:

> *My son, your sins are forgiven.*

Even two centuries later rabbis still agreed that sins had to be forgiven for someone to be cured of an illness. Thus Jesus does not blaspheme when he forgives sins because it does not imply that he is divine. Vermes's theory is that Jesus was one of the Hasidim, The Pious or Devout Ones, whose prayers made miracles occur. He was a charismatic whose powers derived not from magical formulae but from contact with God.

An earlier example was Honi the Circle Drawer, or Onias, the Righteous, in Josephus. In a period of drought about 63 BC just before Jerusalem fell to Pompey, Honi effected a rain miracle by drawing a circle. When he refused to favour either side in a dispute between Hyrcanus II and Aristobulus he was stoned to death by Hyrcanus's followers. Another Hasid contemporaneous with Jesus was Hanina ben Dosa, a Galilaean who was very similar to Jesus. His devotion at prayer was so intense he did not notice a snake bite him, and as a healer he could even cure at a distance.

The other characteristic of the Hasidim besides their working miracles was that they were poor. They lived according to the principle: "What is mine is yours and what is yours is your own". They were not interested in legal matters and matters of ritual but were concerned with moral matters. They were respected for their love and kindness but they were renowned for their miracles. They were men of deeds respected as forming a link between Heaven and earth by their closeness to God. The Hasidim were often Galilaeans because the unsophisticated religious outlook of the people engendered a simple piety and their individual teachings often offended the orthodox such as the Pharisees who respected these men for their devoutness but disliked their individuality, disapproving of the Hasidic disregard for the minutiae of the Law and fearing for the religious order which they had established. The Pharisees did not like the Hasidim's apparent closeness to God and, at the time of Honi, the leader of the Pharisees wanted to have the Hasid excommunicated but dare not. However the organisation of the orthodox eventually prevailed over the individuality and popular appeal of the Hasidim and established Rabbinic Judaism.

Vermes concludes that Jesus was "the just man, the zaddik,...the helper and the healer,...the teacher and leader, venerated by his intimates and less committed admirers alike as prophet, lord and son of God". One has to say that these men sound just like Essenes. Two hundred years before Barabbas the Hasidim had been the movement from which sprang other Jewish parties including the Pharisees and in large measure the Essenes. Were the Galilaean Hasidim an offshoot of the Essenes? Did they have a militant wing? Were they the Galilaeans – the supporters of Judas – of Josephus? Were they the Nazarenes?

Miracles

Jesus dines with a leper on his way into Jerusalem. Today we might do that willingly, knowing leprosy is not highly contagious and that we have ways of treating the disease. But in the society in which he lived Jesus would have done no good encouraging people to fraternise with lepers. You can hardly blame Pharisees or anyone else thinking ill of someone who did this.

It was not a question of hypocrisy but practical hygiene. Leprosy is a horrible and disgusting disease which was incurable. It made sense to avoid lepers and to quarantine those who had the disease. Lepers were forbidden entry into Jerusalem and lived in a leper colony to the east of the city because the prevailing winds were from the west and people thought the disease was transmitted on the winds. If Jesus stayed with Simon the Leper he stayed in a leper colony. It is hardly surprising that the Elders of Jerusalem were annoyed. Of course Jesus was expecting the world to end and God's kingdom to begin at any time, so he might not have been too bothered himself, but that would have been no consolation to those who were not expecting an apocalypse – and they turned out to be right!

Of course Simon was not a leper. The word was code, perhaps for a Nazarene spy or agent, perhaps the man who procured the upper room or the foal and the ass. Perhaps it simply was code for a Nazarene. Who knows? But it is not unusual for clandestine organisations to use code to cover their operations and that is surely what happened here.

At the time of the gospel stories everyone believed in the supernatural and gods were expected to show their supernatural powers. Not that anyone had to see the wonders but that they should be spoken about! Appolonius of Tyana, Jesus's contemporary, was a miracle worker especially noted at the time. The early Christian saints had greater supernatural power than Jesus himself if the stories about them are to be believed. Even Plotinus, a philosopher, performed miracles.

Explaining the miracles at this distance is obviously an uncertain art. We have seen that the gospels are not homogeneous. They were written long after the events they record allowing a lot of time for expansion and exaggeration, and they were heavily altered by later hands. Clearly the miracles also came from different sources. If Jesus were the leader of an apocalyptic band of rebels many miracles can be explained as misunderstood parables. The parables were illustrations used in speeches and were often coded, so that only those with ears to hear could hear. However even if some represent real events they are generally not unexplainable.

When Jesus died, *John* gives no miracles. *Mark* and *Luke* mention the darkness of the sky for three hours and the tearing of the veil in the Temple. The grosser effects – the earthquake, the bursting open of graves and the dead walking – are the product of the fervid imagination of Matthew, one of his sources or a later editor. If any one of these spectacular events really happened, on an occasion as memorable anyway as the death of a god, surely they would have been widely remembered and would have appeared in the other accounts.

The synoptic gospels give six instances of apparent exorcism. The Apostles, the 70 disciples and even a non-disciple were all described as exorcists. Each subject was cured by a firm command, and in one significant incident the demon is told never to go back (Mk 9:25) implying that normally the cures were often only temporary – the demon returned later. Mary Magdalene had had seven devils driven from her – or was it the same one that kept returning? When these cures are not simply Nazarene code, the subjects were probably hysterical. A paralytic was healed and there were twelve other healings (but some were probably the same incident reported twice) in which a simple ritual was used. There were some mass healings and finally there were five instances of non healing miracles – calming a storm, the loaves and fishes, walking on water at night, a large catch of fish, and a catch of a fish with a coin in its mouth just right for paying the Temple tax.

The turning of water into wine must have been based on similar tales told of Dionysus, whose mysteries were widely popular at the time. The date of the event, 6 January, is the date of the festival of Dionysus when a ritual changing of water into wine was enacted as part of the mysteries. The feeding of a multitude with five loaves and two fishes might be copied from Elisha who carries out a similar miracle in *2 Kings* 4, but is most probably a coded incident.

The raising of the dead occurs only in *Luke* and *John*. In *Luke* the son of the widow of Nain is raised, in *John* it is Lazarus. By anyone's standards, raising the dead is no mean feat so it is difficult to understand how *Mark* and Matthew had not heard of them. Such astonishing feats could not have been forgotten and so all subsequent accounts must contain them – they don't so can carry no credibility. If they have meaning it is Nazarene code.

In *Mark* however the daughter of Jairus is raised, not from the dead, from a cataleptic fit. A crisp command breaks the trance, "Girl! Get up!" Other cures fall into the same category – faith healing or psychological techniques which would have seemed miraculous to the ignorant. He would say to the cured person, "Thy faith hath made thee whole". In Galilee where he was known as a local boy people had insufficient faith in him for his faith healing to be effective except in a few cases.

The Idea of Atonement

The doctrine of atonement expressed by St Augustine is that Adam in disobeying God in the Garden of Eden had introduced sin to the world. His punishment was banishment from the Garden and to have to work with the sweat of his brow to survive. Every human being thenceforth was born with original sin. God however eventually relented. He must have decided he had made a mistake, been too cruel on his human products or had punished them enough and he sent his son to suffer a sacrificial death as satisfaction for Adam's crime. Christians are therefore no longer stopped from entering Heaven because of original sin. The joining of a god and man through the sacrifice of the god or one aspect of him and their subsequent communion through symbolic cannibalism is the "at one ment" from which atonement originated.

Today it seems outrageous that a loving god should impose torture and suffering in some propitiatory sacrifice, and the outrage is justified because the sacrifice is pagan. We have seen that pagan gods frequently died for the good of man, and commonly the god sacrificed himself to himself. The source of such beliefs is the cycle of the seasons, the death of nature in winter or the dry season and its resurrection in spring or with the rains.

It was felt by primitive men that nature could be helped in reviving by spilling a little blood with which to fertilise the soil. So human sacrifices were introduced. The victim became identified with the appropriate fertility god so the "god" died for God for the benefit of the people. This practice became the basis of many of the myths noted above. Adonis was killed by a boar but the boar was himself. Mithras sacrificed a bull but the bull was himself. Similarly the goat and bull of Dionysus, the bear of Artemis, and so on. Attis castrated himself to death fulfilling his dual role as Father god and sacrificed son. In the *Epistle to the Hebrews*, Christ is the High Priest who sacrificed himself to put away sin.

In *Isaiah* 53 the prophet speaks of a national figure, not the Messiah, who atones for the sins of the people by his suffering and death. The person represents the nation of Israel itself who have to suffer to be righteous. The scapegoat of *Leviticus* (16:10) carrying the sins of the nation was driven into the wilderness to be eaten by wild animals and atone for the sins of the people. At the time of Christ, sin-offerings of a lamb or a goat were common for the remission of sins. The earliest Christians whether Jewish or gentile must have been primed to accept a sacrificial explanation of Barabbas's death in atonement for the sins of mankind.

What did Jesus have to say on the subject of atonement, a subject of which one would imagine he was conscious? Nothing certain. "The Son of Man came...to give his life as a ransom to many" in *Mark* 10:45 are the words of the author not of Jesus. In descriptions of the Last Supper only in *Matthew* is there any suggestion of the shedding of blood for "the remission of sins" and that is accepted as an editor's gloss.

Ephesians expresses clearly the accepted doctrine and *Hebrews* dwells on the sacrificial nature of the passion – similarly *1 Peter*, thought to be a genuine letter of Peter, the Apostle. The epistle of *James* is quite different, emphasising the importance of works, faith being empty without works. James asks what comfort it is to someone who is naked and starving to be wished well and advised to go in peace. They need sustenance not good wishes:

> *Thus faith, if it have not works, is dead itself.*
>
> Jas 2:17

Bold words by today's standards but more the spirit of Barabbas than Paul who derided works in favour of faith in God's sacrifice. *James* makes no mention of the sacrifice of the crucifixion, and for that reason Luther called it an epistle of straw.

The early Christians accepted the atoning sacrifice uncritically but later theologians were at a loss to understand why the sacrifice should atone for anything if God was "Lord of All". They found an answer with Irenaeus who formulated the "Ransom Theory". With the sins of Adam, Satan had taken the world as his own domain and God, being unable to steal what was another's, had to give his son as a ransom. Satan then brought about Jesus's death on the cross but found he was tricked because the immortal Jesus immediately flew off to Heaven. It was another thousand years before Anselm and Abelard denied that Satan had ever had any rights over mankind. The view of Augustine that Jesus died to relieve all men of eternal torments through original sin was revived.

Peter as Bishop of Rome

Was Peter ever the Bishop of Rome? Catholics believe he was whereas many others do not believe he ever went there.

The church in Rome was already well established when Paul wrote Romans around 57-59 AD. No Apostle founded it. If Suetonius is correct that Claudius banished Jews from Rome because of tumults instigated by Chrestus in 49 AD, it existed before the Council of Jerusalem (~50 AD) yet Peter was still in Jerusalem at that time. In any case Paul would have referred to Peter's role had it been true. In Paul's letter to the Romans Peter is not even mentioned. The audience are Pauline converts, gentiles not Jews, for they are not bound by the Jewish Law and put their trust in faith. The Jews from Rome converted on the day of Pentecost (*Acts* 2:10) must surely have been the founders but following disagreements over "Chrestus" (salvation through faith or works) they were expelled.

According to *Galatians*, Peter spent most of his activity in Jerusalem (1:18;2:1-10) but visited Antioch where he refused to mix with gentile Christians and persuaded Barnabas, Paul's companion, also not to mix, thus antagonising Paul (2:11-21). *Acts* concludes with Paul preaching in Rome but merely says that Peter, after his second release from prison, went to another place. Later he is still in Jerusalem allegedly arguing for Paul's gentile converts not to be bound by the Law. When later documents refer to Peter's martyrdom no place is mentioned. He is claimed to be the first Bishop of Antioch although there is no association of martyrdom with it.

1 Clement, an epistle from the Church of Rome to the Church of Corinth, comparing Peter and Paul, refers to Peter's glorious past but makes no mention of his being in Rome though it does say that Paul came to the limit of the West (Rome) and died there. It seems that Clement did not know of Peter's being in Rome. Ignatius, addressing the Romans, refers to Peter and Paul together as if they had been in Rome. But, although Justin Martyr in about 150 AD talks of Simon Magus being in Rome, he does not mention Peter's supposed polemic against him.

The Bishop of Corinth, writing to Rome about 170 AD, says that both the Church of Rome and the Church of Corinth were founded by Peter and Paul, yet there had been no earlier mention of Peter being at Corinth, though Paul, of course, was. If the bishop was wrong about the history of his own church, is he likely to be right about the history of the Roman one? The author of Romans (Paul) says he has never met the Christians of Rome and this is confirmed in *Acts* where the Roman Christians meet Paul on his arrival. The Bishop of Corinth is taking part in myth building! Soon afterwards Irenaeus says that the Roman church was founded by Peter and Paul.

Later Peter is said to have been in Rome for 25 years and to have founded the church there by himself. This idea grew to strengthen Rome's claims to be supreme of the churches. Bishops were supposed to have been established since the earliest days so it was better to claim the first bishop of Rome as either Peter or Paul. Peter was preferred as the companion of the real life Jesus.

Thus the original conflict between the two Apostles is smoothed, they work together, they actively cooperate in founding churches including the Roman church, then Peter stays 25 years in Rome, becomes the sole founder and the first bishop. In such ways is the good news manipulated: in such ways are myths constructed.

THE GOSPEL ACCORDING TO BARABBAS

...the God of Israel has called out the sword against all the nations, and He will do mighty deeds by the saints of His people.

The War Scroll

Jesus Barabbas had no intention of changing Jewish laws – only expectations. He was a fanatically dedicated Jew of an apocalyptic order, the Nazarenes, who believed that God had begun to create his kingdom on earth. He stoutly defended the Law of Moses as the gospels illogically admit. The Jewish people were fed up and hoping for their enemies to be overcome. Jesus Barabbas was one of many men who thought he could lead his people into the kingdom of God. He could only do this if he believed that he was God sent. He did and accepted the crown of David.

He began by urging people that they should prepare for the coming kingdom just as John the Baptist did. Only the Righteous could enter the kingdom so he invited Jews to sincerely repent and symbolically purify themselves through baptism and prepare themselves for the coming battle. In doing this he was metaphorically casting out evil spirits, making the blind see and healing the sick. Those who were thus purified could enter the kingdom and were the soldiers in the messianic army. He made no claim to be the Messiah.

Jesus believed that God helps those who help themselves. So the kingdom of Heaven has to be won by the Righteous showing that they were ready to take on their enemies, then God would intervene with a miracle. He knew it would not be easy for it was prophesied that those called to the messianic kingdom would have to face the might of the heathen. They had to sustain these tribulations to prove themselves faithful.

Jesus gathered together an army in the desert. He knew that by alerting the faithful and gathering an army he would be also alerting the authorities. He was the Nasi, the Prince. a leader of the Davidic mould who would assert the authority of God's Righteous, and that consequently one "like unto the Son of Man", who the prophet Daniel told would come on a cloud from God, would arrive to institute the kingdom. After some remarkable successes the uprising was a failure, no "Son of Man" appeared, people asked them to leave them alone and Jesus and the disciples had to flee from Antipas's soldiers to Phoenicia.

Jesus hid, then ventured back into Antipas's country. He had come to believe that his mistakes were that God has ordained him the Messiah, the Melchizedek, and that the kingdom of God required him to capture Jerusalem and the Temple. *Then* God would intervene with a miracle. He became transfigured – crowned as Melchizedek. His band proceeded to Jerusalem disguised as Pilgrims. No one could address him by any title that might draw attention to the spies of the authorities. However at the entry into the city he purposely revealed himself by fulfilling the prophesy of Zechariah, captured the city and controlled the Temple. The Roman garrison in the Antonia barracks probably withdrew to await reinforcements from Caesarea.

Pilate's troops counter attack after a few days, kill the Galilaeans in the Temple and batter the Tower of Siloam where some were holding out. The Romans had recaptured the city and still there was no miracle. Jesus and his generals in hiding take a last supper together – a messianic meal of the Essene type. Jesus, convinced that he had done all that God required and that a miracle was still in the offing, says he expects to be eating his next meal in the coming kingdom. He tells his men that they must remain armed. The next day was the Sabbath and also the Passover, a likely occasion for a miracle. They went to the Mount of Olives where, according to prophesy, the miracle would take place and Jesus urged his men to keep watchful – not for the enemy but for signs of God's intervention. It did not occur. A body of the Temple Guard arrived instead and arrested Jesus.

Jesus, the god, and Barabbas, the bandit, were both tried and crucified. Jesus, the god, knew his role in God's plan and as he expired whispered (Jn 19:30):

It is finished.

But Barabbas, the bandit, still believed that God would intervene – until, despairing, he called out with his last breath (Mk 15:34):

My God, My God, Why hast thou forsaken me?

BIBLIOGRAPHY

Allegro, J, *The Dead Sea Scrolls*, London 1964

Baigent, M & Leigh, R, *The Dead Sea Scrolls Deception*, London 1991

Barnes, E W, *The Rise of Christianity*, London 1948

Black, M & Rowley, H H, (Eds), *Peake's Commentary on the Bible*, London 1962

Cruden, A, *Cruden's Complete Concordance*, London 1963

Dodd, C H, *The Founder of Christianity*, London 1971

Douglas, J D (Ed), *New Bible Dictionary*, Leicester 1982

Eisenman, R & Wise, M, *The Dead Sea Scrolls Uncovered*, Shaftesbury, 1992

Forster, W, *Palestinian Judaism in New Testament Times*, London, 1964

Furneaux, R, *The Other Side of the Story*, London 1953

Godwin, J, *Mystery Religions in the Ancient World*, London 1981

Grant, M & Hazel, J, *Who's Who in Classical Mythology*, London 1979

Graves, R & Podro, J, *The Nazarene Gospel Restored*, London 1953

Hutton, R, *The Pagan Religions of the Ancient British Isles*, Oxford, 1991

Maccoby, Hyam, *The Mythmaker: Paul and the Invention of Christianity*, London 1986

Manson, T W, *The Teaching of Jesus*, Cambridge 1951

Pagels, E, *The Gnostic Gospels*, New York, 1979

Renan, E, *The Life of Jesus*, London 1935

Shanks, H (Ed), *Understanding the Dead Sea Scrolls*, London 1993

Taylor, V, *The Formation of the Gospel Tradition*, London 1933

Thiering, B, *Jesus the Man*, London 1992

Toynbee, A, *An Historians Approach to Religion*, London 1956

Vermes, Geza, *Jesus the Jew*, London 1973

Vermes, Geza, *The Dead Sea Scrolls in English*, London 1990

Waterhouse, J W, *Zoroastrianism*, London, undated

Weigell, A, *The Paganism in our Christianity*, London, undated

Wells, G A, *The Jesus of the Early Christians*, London 1971

Whiston, W (Trans), *The Works of Josephus*, London, undated

Wilson, E, *The Scrolls from the Dead Sea*, New York, 1955

About the author

M D Magee was brought up by vociferously Christian parents, one Catholic and one Protestant. He was therefore never indoctrinated into one dogma and was able from an early age to make his own judgements about the Christian religion.

He was born in Leeds, Yorkshire, in 1941.

He attended Cockburn High School in South Leeds in the days when compulsory religious instruction was guaranteed to knock any incipient spirituality from young pupils. He won a studentship to the Royal Military College of Science, Shrivenham, where he graduated with an honours degree in natural science in 1963. He went on to obtain a Ph.D. degree from the University of Aston in Birmingham in 1967 and a teaching qualification from the University of Huddersfield.

He carried out research at the Universities of Aston and Bradford, and at the Wool Industries Research Association, taught in a Further Education College in Devon for seven years and for ten years was an advisor to the UK government at the National Economic Development Office in London.

He has written over a dozen scientific papers on determining the structure of small molecules using microwave radiation and has written or edited some forty publications on microeconomic issues for the government.

Now living in Somerset, he spends his time drinking the fermented juice of the apple and writing for his own amusement. He hopes his observations will also interest others.